CORPORATE STRATEGY

Studies in Management Science and Systems

Editor

Burton V. Dean

Department of Operations Research
Case Western Reserve University
Cleveland, Ohio

VOLUME 8

NORTH-HOLLAND PUBLISHING COMPANY
AMSTERDAM • NEW YORK • OXFORD

Corporate Strategy
The Integration of Corporate Planning Models and Economics

Edited by

THOMAS H. NAYLOR

Duke University
Durham, North Carolina
U.S.A.

1982

NORTH-HOLLAND PUBLISHING COMPANY
AMSTERDAM • NEW YORK • OXFORD

ISBN: 0 444 86331 1

Published by:

NORTH-HOLLAND PUBLISHING COMPANY
AMSTERDAM ● NEW YORK ● OXFORD

Sole distributors for the U.S.A. and Canada:

ELSEVIER NORTH-HOLLAND, INC.
52 Vanderbilt Avenue, New York 10017

Library of Congress Cataloging in Publication Data
Main entry under title:

Corporate strategy.

    (Studies in management science and systems ;
v. 8)
    Bibliography: p.
    1. Corporate planning. 2. Corporate planning--
Mathematical models. I. Naylor, Thomas H.,
1936-   . II. Series.
HD30.28.C69   658.4'012   81-18848
ISBN 0-444-86331-1   AACR2

Printed in the Netherlands

FOREWORD

During the decade of the 1970s, macroeconomists such as Otto Eckstein and Michael Evans did a marvelous job of raising the awareness level of senior executives as to the importance of macroeconomic information in strategic planning. Unfortunately, microeconomists have not done nearly such a good job of pointing out that the "economic theory of the firm" is an extremely useful conceptual framework through which to view a company as a whole. This is particularly true if the company consists of a portfolio of strategic business units, some of which may be interdependent with regard to production, marketing, or distribution.

Under the assumptions of microeconomics, the firm attempts to make a set of product-output decisions and factor-input decisions that are consistent with its overall objectives in light of information available on product demand, factor supply, and production technology. But that is precisely what strategic planning is all about. It deals with the selection of business strategies that will enable management to achieve its long term objectives based on limited information about the company's macroeconomic, competitive, regulatory, technological, and factor supply environments. Corporate planners and microeconomists should spend more time listening to each other - they both might stand to benefit from the experience. The aim of this book is to improve communication among corporate economists, corporate planners, and corporate executives who are the principal users of the services of corporate economists and corporate planners.

This book contains a collection of fourteen papers by leading corporate economists, corporate planners, and academicians. These papers were originally presented at an international symposium held at Duke University on 4-5 December 1980, which was attended by nearly 200 corporate executives. The objectives of this symposium were: (1) to examine the interfaces between corporate simulation models, analytical portfolio planning models, and portfolio optimization models as strategic planning tools; (2) to develop an approach for integrating these methodologies into the strategic planning process; and (3) to explore the possibility of making microeconomics the language and conceptual framework for strategic planning and modeling.

The paper by William F. Hamilton and Michael A. Moses entitled "An Optimization Model for Corporate Financial Planning," was originally published in *Operations Research,* Volume 21, Number 3 (May-June 1973), and has been reprinted with the permission of The Journal of the Operations Research Society.

Michele H. Mann not only organized the original Duke Conference at which the papers were presented, but she also edited the entire manuscript and supervised its preparation for publication. Without her valuable assistance both the conference and this volume would have been impossible.

Durham, North Carolina   Thomas H. Naylor
September, 1981

TABLE OF CONTENTS

ECONOMICS: THE LANGUAGE OF STRATEGIC PLANNING

BIBLIOGRAPHY

STRATEGIC PLANNING MODELS

AN OVERVIEW OF
STRATEGIC PLANNING MODELS

Thomas H. Naylor

Department of Economics
Duke University
Durham, North Carolina
U.S.A.

INTRODUCTION

During the decade of the 1970s, three alternative approaches to strategic planning modeling evolved: (1) corporate simulation models, (2) analytical portfolio models, and (3) optimization portfolio models. In this paper we shall review the state of the art of strategic planning modeling from each of the aforementioned perspectives. We shall focus our emphasis on the complementarity of the three approaches rather than on their differences. We conclude the paper with some speculations about where we see the field of strategic planning and modeling going in the decade of the 1980s.

CORPORATE SIMULATION MODELS

Although there was a handful of corporate simulation models in existence prior to 1965, we shall define first generation models as those developed between 1965 and 1973. Second generation models are those which appeared between 1974 and 1979. Third generation models are those developed in the 1980s.

First Generation: 1965-1973 [19]

In March 1970 the TIMS College on Simulation and Gaming sponsored the first symposium ever held on "Corporate Simulation Models" at the University of Washington in Seattle [19]. Over 250 people attended and heard 25 speakers describe the corporate simulation models of such companies as Dow Chemical, Boeing Aircraft, AT&T, Sun Oil, Wells Fargo Bank, Boise Cascade, Weyerhaeuser, New York Life Insurance, Xerox, IBM, Honeywell, and Deere.

Almost without exception these early corporate simulations were essentially financial planning models capable of generating proforma financial statements. Furthermore, most of them were written in FORTRAN and were run in batch mode on the company's in-house computer. Some of these models were quite large and took a long time to develop. For example, the Sun Oil model, probably the most widely publicized model ever developed, took 23 person-years and over 3 1/2 years elapsed time to build. For all practical purposes, the model was really never even used by Sun's management.

By the early 1970s two important developments were underway. First, conversational computing became available, thus giving rise to commercial timesharing bureaus. Second, a number of first generation corporate simulation languages emerged to facilitate the coding of corporate simulation models. Among the early corporate simulation languages were PSG, FP-70, FORESIGHT, and PROPHIT II. Even though these simulation languages were primarily financial report generators with limited modeling capabilities, they did permit non-technical managers and analysts to develop their own corporate financial simulation models.

The first generation models tended to be stand-alone financial models with limited marketing and production components. Virtually all of these models were "What If?"

3

models.   There were no optimization models being used for overall corporate
planning. All of the early models were deterministic.

Second Generation: 1974-1979 [14-15]

Between 1974 and 1979 the number of companies using corporate simulation increased
dramatically.   By 1980 nearly all of the Fortune 1000 companies were routinely
using some form of corporate   simulation model, and many smaller firms were
starting to use them as well.   This period in the evolution of corporate simulation models was characterized by (1) the development of integrated planning
models, (2) attempts to integrate planning models into the planning process,
(3) increased attention focused on the human aspects of corporate simulation
modeling, (4) the introduction of a number of very powerful new corporate simulation languages, and (5) a substantial increase in the use of econometric models
to link corporate   simulation models to product markets and to the national
economy.

During this period, companies like Eli Lilly, Ross Labs, Monsanto, The New York
Times, Pennzoil, AVCO, and Wisconsin Power & Light developed business simulation
models characterized by the fact that finance, marketing, and production modules
were all integrated into one model. Others like United Air Lines, Lever Brothers,
Hercules, Allis-Chalmers, Kraft, and Springs Mills developed the capability to
develop business planning models for many different divisions and then to consolidate them into a single corporate model. Figure 1 contains a flow chart of a
typical corporate simulation model.

Most of the second generation models were strictly "What If?" models.   However,
there were a few exceptions.   North Carolina National Bank linked a portfolio
optimization model to its integrated bank planning model [15].   Ross Labs developed an integrated model which included a linear programming optimization model
to minimize production and distribution costs over multiple plant locations [15].

No longer were corporate simulation models merely appendages to the planning process, for companies such as The New York Times, Monsanto, and AVCO made substantial progress towards integrating their models into the planning process.   Many
companies began to obtain a better understanding of the politics of corporate
planning and modeling.

During this stage of development there was a significant shift away from scientific programming languages such as FORTRAN, PL/1, and APL in favor of several
powerful and quite flexible corporate planning modeling languages such as EXPRESS,
SIMPLAN, and XSIM [12,14].   These software systems typically included: (1) a
database, (2) a report generator, (3) graphics, (4) a security system, (5) the
ability to solve linear, non-linear, recursive, and simultaneous equations,
(6) risk analysis, (7) time series forecasting, and (8) econometric modeling.
They were available on commercial timesharing bureaus and could also be installed
on the client's in-house computer.   Some of them could be linked to external
econometric models and economic databases as well.

As recently as 1970, the number of companies with corporate econometric models was
probably in the order of magnitude of less than 100.   By 1980, if one considered
the clients of Chase Econometrics, DRI, and Wharton, then one could conservatively
estimate the number of companies using econometric models to be somewhere between
750 and 1,000.

ANALYTICAL PORTFOLIO MODELS

Assume that a company has a collection or portfolio of businesses, products, or
profit centers, and must decide how to allocate its scarce financial resources
across the portfolio.   Which businesses should be stimulated by investment in
the hopes of producing growth and eventually increased cash flow? Which businesses

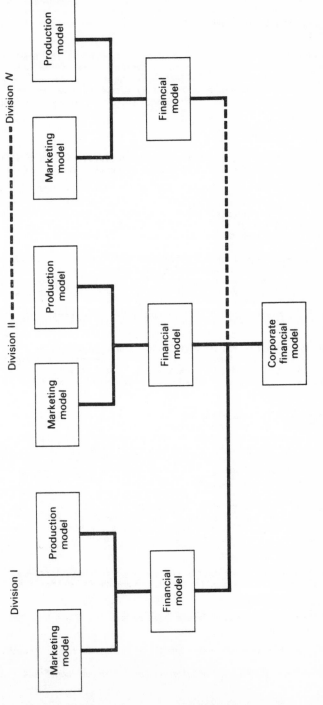

Figure 1. A Corporate Simulation Model

should be retained, but maintained at present levels of investment? Which businesses should be purged from the portfolio altogether, since they offer little promise of either growth or cash? These are all examples of the problem of portfolio planning.

In the early 1960s, under the leadership of Fred J. Borsch, the General Electric Company pioneered in the development of an analytical framework to facilitate this type of strategic decision making. Collectively these tools are called analytical portfolio models. They have been popularized by a number of management consulting firms, including the Boston Consulting Group (BCG), McKinsey and Company, and Arthur D. Little.

Boston Consulting Group (BCG) [8]

By far the most popular of the analytical portfolio models is the BCG model. The BCG approach is based on two relatively simple concepts - the growth share matrix and the experience curve.

The basic idea of the growth share matrix is that a company can be divided into component products or businesses, each of which is separable from the others. Specifically, each business is characterized as having either a high or low market growth rate and either a high or low market share. (See Figure 2.)

Products or businesses with high market share and low growth, which frequently generate large amounts of cash, are called cash cows. The excess cash generated by such products should not be reinvested in the products. Indeed, if the return on investment (ROI) is greater than the market growth rate, the cash cannot be reinvested indefinitely without reducing the ROI. The appropriate strategy is to protect the current position of the cash cow while generating cash invested in other projects.

A business that is characterized by high growth and high market share is called a star. It usually shows positive profits but it may or may not produce positive cash flow. If the star remains a market leader then it will eventually evolve into a cash cow, when growth is reduced and reinvestment requirements decline as well.

The problem child is a business that has high market growth and low market share. The problem child has an inferior market position, and typically requires more cash than it can generate. If cash is not provided, a problem child may fall behind and drop out of the market. However, even if cash is provided, the product may become a "dog" when the growth slows. Problem children require large injections of cash to buy market shares. Such products are likely to be liabilities unless they can become market leaders.

Finally, products or businesses with low market share and slow growth are called dogs. Although dogs may show a positive profit, the profit must consistently be reinvested simply to maintain market share. Dogs are worthless, and evidence of the failure to achieve a position of market leadership or to cut losses when faced with a "no win" situation.

In summary, the BCG growth share matrix represents a conceptual framework on which portfolio investment decisions can be based. A balanced portfolio of businesses calls for:

1. Heavy investment in stars, whose high market share and high growth insure the future.

2. Protection of cash cows that supply the funds for future growth.

3. Selective investment in problem children to be converted into stars.

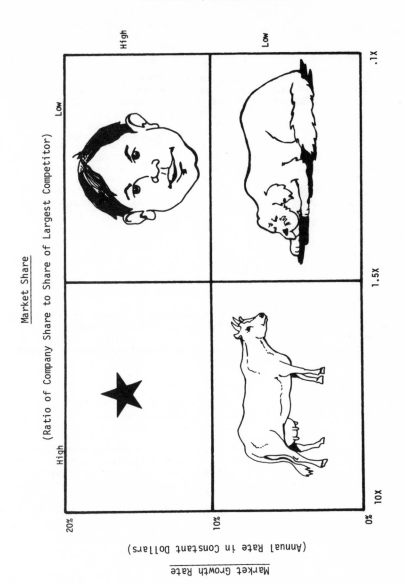

Figure 2. A Growth Share Matrix

4. Liquidation of dogs.

The second major concept of the BCG is known as the experience curve. According to the BCG, the unit cost (in real terms) of manufacturing a product declines approximately 20% to 30% each time accumulated experience is doubled. Examples where the experience curve seems to apply include automobiles, integrated circuits, semiconductors, crushed limestone, gas ranges, polyvinylchloride, and steam turbine generators, to mention only a few. (See Figure 3.)

As we previously indicated, the growth share matrix and the experience curve have been widely used by a number of major corporations during the decade of the 1970s. A limited number of companies, such as Monsanto, can now produce growth share matrices and experience curves as outputs of their corporate simulation models. It seems likely that this approach will be widely emulated among users of third generation strategic planning models. Two other consulting firms, Arthur D. Little and McKinsey and Company, offer portfolio planning models that are virtually identical to those of the Boston Consulting Group.

PIMS

The PIMS (Profit Impact of Market Strategy) Program of the Strategic Planning Institute (SPI) represents a second type of portfolio planning model that is used by a number of large companies in the United States and Europe. It has its historical origins in the General Electric Company.

Utilizing a database of strategic information on over two thousand product-line businesses, the objectives of the PIMS Program are "to discover the general 'laws' that determine what business strategy, in what kind of competitive environment, produces what profit results," and "to produce reports for the managers of each business unit, which they can use as a basis for decision making" [16].

Methodology

The basic methodology underlying most of the research findings of PIMS is multiple regression analysis. Using the PIMS database on approximately two thousand businesses, SPI has developed a single-equation econometric model that explains about 75 percent of the variation in return on investment among these businesses in terms of 28 "profit-influencing" factors. A similar model has also been developed that explains 70 percent of the variation in cash flow among these same businesses in terms of 19 "cash flow-influencing" factors. In each of the aforementioned models, the profit-influencing and cash flow-influencing factors are identified (on the basis of statistical significance) and discussed in some detail. Among the factors identified as influencing profitability are rate of growth, degree of market concentration, market share, product quality, and productivity of capital and labor. The PIMS methodology is based on the assumption that while there are differences among businesses, it is possible to identify common factors that cut across all businesses.

PIMS Reports

Participants in the PIMS Program receive a number of reports. These include Par reports, strategy reports, and portfolio reviews.

The Par ROI report specifies the return on investment that is normal for a business, given its market attractiveness, competitive position, degree of differentiation from competitors, and its production structure. The report also quantifies individual strategic strengths and weaknesses, as indicated by the impacts of key profit-influencing factors.

The strategy reports are said to answer the following questions: (1) If this business continues on its current track, what will its future operating results

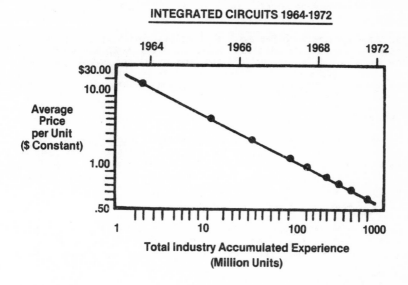

Figure 3. The Experience Curve for Integrated Circuits

be? (2) What changes in market share, investment intensity, and vertical integration are likely to produce better results?

Finally, the PIMS portfolio reviews are an attempt to answer the following kinds of questions: (1) Has the strategic position of the portfolio improved over the last few years? (2) Is the portfolio performing well or badly, given its strategic position? (3) Will proposed business plans strengthen the portfolio? How much? (4) Which plans deserve the most detailed review? (5) Which businesses are potential divestment candidates?

Research Findings

Derek F. Abel and John S. Hammond, in their book Strategic Market Planning [1] have succinctly summarized the important research findings of the PIMS project. They are listed below as determinants of ROI and determinants of cash flow.

Determinants of ROI

1. Investment Intensity

    a. Large investment and high marketing intensity equals poor ROI.
    b. Capacity utilization is vital when fixed capital intensity is high.
    c. High capital intensity and small market share equals disaster.

2. Market Share

    a. Market share is most profitable in vertically integrated industries.
    b. High research and development spending depresses ROI when market share is weak.
    c. Capacity utilization is most important for low share businesses.
    d. Heavy marketing depresses ROI for low share businesses.
    e. Market share and quality are partial substitutes for each other.

3. Market Growth Rate

    a. A rapid rate of new product introduction in fast growing markets depresses ROI.
    b. Research and development is most profitable in mature, slow growth markets.

4. Life Cycle Stage

    A narrow product line, in the early or middle stage of the product life cycle, is less profitable than at the later stage.

5. Marketing Expenses

    a. High research and development expenses plus high marketing expenses depress ROI.
    b. High marketing expenses depress ROI, especially when quality is low.

Determinants of Cash Flow

1. Investment Intensity

    a. Low or medium growth, coupled with low investment intensity produces cash; high growth coupled with high investment intensity is a cash drain.
    b. Harvesting share when investment intensity is low produces cash; building share when investment intensity is high is a cash drain.
    c. Investment plus marketing intensity results in cash drains.

    d. Few new product introductions, coupled with low investment intensity, produces cash.

2. Relative Market Share

    a. High relative share improves cash flow; high growth decreases it.
    b. High share and low investment intensity produce cash; low share and high investment intensity result in cash drain.
    c. High relative share produces cash--especially when marketing intensity is low.

A Critical Appraisal of PIMS

Although some economists have criticized the methodology of PIMS on the grounds that it places too much faith in single-equation econometric models, the real value of PIMS lies in its database, containing extensive time series and cross-sectional data on finance, marketing, and production operations for over two thousand strategic business units. The research potential of the PIMS database remains virtually untapped by corporate and academic economists.

OPTIMIZATION PORTFOLIO MODELS

For over one hundred years economists have been proposing the use of optimization models as planning tools for the firm. The dream of the C.E.O. sitting in his or her office managing a portfolio of businesses according to some optimization model has yet to occur. Although the decade of the 1970s witnessed the growth of the use of corporate simulation models and analytical portfolio models, such as the BCG model and the PIMS model, we cannot identify a single firm that currently uses optimization as a strategic planning tool.

However, we believe that the experience gained by firms in the 1970s with analytical portfolio models and corporate simulation models has laid the groundwork for the introduction of optimization models as strategic planning tools in the 1980s. In this section we shall describe three portfolio optimization models that have been proposed for strategic planning. The Boston Consulting Group "Strategy Based Resource Allocation Model" [3] and the Hamilton and Moses [7] "Optimization Model for Corporate Financial Planning" are both deterministic models. The capital-asset pricing model [9,20] extends the concept of risk analysis to portfolio optimization models.

Boston Consulting Group Model

The BCG has defined a set of six major decisions that are the heart of a company's strategic resource allocation problem:

1. What businesses should be supported for growth?

2. Which businesses should be managed for greater cash generation?

3. What should be the level of dividends to shareholders?

4. How much debt should the company use to finance its growth?

5. Should the company seek acquisitions, and if so, what should be the nature of these acquisitions?

To aid in the difficult task of managing a large number of different businesses in a complex competitive environment, the BCG has developed a strategy-based resource allocation model [3]. The model is a linear programming model which helps management choose either a growth strategy or a cash strategy for each business in the company's portfolio, thus allocating as optimally as possible the company's scarce resources.

For each business, the model indicates which strategic option maximizes the company's growth or long run earnings, subject to a set of financial constraints. The strategic option selected takes into consideration the necessary tradeoffs between growth and return over a specific planning horizon, say five years. Both the cash plan and the growth plan for each business are based on the following financial forecasts for each business: return on assets, growth in sales, growth in assets, and growth in earnings.

In the process of formulating growth and cash plans for the specific businesses, the model maintains a balance between cash inflows and outflows. The major sources and uses of funds to express these cash balances include:

Sources of Funds

1. Operating income
2. New debt
3. Reduction of working capital assets or sale of fixed assets
4. Other cash inflows

Uses of Funds

1. Interest payments
2. Dividends
3. Investment in new assets
4. Other cash outflows

In summary, there are two alternative versions of the BCG resource allocation model. In the first case the objective is to select a portfolio of cash and/or growth plans which will maximize growth, which is defined to be assets at the end of the planning horizon. In the second case the objective is to maximize earnings, which are defined as net income after interest at the beginning of the planning period. In both cases the selection of strategic options is constrained by the following three cash constraints assuming a five-year planning horizon:

1. Five yearly cash balances reflecting yearly minimum cash requirements and maximum cash availabilities (other than from operations and financial policies).

2. Four minimum yearly growth rates in earnings per share.

3. A five-year minimum cash balance requirement, averaging over the entire planning period the cash flows from operations and financial decisions.

There are several obvious limitations to the BCG optimization model, which may explain why this particular model is not widely used by corporate executives. First, the assumption that all strategic decisions can be reduced to the dichotomy of cash versus growth is an over-simplification of the planning problem. Second, the BCG model unduly restricts the firm's investment options. Third, the methodology is completely incapable of handling interdependent businesses. Further, to some extent this model assumes away the problem of strategic planning by virtue of the information required to feed it. Although the BCG model is a step in the right direction, it is understandable why so few firms have embraced this approach to portfolio planning.

Hamilton and Moses Model

Perhaps the best known portfolio optimization model is a model published by Hamilton and Moses [7] in 1973. The model was designed specifically for strategic planning in a large diversified company. The model includes a full range of financial decisions, including internal capital budgeting, acquisitions, divestments, debt creation/repayment, stock issue/repurchase, and dividend payout. The model employs mixed integer programming to select optimal investment and financing strategies over a multiperiod planning horizon.

Like the BCG optimization model, this model also permits two different types of strategy options - momentum strategies and development strategies. Momentum strategies represent a continuation of present activities in current lines of business. Development strategies reflect proposed changes in the nature or level of present activities. The objective of the firm is to maximize earnings per share subject to a set of goal constraints, corporate constraints, and group constraints.

Unfortunately, there is little evidence to suggest that either the BCG Model [3] or the Hamilton and Moses Model [7] have been used very extensively as strategic planning tools. However, they do represent interesting conceptual frameworks from which to view the problem of strategic portfolio planning.

Capital-Asset Pricing Models [21]

The modern literature on finance [21] abounds with applications of the capital asset pricing model (CAPM) which was first developed by Sharpe [20] and Lintner [9] and is based on the earlier work of Markowitz [11]. Until recently, most of the applications of the CAPM were oriented towards the problem of an individual investor involved in the selection of a portfolio of securities under conditions of risk.

Markowitz [11] showed that the variance of the return on a portfolio of financial securities depends not only on the riskiness of the individual securities in the portfolio, but also on the relationship among these securities, i.e., on the covariances between the respective securities in the portfolio. He showed that the variance of a portfolio of securities may be less than the smallest variance of an individual security if there are sufficient negative covariances among the securities. (A negative covariance between two securities can be interpreted to mean that when the return from one security is above its average value the return from the other is below its average value.) The optimum portfolio involves selecting that combination of securities that yields the best combination of expected return and risk which, of course, depends on the investor's utility function.

It can be shown that there is an implied equilibrium relationship between risk and return for each security. In equilibrium, a security will be expected to yield a return commensurate with its unavoidable risk. This is simply the risk that cannot be avoided by diversification. The greater the unavoidable risk of a security, the greater the return that the investor will expect from the security. The relationship between expected return and unavoidable risk, and the valuation of securities in this context is the essence of the capital asset pricing model.

Among the numerous financial applications of the CAPM described in the literature are included: (1) valuation of a firm's common stock, (2) capital budgeting, (3) merger and acquisition analysis, and (4) the valuation of warrants and convertible securities. Recently, two management consulting firms, Marakon Associates and Strategic Planning Associates, have proposed the possibility of employing the CAPM not only as a decision making tool for investors with a portfolio of financial assets, but also as a planning tool for corporations that manage a portfolio of businesses, divisions, strategic business units, etc. In the latter case, the portfolio consists of tangible assets while the former case consists only of financial assets.

The CAPM is based on the following seven assumptions: (1) All investors in securities are single-period (say one year), expected utility wealth maximizers who choose securities on the basis of mean and variance of return; (2) Investors can borrow or lend funds at risk-free interest rate; (3) Investors have identical subjective estimates of the means, variances, and covariances of all securities; (4) The market for financial securities is perfectly competitive and all investors are price takers; (5) The quantity of securities is fixed; (6) All securities are perfectly divisible and liquid, i.e., they are marketable without significant transaction costs; (7) There are no taxes. The CAPM attempts to determine how an investor's financial assets are valued when the behavior of all investors in the stock market is taken into consideration. To extend the CAPM to the case of a corporation that owns a portfolio of businesses, we must assume that the businesses have the same properties as securities.

A complete treatise on capital asset pricing models is beyond the scope of this paper. For a more complete treatment of the possible application of capital asset pricing models as a strategic planning tool, the reader should see the recent paper by Naylor and Tapon [17].

THIRD GENERATION STRATEGIC PLANNING MODELS: METHODOLOGICAL CHALLENGES OF THE 1980s

Strategic Business Units: A Critical Appraisal

Underlying each of the portfolio models described in this paper is the concept of the strategic business unit of the SBU. The firm is assumed to own or control a portfolio of SBUs. Indeed, the entire literature on analytical and optimization portfolio models assumes the existence of well defined SBUs. Increasingly, the whole concept of the SBU has come under attack from a variety of different points of view.   The article by Abernathy and Hayes [2] contains a number of these criticisms of SBUs. Below we shall outline some of the relevant issues involved:

  1. There is no scientific definition of a strategic business unit. A number of different definitions based on markets, technology, organizational structure, and SIC codes has been proposed. In all too many cases these definitions are inconsistent and arbitrary.

  2.   With the exception of the capital-asset pricing models, there is the implicit assumption that SBUs are independent of one another. Yet many SBUs are not at all independent. Take, for example, the case of international oil companies, which have attempted to define strategic business units around specific regions of the world. SBUs might be defined for integrated oil companies within say, the United States, Europe, and the Far East. The only problem is that most international oil companies have a world-wide crude oil supply system in which crude allocation decisions are made at the corporate level rather than at the SBU level.   The portfolio models are simply not able to cope with such interdependencies in their present form.

  3.   Another completely different line of attack on the SBU has focused on the behavioral implications of SBUs. According to this point of view, general managers of SBUs are placed under such great pressure to produce short term profits that they devote little or no attention to strategic planning which may ensure the long term profitability of the business.

  4.   Somewhat related to the previous criticism is the argument that the whole philosophy of SBUs is producing a generation of risk averse managers who lack entrepreneurial drive and the desire to innovate. According to this school of thought, many of American industry's productivity problems are by-products of the problems outlined above.

It seems clear that the concept of the SBU needs a lot more theoretical and empirical research. The PIMS database described above contains a gold mine of data for this type of research.

The Complementarity of Alternative Strategic Planning Models

Although corporate simulation models, analytical portfolio models, and optimization portfolio models were developed independently in the 1970s, we believe there will be many attempts to exploit their complementarity in the 1980s. Growth share matrices and experience curves are obvious outputs of corporate simulation models. Linkages between the PIMS database and individual corporate simulation models are also likely. As previously stated, some companies using simulation models will extend them to include some type of optimization.

The Role of Industrial Organization as a Strategic Planning Tool

The recent book by Michael E. Porter entitled Competitive Strategy [18] has opened up a whole new field for corporate economists and corporate planners. Heretofore, industrial organization specialists concentrated their efforts on questions of anti-trust, monopoly, and government regulation. Porter has demonstrated the applicability of industrial organization as a tool of corporate strategy.

Decision Support Systems

1. Modular. Second generation decision support systems for strategic planning were characterized by an attempt to cram as many planning and modeling features as possible into a single computer software system -- risk analysis, econometric modeling, Box-Jenkins, optimization, and multi-color graphics, to mention only a few. We believe there may be an upper limit to the number of bells and whistles that can be integrated into higher level planning and modeling software systems such as EXPRESS, SIMPLAN, and XSIM. In other words, in terms of analytical power, it is difficult to envisage a substantial number of new techniques to be included in third generation planning and modeling software systems.

It seems likely that many of the existing planning and modeling software systems will adopt a modularized approach. That is, it will become possible to acquire the database management capabilities and report generation of a particular planning system without purchasing some of the more sophisticated modules including econometric modeling, risk analysis, and optimization. As the user's level of experience and sophistication increases, additional modules can be acquired as they are needed.

2. Interfaces. Third generation decision support systems will reflect, and indeed, exploit the complementarity of corporate simulation models, analytical portfolio models, and optimization portfolio models. Various linkages among these alternative approaches to planning modeling will be provided by third generation planning and modeling software systems.

3. Graphics. There will be a continuation of the trend established in the late 1970s to produce a wide variety of different types of graphical output from decision support systems.

4. Mini-Computers. Third generation planning software systems and databases will be available on most mini-computers, and in the not-too-distant future possibly available even on micro-processors. This will mean that strategic planning modeling will no longer be restricted to the really large corporations, but rather that quite small companies will find it economically feasible to use these types of tools.

5. Ease of Use. There is every indication that third generation planning and modeling languages will become even easier to use than in the past. Some vendors will use "canned models" to introduce unsophisticated users to their systems, thus permitting the user to start with very simple and restricted applications, but then to switch over to the full power of the planning and modeling system as experience is gained with the system.

REFERENCES

[1]   Abel, Derek, F. and John E. Hammond. Strategic Market Planning. Englewood
      Cliffs, N.J.: Prentice-Hall, 1979.

[2]   Abernathy, William J. and Robert H. Hayes. "Managing Our Way to Economic
      Decline," Harvard Business Review (July-August, 1980), pp. 67-77.

[3]   Boston Consulting Group.   "A Strategy-Based Resource Allocation Model"
      (unpublished, undated report). Boston, MA: The Boston Consulting Group.

[4]   Coate, Malcolm G. The Boston Consulting Group's Strategic Portfolio Planning
      Model: An Economic Analysis.   (Unpublished Ph.D. dissertation.)   Duke
      University, 1980.

[5]   Cohen, Kalman J. and Frederick S. Hammer. "Linear Programming and Optimal
      Bank Asset Management Decisions," Journal of Finance, XXII, No. 2 (May,
      1967), pp. 147-165.

[6]   Gale, Bradley T.   "Planning for Profit," Planning Review (January, 1978).

[7]   Hamilton, W.F. and M.A. Moses. "An Optimization Model for Corporate Finan-
      cial Planning," Operations Research (May-June, 1972), pp. 677-692.

[8]   Jenderson, Bruce D. Henderson on Corporate Strategy. Cambridge, MA: Abt
      Books, 1979.

[9]   Lintner, John.   "The Valuation of Risk Assets and the Selection of Risky
      Investments in Stock Portfolios and Capital Budgets," Review of Economics
      and Statistics, XLVII (February, 1965), pp. 13-37.

[10] Lorange, Peter and Richard F. Vancil. Strategic Planning Systems. Engle-
      wood Cliffs, N.J.: Prentice-Hall, 1977.

[11] Markowitz, H. Portfolio Selection. (Cowles Foundation Monograph No. 16.)
      New York: John Wiley, 1959.

[12] Mayo, R. Britton.   Corporate Planning Models with SIMPLAN.   Reading, MA:
      Addison-Wesley, 1979.

[13] Naylor, Thomas H. (editor). The Politics of Corporate Planning and Modeling.
      Oxford, OH: Planning Executives Institute, 1978.

[14] Naylor, Thomas H. Corporate Planning Models. Reading, MA: Addison-Wesley,
      1979.

[15] Naylor, Thomas H. (editor).   Simulation Models in Corporate Planning.   New
      York: Praeger, 1979.

[16] Naylor, Thomas H.   Strategic Planning Management.   Oxford, OH: Planning
      Executives Institute, 1980.

[17] Naylor, Thomas H. and Francis Tapon.   "The Capital Asset Pricing Model:
      An Evaluation of its Potential as a Strategic Planning Tool," Corporate
      Economics Program Working Paper Number 6, Duke University, 1 April 1981.

[18] Porter, Michael E.   Competitive Strategy.   New York: Free Press, 1980.

[19] Schrieber, Albert N. (editor).   Corporate Simulation Models.   Seattle:
      University of Washington, 1970.

[20] Sharpe, William F. "Capital Asset Prices: A Theory of Market Equilibrium under Conditions of Risk." Journal of Finance, XIX (September, 1964), pp. 425-442.

[21] Van Horne, James C. Financial Management and Policy. Englewood Cliffs, N.J.: Prentice-Hall, 1980.

CORPORATE SIMULATION MODELS

Leonard Forman

The New York Times
New York, New York
U.S.A.

INTRODUCTION

The transformation of corporate goals and objectives into policies that will achieve them in an environment characterized by risk and uncertainty is the essence of planning. That process typically involves establishing goals and objectives; assessing probable economic, political, social, competitive and market trends; identifying potential opportunities and problems; and developing strategies and policies to take advantage of opportunities and deal with problems.

Experience has taught us, however, that many companies fail to meet their objectives. Most often planning, despite the elaborate mechanisms of many corporate planning systems, is an exercise in "seat of the pants" judgment, where intuition is the prevailing mode of decision making.

The complexity of the corporation operating in an environment characterized by rapid change precludes intuitive decision making. The complex interrelationships among a corporation's financial, marketing, and production activities necessitate the use of computer-based planning simulation models. The rationale underlying the use of such a tool is identical to the rationale for corporate planning. Models cannot predict the future, but they can help management cope with a wide variety of problems and opportunities which create risk and uncertainty.

Suppose we define a corporate planning model as a structural system of mathematical and logical time-dependent relationships which depict the financial, marketing and production activities of the corporation, and the linkages between these activities. If we further define simulation as the mathematical solution of this system of equations then, by a judicious use of simulation, management can evaluate corporate performance under a wide variety of alternative futures. More importantly, because we are incapable of mentally evaluating more than a few of the interactions between changes in the environment, decisions which are made as consequence of those changes, and the results of those decisions, models are required for strategy and policy design if the pitfalls of intuitive decision-making are to be avoided.

The topic of this paper, corporate simulation models, is nearly as broad as the number of models which are identified as corporate simulation models. To help reduce that breadth, my discussion focuses on one class of such models, corporate planning models. There is a consistent theme which threads its way throughout the paper: if planning models are to prove useful to strategic planners, they need to be more than simple number crunchers.

Strategic planning is a dynamic process. Indeed, conceptually the process can be viewed in modeling terms as a feedback and control system. Planning--goal setting, information gathering, environmental appraisal, and the development and execution of plans--includes information exchange and feedback between many groups during the planning cycle. To represent such a process, a planning model must include

not only financial relationships but the physical stocks and flows which produce
the financial data.

Financial information is a performance measure--the super structure of the corporate system--it suggests what is happening, not why it is happening. A complete dynamic representation should also include the physical stocks and flows
generated by production and marketing: information, material, orders, workers,
capital goods and inventories. Accounting, production, marketing, finance, personal relations, and economics have typically been dealt with as if they were
unrelated subjects. Only at the top of the management hierarchy do managers need
to integrate these separate functions. Corporations are such large and complex
systems that a knowledge of the parts by themselves is not very informative. In
management as in most complex systems, the dynamic relationships between system
components often produce results that are counterintuitive. An understanding of
those linkages are often more important than the individual components themselves.

The Adequacy of Conventional Microeconomic Theory

As a Guide to Modeling the Firm

All modeling efforts require a theoretical structure to provide a framework for
design and construction. Economists look towards microeconomic theory to provide
that framework. However, corporate model builders have been reluctant to adopt
economic theory because the behavioral assumptions and the decision rules of the
firm in their theory bears little resemblance to the firm of the real world. If
corporate planning is concerned with long term decision making in an environment
which is uncertain as well as subject to rapid and continual change, formal
microeconomic theory focuses on equilibrium conditions in a world with little or
no uncertainty.

The theory of the firm can be organized conceptually around four elements: goals,
information, decision making, and the production process. The assumptions which
the traditional model makes about each of these elements are well known:

1. A total revenue function which relates the output quantities of the firm's
    products to total revenue. This function is fixed and known.

2. A total cost equation is defined which relates the input quantities of the
    firm's variable factors to total cost. This function is fixed and known.

3. The objective of the firm is to maximize profit subject to the technical con-
    straints imposed by its production function.

4. A continuous production function exists which relates the set of independent
    product variables. This function expresses the most efficient input-output
    configuration.

5. The exact nature of the firm's production function has been predetermined by a
    set of technical decisions by the firm's engineers and technicians.

6. The production function is characterized by a decreasing marginal product for
    all factor-product combinations, a decreasing rate of technical substitution
    between any two products.

7. All of the firm's factors and products are perfectly divisible.

8. The parameters which determine the firm's total revenue function, production
    function, and total cost equation will not change over the planning period.

Despite its acceptance by economists, the traditional model has come under vigo-
rous attack from a variety of groups for its lack of realism and its excessive

abstraction for real world decision making. The mathematical assumptions as well as the type of firm implied by the traditional model bears little resemblance to the business firm of the real world. Within the profession, a number of economists have begun to explore alternative models of price, investment, production, and other behaviors.

Goals

The assumption that firms maximize profits is the fundamental behavioral assumption in the traditional model. There have been a number of challenges to this assumption: from the argument that firms have multiple objectives--inventory goals, sales goals, growth goals, market share goals, personal goals of management, etc.--to the argument that firms are non-rational. Firms frequently select strategies which do not maximize their objective function. In the world of the megacorp, the simple profit maximization rule followed by the firm which produces a homogenous product operating in a perfectly competitive market does not hold.

Corporate simulation models liberate the model builder from this constraining assumption. Given a model which describes the firms structure - a systems view of the firm which captures the dynamic linkages between the various components of the firm such as production, financial and marketing activities and an understanding of the crucial decision rules and decision variables, the decision maker's criterion or utility function need not be explicitly defined. The model can then be used to indicate the likely consequences of those implicit or explicit decision rules. Decision makers can then choose the policy or strategy which is compatible with their utility function.

The likelihood of multiple objectives, some of which may be inconsistent with one another forces the decision maker to often choose second best solutions which can only be selected through the judicious use of a realistic simulation model. For example, many firms have both cash flow and earnings per share objectives. Often an investment which might positively affect cash flow will reduce earnings per share. A public company needs to be mindful of earnings per share dilution because of potential adverse effects on its stock price which might hamper the financing of future investment decisions. Since this trade-off is only one of a multiplicity of objectives, an analytical model which requires the exact parametric representation of the firm's criterion function would be difficult if not impossible to construct. In the future, non-linear optimal control models, which have not yet yielded fruitful results, may provide the necessary analytical solution. Until then, simulation models provide the only real alternative to the textbook model which currently provides little help to the decision maker in the real world.

Information

The traditional model assumes that the firm possesses perfect information about its market, its costs, its competitors, the economy, etc. In the real world, however, the lack of perfect and/or distorted information is the rule, not the exception. Corporate simulation models do not require the assumption of perfect information.

The traditional model's assumption of perfect knowledge and complete certainty with regard to market, cost and production functions eliminate any need for real decision making. Indeed, a decision maker simply needs to follow the rules of the marginal calculus in order to maximize profits. Marginalism in this model eliminates competitive conflict as well as the need for a creative entrepreneurial spirit. The decision maker is emasculated.

Decision Making

The assumptions of the traditional model eliminate the most critical problem confronting management in the real world: decision making in an environment characterized by risk and uncertainty. Risk of course can be introduced by assuming stochastic rather than deterministic variables, and assigning predetermined probability distributions to the variables. Keynes and Frank Knight, over 40 years ago, however, distinguished between risk and uncertainty. They were concerned with the effect of uncertainty on decision making in a production-monetary economy set in historical time.

While risk is a statistical concept which can be quantified through the application of the probability calculus, uncertainty cannot be measured. Uncertainty implies that the future is unpredictable. It cannot be described in terms of probability. To use probability distributions to determine economic outcomes--that is, to replace the concept of uncertainty with the concept of risk--is to assume that most people have knowledge that they are actually unlikely to possess. Risk and probability imply a sampling of repetitive events and a specified outcome occurring with a given frequency. Most real world decisions, however, are not capable of being repeated. They are unique in terms of the events which necessitated a decision and the changes in physical and psychological states which result from that decision. According to Keynes, "the one way traffic of human history allows no repetition of the kind of experiments that change men's ideas. They are self-destructive experiments."

Since the future is logically unknowable, the choice of future alternatives is fundamentally uncertain. Probabilities cannot be calculated by sampling the future. Consequently, problems of uncertainty are incapable of being reduced to problems involving risk.

As Keynes pointed out, uncertainty pervades economic life because the economy exists in historical time, not logical time. The economic system is indeterminate. The problem is "to make rational dispositions in the face of an uncertain future. It is a problem that is insolvable. But, decisions need to be made. Usually present conditions and majority opinion are assumed to be a serviceable guide to the future. But such opinions are flimsy, without solid foundation, subject to sudden and violent change." Decisions which affect the future cannot possibly depend on strict mathematical expectations because the basis for making these calculations does not exist. This provides a rationale for the use of corporate simulation models which overcome uncertainty not by eliminating it but by giving management a "feel" for the consequence of potential.

Production

The traditional model assumes a continuous, strictly concave production function that is completely determined by the firm's engineers. All factors are perfectly divisible. The marginal approach to production relationships has been an unreliable guide for model builders who have embraced the conceptual framework of activity analysis for their production models. However, because of the difficulties associated with specifying criterion functions, such production models have typically not been well integrated into corporate models. The New York Times model described below offers one possible solution which integrates simulation techniques within the methodological framework of activity analysis.

THE CORPORATION AS A DYNAMIC SYSTEM

It is convenient to visualize the corporation as a dynamic system composed of numerous interrelated components. This is a useful way of characterizing the corporation because it formalizes the linkages between the functional departments of a corporation such as accounting and finance, production, marketing and personnel, as well as the linkage between the corporation and its environment. The complexity of such a system, with its many interactions among component parts, precludes consistent, effective planning which relies solely on intuition.

Several years ago, Jay Forrester, in his book, <u>Industrial Dynamics</u>, suggested that in a complex system, decision makers who depend on intuition will more often than not, select the wrong solution. Most intuitive responses have typically been developed when cause and effect were often closely related in space and time or what Forrester calls first order negative-feedback loops. For example, as Forrester points out, warming one's hands next to a stove is such a process. If you get too close, you burn your hands. If you are too far away, you receive too little heat. Intuition tells you that cause and effect are closely related in both time and space. Temperature depends on distance from the stove and the relation of cause and effect is immediately clear.

Complex systems do not contain such clearly defined cause-effect relationships, but contain a multiplicity of interacting negative and positive feedback loops which are often interrelated in a highly nonlinear fashion. Thus causality may not be observed from the symptoms, and may be derived from a completely different part of the system.

Corporations are complex, dynamic systems. Sales, profits and market share all change over time. They may oscillate, grow smoothly in a exponential pattern, decline exponentially or exhibit some combination of all three patterns. The dynamic behavior of a corporation is summarized in the movement over time of such performance measures.

Such behavior may result from the actions of the corporation itself, the actions of its competitors, or changes in the economic, political or social environment. The essence of dynamic change is the feedback relationships which occur internally between the functional areas and externally between the corporation and its environment. Feedback occurs whenever an event gives rise to an action which produces a result which in turn has an effect on the initiating event. Figure 1 depicts a flow diagram illustrating the dynamics of a publishing firm. This visual model is the conceptual basis for magazine and newspaper planning models at the New York Times.

The economics of newspaper and magazine publishing are complicated by the fact that its revenues come from two different but related sources: advertising revenues and circulation revenues. They are related by the number of readers of the magazine. Circulation revenues are obviously directly related to readership. Advertising revenues on the other hand are indirectly related to readership since the price that advertisers are prepared to pay for magazine advertising space depends to a large extent upon the exposure of their advertisements, i.e., the number of readers. Also if companies tend to finance readership growth out of current revenues, then the readership level is also dependent over time upon itself. This suggests that a publishing firm can be viewed as a rather complex system of parts dynamically related over time.

The model can be thought of as expressing the dynamic interrelatedness between the financial accounts, measures of performance based on the accounts, management's decisions based upon the measures of performance, and the reaction of the marketplace to those decisions. For example, imagine that management's response to an unsatisfactory reported profit is to increase the circulation price of its daily newspaper. At the end of the year, profits prove to be satisfactory but circulation sales revenue has declined or not grown as fast as was expected because the increase in price has caused some erosion in the physical units sold. (Rational decision making implies that before instituting a price increase, management would have some knowledge of the appropriate price elasticities. Unfortunately, this is not always the case.) This would prove worrisome since advertisers might be reluctant to pay the same or higher rates in order to reach fewer readers. In response, the management decides to increase sales promotion activities. At the end of the next period, circulation sales have increased to a satisfactory level, but this extra expenditure on sales promotion has reduced the profit, and so on. It is the latter aspect of the dynamic relationships between the financial ac-

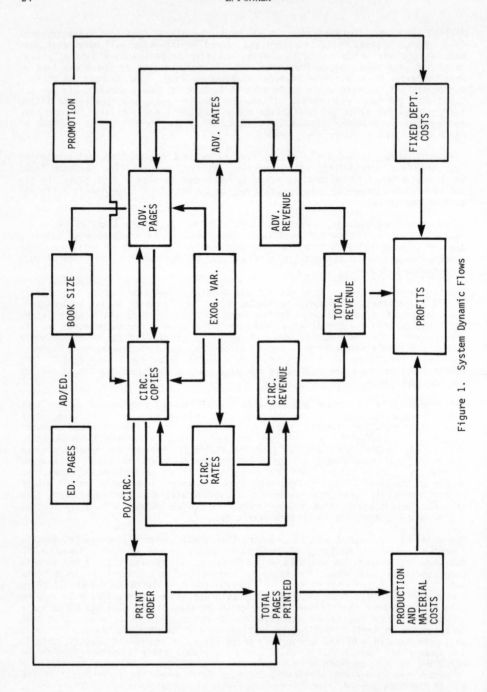

Figure 1. System Dynamic Flows

counts, measures of performance based on the accounts, management's decisions based upon the measures of performance, the reaction of the firm's environment to those decisions and the results of this interchange as reflected in the accounts which best illustrates the publishing firm as a complex dynamic system.

Many other feedback interactions could be described. Nevertheless, the diagram illustrates how change or dynamic behavior is created by feedback interactions involving company policies and decisions. Different policies produce different behavior.

PLANNING MODELS: A TAXONOMY

The earlier discussion defined a planning model, as a system of mathematically time dependent relationships which depict the financial, marketing, and production activities of the firm and the linkages between these activities. This is unquestionably an ambitious definition of a planning model, a definition which in practice most models fall short of. Typically most planning models are accounting or financial models which portray in a static framework only the financial relationships and not the physical stocks and flows which determine corporate behavior. Given some assumptions about sales, financial and accounting identities are used to generate income and balance sheet statements.

Although financial models can be useful in minimizing the costs of computing and evaluating a firm's financial position as well as answer some basic "what if" questions, there is a danger in expecting such conceptually simple models to produce answers to sophisticated questions. Structural and behavioral relationships are absent. Typically, such models are based on simple financial ratios which remain constant over the planning horizon, implicitly assuming static and linear relationships. In reality, causal relationships which describe corporate behavior contain many interacting feedback relationships which are undoubtedly related in some highly non-linear manner.

A good illustration is the usual treatment of the receivables-sales relationships in most financial models. Receivables are specified as a constant percentage of sales, the percentage calculated as the average value of the ratio of receivables to sales over a period of years. However, it is well known that receivables-sales ratios are not constant but vary over the business cycles. Corporate cash managers, trying to maximize profits, often stagger their accounts payable, i.e., someone else's receivables, depending on their cash position, market interest rates, etc. At a minimum one should try to allow for cyclical movements in this ratio. Thus the ratio might depend on changes in real GNP, or some characterization of the business cycle. This is only part of the explanation for fluctuations in these ratios. Receivables ultimately depend on the shipment of goods and these physical flows often produce the most interesting behavior. Receivables depend on the dollar amount of goods invoiced out, the payments received for goods shipped previously, the volume and average prices of the goods shipped, production and consumer orders, etc. These relationships are not static. The intermediate steps which causally connect receivables and sales involve a complex time pattern, best handled as a convolution of distributed lags.

Fluctuating receivables-sales ratios only begin to make sense when the underlying dynamics are imbedded in the model. In the static financial model, a change in sales produces an instantaneous adjustment in receivables so that the ratio does not change. In a dynamic model, however, a change in sales brought about by a one-time shift in customer orders is likely to produce fluctuations in the ratio because of the time lags involved. Only after a considerable delay would the ratio return to its equilibrium level. Since in reality customer orders are not smooth, the receivables-sales ratio would tend to fluctuate considerably, a result consistent with actual ratios.

To summarize, accounting models do not capture the dynamic behavior of the corporation in any meaningful way and must be used with care because of their obvious limitations. The most important aspect of model building is studying the system behavior and underlying feedback mechanisms.

A Conceptual Framework for Micro Economic Planning Models

A corporate planning model is an abstraction of the complex dynamic interrelationships among a company's financial, marketing and production activities usually expressed as a system of linear and nonlinear difference--differential equations and logical relationships. The system of equations usually contains simultaneous and recursive blocks with dynamic linkages between blocks and between components in the same block expressed as a system of first and higher order positive and negative feedback loops. In the language of econometrics the model is a disequilibrium model in which adjustment process goes beyond the simple first-order exponential delay of the stock adjustment scheme to include pascal and rational distributed lag mechanisms. It represents, not, an idealized conception of behavioral relationships which describe how decisions are made in the homogeneous firm of the perfectly competitive market place, but actual behavioral relationships of a real firm in which decisions are made in an environment characterized by risk and uncertainty.

Suppose, for example, that a firm can be symbolically represented by a dynamic structural system of the following sort:

$$AX_t + BY_t + \sum_{i=1}^{m} C_i Y_{t-i} + DZ_t = U_t$$

X_t is a vector of exogenous variables (variables which are not explained by the model such as economic, demographic, or political); Y_t is a vector of endogenous variables (variables whose values are determined by the model such as revenues, output, costs, profits); Y_{t-i} is a vector of lagged endogenous variables, Z_t is a vector of control of managerial decision variables (such as prices, wage rates, promotion expenditures); U_t is a vector of random variables; and A, B, C, D are coefficient matrices whose parameters have been empirically estimated. The model is dynamic because the variables are time dependent and at least one of the endogenous variables appears as an explanatory variable somewhere else in the system. It is this latter condition which produces the feedback linkages described earlier.

Such a model liberates the user from having to assume knowledge of the firm's objective (criterion) function or targets of the decision maker. The system is solved for the time pattern of the variables in Y_t in terms of X_t, Y_{t-i}, Z_t and U_t. The solution to such a system, what economists call "the reduced form" is determined analytically in the case of a linear system and by an iterative method in the case of non-linear systems.

For any given values of the managerial decision variables, the time paths of the endogenous variables can be generated. Management can change the environmental assumptions implicit in the values of the exogenous variables, simulate to assess corporate performance and then choose that set of managerial decision variables which achieve the desired goals.

For a given corporation, division of a company, or strategic business unit, the financial, marketing and production relationship can be conveniently expressed as an integrated system. This framework is illustrated in Figure 2.

Each unit has a marketing model which corresponds to but goes beyond the demand equations of the traditional model. Within this block are the demand equations for the unit's products, the price equations and the revenue functions. Firms are not assumed to be price takers. Prices are control variables for the firm. Their

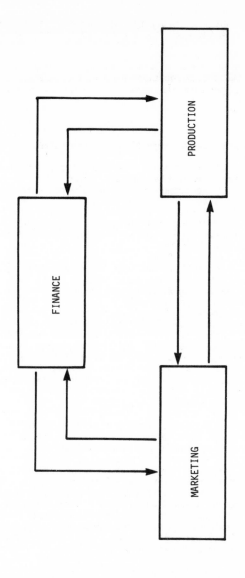

Figure 2. An Integrated Planning Model

values depend on both unit costs and operating margins. Demand considerations
enter price decisions through the size of the mark-up of over costs and investment
financing needs.

The marketing model is the key block in the corporate planning model. The potential output derived from the demand equations becomes the inputs to the production
block which, if feasible, generate the associated costs which are then used to
compute output prices.

The links are as follows:

1. Starting values for all control variables are generated, including prices.

2. The demand equations contain variables designed to capture the influence of
    relative prices and other competitive factors, advertising, personal incomes,
    economic activity, etc. The output prices which appear are computed on the
    basis of a mark-up over costs.

3. The mark-up reflects the firm's profit objectives tempered by the price elas-
    ticity of demand and market activity, and long term liquidity considerations
    in light of investment requirements.

4. Given the potential outputs calculated from the demand equations, production
    costs are computed. These production costs become inputs into the marketing
    block where output prices are recomputed.

5. Both costs and revenues generated from the marketing and production blocks are
    used to produce a statement of profitability. This profit and loss statement
    is an important part of the finance model which also contains equations to
    generate the unit's balance sheet and cash flow statement. Given the output
    and price linkages between the marketing and production models, the model is
    simulated until a desired time path for the systems criterion variables:
    profits, cash flow, etc. are produced and the resulting output and price
    configuration is a feasible one with regard to both internal production
    constraints and market and competitive constraints.

As Figure 3 indicates, a consolidated corporate planning model is driven by a
series of integrated business unit planning models describing the individual
businesses of the company. These models may be used either on a stand-alone basis
at the business unit or as a component of a larger model describing the activities
of the corporation. The corporate planning model itself consists of the sum of
these individual integrated business unit models summarized by the box which reads
Corporate Financial Model. Figure 3 also illustrates the importance of regional
and macro models which provide the values of many of the exogenous variables in
the integrated models. In particular, the demand equations in the marketing
models depend on local and national economic and demographic variables, the values
of which are supplied by these satellite models. The linkage between the corporate planning model and the regional model is a crucial one in corporate planning.

An Application: The Elements of a Newspaper Model

The New York Times model is structurally composed of two major blocks: a demand
model and a production, cost, and revenue model. The demand model, the heart of
the model, is a set of simultaneous non-linear econometric equations which forecast physical volume, approximately 35 categories of advertising lines and 10
categories of circulation. The second block is recursive and contains roughly 300
equations, some of which are stochastic behavioral equations. This block converts
the volume forecasts into paging, newsprint consumption, newsprint distribution,
and labor requirements. These physical flows are then monetized, using price and
wage forecasts, to produce estimates of revenue, fixed and variable costs, and
operating profit.

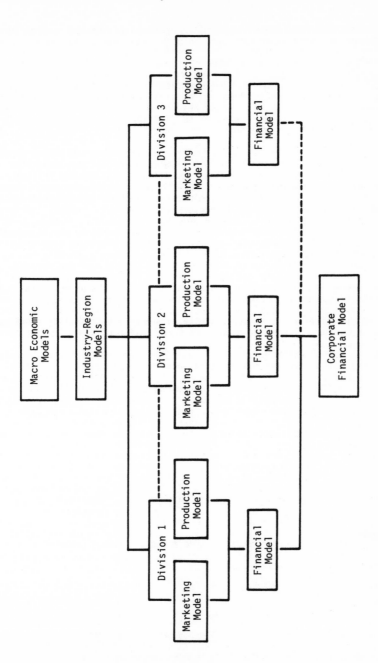

Figure 3. A Conceptual Framework for Corporate Models

A newspaper produces two different products and sells them in two different markets. It sells copies to readers and space to advertisers. By itself, there is nothing unusual in this. However, for newspapers, this joint product presents unusual marketing problems. The demand for advertising space is greatly affected by the sale of copies. There is also evidence of reverse causality although the relationship is weaker. A newspaper becomes a more attractive vehicle for advertisers the larger its circulation base. Similarly, many people purchase a paper for its advertising content which provides readers with an information alternative to new content. It is even more unusual to find that the demand for space is affected by the character of the newspaper's readers. In this case, class does matter.

Newspaper planning models typically include demand equations and production and technical relationships. There are demand equations for advertising lines and circulation copies. The news department is allocated space by assigning them a percentage of total space above a fixed minimum commitment. Above that minimum level, news linage allocated varies linearly with advertising linage. The allocation is based on production--newspaper make-up requirements, product quality considerations and profitability requirements. At the New York Times newspaper, product quality takes precedence over profitability. The organizational structure is evidence of this. The executive editor of the newspaper reports directly to the CEO and has the same status as a group vice president for the corporation.

Closing the demand block are circulation and advertising rate equations. The advertising "rate card" is exceedingly complex and can be conceptualized as a three dimensional grid. Rates vary across categories as well as within each category. In the latter case, rates vary with time and space. That is, they vary by category, by volume and by the number of days an advertisement appears in the paper.

The demand model is a simultaneous block of non-linear equations for advertising lines and copies sold. Both outputs are sold in oligopolistic markets with varying product differentiation and intense non-price competition. Because the Sunday and daily papers are distinct products, Sunday and weekday advertising and circulation are treated separately. Conceptually, the demand for each output is treated as a function of its price, the price of its competitors, indicators of market activity, and equality. Symbolically, the demand for circulation looks like the following:

$$CIRC_{ti} = F_3 (P_i, P_{ji}, Prom, M_n, Q)$$

where $CIRC_{ti}$ = average circulation in period t for the ith market

   P_i = the unit price per copy in the ith market

   P_{ji} = the price of the competitive product in the ith market

   Prom = promotion expenditures

   M_i = indicator of market activity

   Q   = quality

The variable quality is a measure of the appeal of the paper to its readers. Potential readership depends on attitudes which in turn depend on education, household income, occupation, orientation to New York City, politics.

Similarly, the demand for advertising lines;

$$L_{ti} = F_4 (P_i, P_{ji}, Prom, Q, M_1, ...M_n)$$

where all variables are defined as above and L_{ti} is advertising lines for the ith category in period t. The variable Q represents the quality of a unit of linage to the advertiser as measured by the purchasing power of its readers, prestige of the newspaper, and readership. Generally, circulation demographics can be used as a proxy variable for advertising quality.

Figure 4 shows the model in terms of its financial flows. The dotted and solid lines represent the linkages between sectors. Of course, the dynamics are best revealed in diagram 1 where the system's dynamics rather than the financial flows are shown.

The dotted lines are an attempt to surface the underlying dynamics. The solid lines represent dollar flows while the dotted lines portray the interaction between these dollar flows. The arrows indicate the presumed direction of the interaction. For example, expenditures for promotion influence advertising and circulation revenues by impacting sales volume. Conversely, advertising and circulation revenues constrain the dollars available for promotion expenditures.

The production process is a modification of activity analysis. Given the difficulty of reducing corporate objectives to a single objective, no attempt is made to optimize with respect to production costs. Instead, an experimental approach is adopted where alternative production plans are evaluated through the use of simulation.

The production function for a newspaper is vector valued with output defined as the number of copies produced and the number of pages per copy or:

$$Q_t = \begin{bmatrix} C_t \\ P_t \end{bmatrix} = F(K_t, L_t, TC_t, M_t)$$

where

$\quad Q_t \quad = \quad$ output

$\quad C_t \quad = \quad$ copies produced

$\quad P_t \quad = \quad$ pages per copy

$\quad K_t \quad = \quad$ capital stock

$\quad L_t \quad = \quad$ labor

$\quad TC_t \quad = \quad$ technological change

$\quad M_t \quad = \quad$ materials (newsprint, ink)

Pages per copy is built up by combining the number of pages of advertising with the number of editorial pages, both derived from the demand model. Costs are computed in a two step procedure as follows:

First a resource requirements vector is computed by post-multiplying the final demand vector (pages, copies) by an estimated input-output matrix:

$$R = A * Q$$

where

A = input-output matrix whose elements denote the quantity of input; required to produce output j

Q = Vector of Outputs

R = Vector of Resource Requirements

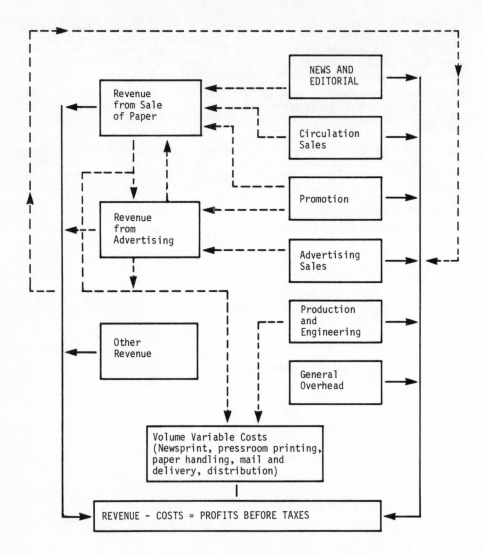

Figure 4.   Simulation Model: Conceptual Framework

Q, the vector of outputs, is disaggregated into a number of components depending on whether the element in the vector represents daily or Sunday circulation, area of distribution, section of the paper.

Each component is vector valued. That is, each component consists of total copies produced and pages per copy. Costs are computed by the following identity:

$$C = P * R$$

where

P = resources price vector

C = costs associated with P * R

Given alternative assumptions about regional and aggregate economic activity, generated by simulating the regional and macro models, a variety of planning scenarios can be generated to provide management with a set of strategic alternatives upon which to base their plans.

CONCLUSION

Experience indicates that most managers are able to specify, at least in a qualitative way, the detailed relationships between corporate policies, company performance, and the market and competitive environment. That is, they can identify the single equation relationships. However, the linkages between equations and the dynamic behavior implied by those relationships are almost impossible to cope with.

Successful planning requires an understanding of the consequences of corporate decisions and actions, the evaluation of corporate performance as a result of changes in the business environment and the ability to do numerous calculations which trace through the impacts of such changes. Given the size and complexity of most firms, the requirements for effective planning limit success if planning is based solely on intuition and experience.

Corporate planning requires the use of planning models. Models allow decision-makers the freedom to examine numerous factors, either individually or simultaneously which might impact the firm. They provide a means of assessing the impact of different corporate policies on corporate performance under a wide variety of operating and environmental assumptions. While models cannot predict which events will eventually unfold, they can give managers a feel for the consequences if they do occur. The design of policies and contingency plans can be dramatically enhanced through the judicious use of a planning model.

PRODUCT PORTFOLIO MODELS

Joel Huber and John McCann

Fuqua School of Business
Duke University
Durham, North Carolina
U.S.A.

This paper is about portfolio models. The portfolio models with which we will be dealing have as their goal the allocation of resources at the corporate level among the various business that makes up a firm. As the name "portfolio" suggests, the resultant mix of business is balanced with respect to variables such as cash flow, managerial needs, or risk.

There appears to be a bewildering array of these portfolio models. These models take different forms that are applied differently in different companies. Like the stars in the heavens, they take various shapes depending on the observer. Our perspective is more like that of a star gazer than an astrologer -- we neither identify constellations nor make our living from deriving predictions from their shapes. Still we would like to know which astrologer to trust, and whether that rising constellation is really a bear or a bull.

For the sake of simplicity, we will concentrate on three models that have perhaps received the most attention--the Boston Consulting Group's [4] growth/share matrix; the industry attractiveness/business position matrix, first developed as G.E.'s Business Screen (Abell and Hammond [1]), and the PIMS model (Strategic Planning Institute [19]). We had originally planned to evaluate all three models on the same criteria. We found, however, that the models have different orientations and ultimately different criteria by which they are appropriately judged and used. Thus the business screen is seen as primarily a process oriented model, in contrast to the BCG model which can be characterized as a hypothesis whose usefulness depends on the appropriateness of its assumptions to the firm. Finally, the PIMS model differs from these in being an empirical model whose validity depends on the correspondence between the estimated coefficients and the conceptual phenomena under study. While these characterizations are admittedly caricatures, the differences across models are great enough to render inappropriate the use of identical evaluative criteria for each model.

BUSINESS SCREEN: A PROCESS MODEL

When one examines the BCG and the Business Screen Portfolio models (Figures 1 and 2) for their testable truth content, an interesting difference emerges. While the BCG model has several testable consequences, there are far fewer testable consequences to the general Business Screen. This distinction can be seen in Figure 3. The models differ with respect to their inputs, orientations, and finally, the criteria by which they should be judged.

In terms of inputs, for the Business Screen the members of the firm typically determine the location of various businesses with respect to industry attractiveness and business position on subjective scales. For example, the size of a business (one component of Business Position) might be rated as one of three categories: High = 1.0, Medium = 0.5, Low = 0.0 (Abel and Hammond [1, p. 219]). Furthermore, even if the score on a component is determined objectively, the weight it is given with respect to business position is determined subjectively. By contrast, for the BCG model, once market boundaries have been determined, the

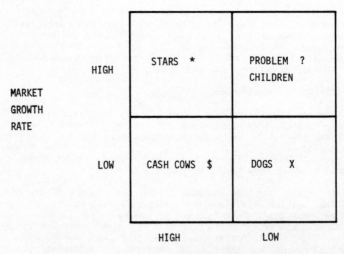

```
                              ┌─────────┬─────────┬─────────┐
                       HIGH   │ INVEST  │  SHARE  │  HOLD   │
                              ├─────────┼─────────┼─────────┤
INDUSTRY                      │         │         │         │
                       MED.   │  GAIN   │         │  STARVE │
ATTRACTIVENESS                │         │         │         │
                              ├─────────┼─────────┼─────────┤
. MARKET GROWTH               │         │         │         │
                       LOW    │ SELECT  │ DIVEST  │         │
. MARKET SIZE                 └─────────┴─────────┴─────────┘
                               STRONG    MEDIUM    WEAK
. MARKET CYCLICITY

. MARKET CONCENTRATION

. TECHNOLOGICAL               BUSINESS POSITION
  MATURITY
                              . ADVANTAGE IN TECHNOLOGY
. COMPETITIVE
  CONCENTRATION               . ADVANTAGE IN MARKETING

                              . ADVANTAGE IN PRODUCTION

                              . SIZE

                              . MARKET SHARE
```

Figure 1. Business Screen

```
                              ┌───────────────┬───────────────┐
                              │               │               │
                     HIGH     │  STARS    *   │  PROBLEM   ?  │
                              │               │  CHILDREN     │
        MARKET                │               │               │
        GROWTH                ├───────────────┼───────────────┤
        RATE                  │               │               │
                              │               │               │
                     LOW      │  CASH COWS $  │  DOGS     X   │
                              │               │               │
                              └───────────────┴───────────────┘
                                 HIGH            LOW
                                RELATIVE MARKET SHARE
```

Figure 2. The Boston Consulting Group Growth/Share Matrix

Figure 3

DIFFERENCES BETWEEN PROCESS AND

NORMATIVE PORTFOLIO MODELS

EXAMPLE	. G.E.'s BUSINESS SCREEN	. B.C.G.'S GROWTH/ SHARE
INPUTS AND RELATIONS AMONG VARIABLES	. SUBJECTIVELY DETERMINED	. OBJECTIVELY DETERMINED
ORIENTATION	. BOTTOM-UP	. TOP-DOWN
	. PROCESS	. REDIRECTION
CRITERIA FOR EXCELLENCE	. CONSISTENCY	. APPLICABILITY OF ASSUMPTIONS
	. HARMONY	. REASONABLENESS OF RECOMMENDA- TIONS

position of each of the businesses and the strategic implications of these positions are quite fixed.

This difference in inputs affects both the orientation of the models and their
testability as scientific hypotheses. The orientation of the business screen is
with respect to the process of planning. It would be virtually impossible to
implement without rather elaborate information from the businesses themselves.
Further the process of deriving the subjective positions and weights is amenable
to averaging and identification of conflicts among raters. Thus the method has a
way to identify conflict so that consensus is possible, and a way to average to
produce compromises.

By contrast, the lack of subjective inputs in the BCG model enables it to have a
more top-down orientation. It can be used to justify changes without extensive
input from middle management. Of course, this relative lack of involvement of the
BCG approach could be either an advantage or a disadvantage depending on the
managerial style of the company.

To the extent that portfolio models represent processes rather than hypotheses,
they cannot be tested for truth content in the normal sense of that phrase.
Indeed, the very flexibility of the Business Screen renders it inappropriate as
testable hypothesis, since only the recommendations from particular implementa-
tions can be tested, not the general procedure. The procedure can however be
evaluated in terms of efficiency--whether it results in consistency and harmony
with the firm.

The assumptions and predictions in the Business Screen are determined by the
members of the firm in estimating the positions of the businesses and the weights
of the characteristics. If these inputs are wrong, the process will produce poor
results, but the process is not true or false, any more than the process of
democracy is true or false.

Thus, whether a process oriented model should be used in a firm depends on whether
one believes that the members of the firm can collectively determine the best
strategy for themselves. Generally, strategies evolving out of models such as
the Business Screen can be expected to be somewhat more conservative, effecting
relatively small marginal changes from the status quo. However, one can also
expect that both the incremental nature of the recommendations and the consensual
nature of the process will increase the likelihood that the final strategy will be
implemented. In terms of deciding which consensual model to use, we must defer to
the organizational theorists, and they have been remarkably mute on the issue.

THE BCG MODEL: RECOMMENDATIONS AND ASSUMPTIONS

The preceding has intentionally made a distinction between the BCG approach and
the Business Screen approach. In point of fact, the actual implementation of both
models may be far more similar than was suggested. A great deal of bottom-up
thinking may go into the formulation of a BCG strategy. Indeed, the hidden agenda
of any BCG exercise may be the determination of the market boundaries since the
results depend so critically on that framing. Furthermore, in spite of its
bottom-up orientation, the Business Screen can certainly be manipulated by top
management to achieve their goals under the guise of participative management.

But the BCG model is unique in having a set of relatively firm recommendations
that follow from a set of assumptions. Furthermore, the lack of a consensual base
for the BCG precepts makes it even more important that the model be validated
outside the firm. Thus we shall consider the reasonableness of its recommendation
in the context of the validity of its assumptions.

The precepts of the BCG model follow a simple and intuitively pleasing barnyard
metaphor, which in itself has been a factor in the success of the model. There

are four recommendations:

1. Milk Cows

   Take excess resources from high share/low growth and put them into high growth businesses.

2. Support Stars

   Sustain share in high growth and high market share businesses.

3. Breed Selected Heifers

   Choose from among those that are high growth and low share and breed only those whose offspring will come to have high share.

4. Starve Dogs

   Sell, or starve those businesses that are low growth and low share. Alternatively you may sic the dogs on your competitor.

Thus BCG advocates that one Milk Cows, Support Stars, Breed Selected Heifers, and Starve Dogs. We will here examine three assumptions that underlie these precepts. These three are (1) the experience curve, (2) that market share is easier to attain earlier in the life cycle rather than later and (3) corporate communism.

Assumption 1: The Experience Curve

As developed by the Boston Consulting Group (1972), the experience curve provides a unifying justification for their precepts. If costs are a decreasing function of total experience and the market has been relatively stable (so that market shares are a good surrogate for total experience) then the experience curve gives a good explanation for the empirically found association between profitability and market share. Then, if one allows that growing companies need more cash than those that are not growing, a simple cash constraint leads to the four precepts just given.

While one may question the validity of the experience curve (Abernathy and Wayne [2]), it is also possible to acknowledge its reality and claim its inappropriateness for many industries. Consider consumer goods companies such as General Foods or Proctor and Gamble. While the experience curve may apply to a new production technology, such aspects tend to reflect a very small part of value added for consumer goods companies. Instead, much of value added is carried in the distribution and promotion function, activities quite far down the experience curve. It has been argued (Sherer [17, p. 251]) that the experience curve has less strategic importance for such mature corporate functions. The fluidity of employees, ideas and techniques means that the advantage enjoyed by the most experienced firm will be less than implied by experience curve. Indeed, in advertising one might argue that too much experience leads to creative atrophy rather than more efficiency. Put simply, the experience curve is generally not an important strategic issue for consumer goods companies. What drives the correlation between share and profitability in such companies instead are scale economies and shared costs across the different businesses.

The implications, however, of the cost-profitability relationship being driven by shared costs and economies of scale are very different from one driven by experience. If a company is behind a competitor with respect to accumulated experience, it is very difficult to ever catch up. The more experienced competitor can simply match any attempts to gain share. Because of a more favorable cost structure, the experienced competitor will be more viable in a sustained struggle to gain share. By contrast, assuming a "U" shaped cost curve, economies of scale can be bought by simply purchasing or building a plant of sufficient size, while the promotional and distribution costs can be shared with other brands the company offers.

An example of such a successful move in the face of competitor's experience is the thrust of Proctor and Gamble into paper products. They purchased the paper-making facilities, invested in new technology, and within ten years were able to become the market leader in diapers (Pampers), premium toilet tissue (Charmin), and paper towels (Bounty). This occurred in spite of the fact that their major competitor, Scott Paper Company, had far more accumulated experience in paper products.

Thus, while the experience curve might be a good justification for applying the BCG precepts for certain high technology products, it breaks down with products where the value added is for aspects of the offering that are far down the experience curve.

Assumption 2: Market Share is Cheaper to Buy in High Rather Than Low Growth Industries

This assumption is crucial if one advocates shifting funds from low to high growth businesses within a firm. If the assumption does not hold then one would advocate buying share in the mature stages of the product life cycle.

Where the experience curve is an important force, the built-up experience of competitors could be said to deter attempts to shift market share later in the product life cycle. Furthermore, the large investments in plant and equipment found in so many producer goods companies result in strong competitive price reactions to avoid underutilization of capital equipment. For consumer goods, particularly frequently purchased ones, as we have argued, the experience curve is less of an issue. Further, over-capacity may be less of a problem to the extent that plants are adaptable to produce other consumer goods.

However, for consumer goods Assumption 2 is probably justified because of the hardening of consumer tastes and distribution channels over time. For frequently puchased non-durables, purchase habits once developed are difficult to change. Similarly, distribution patterns become fixed so that a new entry may have great difficulty getting shelf space or promotional support from channel numbers.

Thus the assumption that share is easier to get in high rather than low growth markets is probably justified (for a contrary view see Dhalla and Yuspeh, 1976) but the source of that justification differs somewhat in consumer and producer markets.

As an ominous aside, the situation could be reversed in the future, ironically following from firms using the BCG framework. Suppose a firm sets in motion the transfer of funds from cash cows to stars or selecting heifers; this action might provide a competitive opening against a relatively weakened cash cow. One could conjecture that the successful attack of Phillip Morris on the cigarette business was possible, in part, by R.J. Reynolds' practice of making corporate acquisitions with funds from its mature cigarette business.

Assumption 3: Corporate Communism

Almost all of the portfolio models, by virtue of their goal of re-allocating resources across businesses within a firm, echo Carl Marx's dictum that resources should flow to each according to needs and from each according to ability. Those with needs, of course, are high growth business requiring cash, while those with abilities are the low growth business being divested or milked for funds. The arguments against such corporate communism are painfully similar to those against transfer payments in any social system -- that the fruit of success should be consumed by those who generated it or there will be less motivation for succeeding.

In a corporate environment where success is measured in terms of control over resources then taking away such resources from those who gain them will be perceived as unfair and may ultimately act as a deterrent to taking risks.

In particular, the implementation of portfolio models can be expected to conflict with both the motivational effects and the assigned responsibility of a strong profit center orientation.* With respect to motivation, a manager asked to strip cash from a low growth/low share business is being asked to reduce the power and influence of that position. In terms of responsibility, restricting the degree to which a manager can reinvest earnings from a high share business provides an excuse for lessened performance.

By relating corporate communism to the political system we are not implying there is any inconsistency in espousing a free market across firms but transfers within a firm. Certainly, the nuclear family is a kind of communistic unit -- where each element contributes according to abilities and benefits according to needs -- but people believing in the family would not generally be considered procommunist. The issue is whether the family model works in a corporation, a question less of ideology than practicality. To the extent that a profit center philosophy is needed to motivate and orient the managers within a firm, this philosophy will conflict with any portfolio model.

In summary, the issue of the validity of the two portfolio models was first related to the degree of falsifiable content in the model. Those aspects of models which, in their implementation or design, are largely reflections of managers' beliefs are difficult to test, and indeed "truth" may be the wrong criterion relative to the ability of the portfolio model to achieve consensus and consistency of action within the firm. By contrast, those aspects of portfolio models that result in normative recommendations are important to validate. We have just considered the validity of three assumptions. These limit the applicability of the BCG model to businesses where the experience curve is a significant competitive factor, where market share is cheaper to buy earlier in the product life cycle, and where the profit center orientation is not primary in the firm.

PIMS: AN EMPIRICAL MODEL

By contrast to the process oriented Business Screen or the normative BCG model, the PIMS model can best be characterized as an empirical model. The inputs, coming from the PIMS questionnaire, are relatively objective, like BCG, once the product market has been determined. The relationships, however, are empirically derived from a cross-sectional analysis of a large sample of businesses, rather than flowing from managers' beliefs or from a theoretical construct such as the experience curve. The detail of the ROI and cash flow models allows the model to be used as a simulation tool. For portfolio planning the model simulates the ROI and cash flow implications of actions on different businesses. When aggregated the effect of different allocation decisions across businesses can be estimated (Strategic Planning Institute [19]).

To assess the validity of the PIMS model for portfolio planning, we must examine the model itself. Schoeffler [16, p. 111] asks us to consider three tests: (1) is the explanatory variable statistically significant, (2) does the model conform to available theory, and (3) does it make sense to knowledgeable businessmen? How-

---

*A profit center orientation is to be distinguished from a profit center accounting system. The former works on the model of an independent businessman, responsible for actions, and the primary recipient of the outcomes. Portfolio models can be implemented by accounting conventions (assigning one manager to minimize costs, one to maximize sales, another to maximize long run profit), but these generally have a dampening effect on a profit center orientation.

ever, we have chosen to ask a somewhat different question, namely, "Do the coefficient estimates measure the conceptual phenomenon under study?" In using the
PIMS model as a portfolio planning tool, the manager is assessing the impact of
such strategic moves as increasing the marketing expenditures of business A versus
increases in the R&D budget of business B. To provide accurate answers to such
questions, the model must contain valid coefficient estimates of the impact of
the strategic and environmental variables on ROI. Whereas Schoeffler would rely
on statistical significance and the sign of the coefficient (theory and business
knowledge rarely go beyond the sign of the relationships), we propose that we examine the degree to which single-equation estimates obtained from cross-sectional
data can be utilized to ascertain the impact of strategic moves which must occur
over time.

SIMULTANEOUS RELATIONSHIPS

First, we will examine the problems associated with using a single regression
equation to model a very complex world involving many factors. The PIMS ROI model
relates Return-on-Investment (ROI) to 37 explanatory variables plus a large array
of cross-product terms [16]. The model parameters are estimated via Ordinary
Least-Squares (OLS), with the usual set of assumptions about the variables and
disturbance term. Implicit in the use of OLS is the assumption that the direction
of influence is from the "explanatory variables" to ROI, and that the level of ROI
does not have a simultaneous influence on at least some explanatory variables.
Such an assumption may not be justified, as would be indicated by the work of
other researchers. Elliott [8], in a study of the factors influencing marketing
expenditures, found that the ratio of marketing expense to sales was related to
the firm's discretionary income, i.e., discretionary income impacts marketing
expenditures. Schendel and Patton [15] found that not only did market share
influence ROI, but ROI seemed to impact attained market share. The simultaneous
nature of the various factors termed "explanatory variables" is confirmed in
studies by Tsurumi and Tsurumi [20], Mueller [13], and Elliott [9].

If such simultaneity exists and is ignored in the model, then the estimates of
the parameters will be both biased and inconsistent [11]. This latter property
means that increases in the number of businesses in the PIMS database cannot
overcome the difficulties with the model, i.e., the large sample will not permit
the "delineation of very complex patterns", as claimed by Schoeffler [16, p. 111].
Hence, unless the simultaneous nature of markets and decision-making is incorporated into the PIMS models, portfolio recommendations may not be valid due to
the use of models with biased coefficients.

USE OF CROSS-SECTIONAL MODEL FOR TIME-ORIENTED APPLICATIONS

One of the original purposes of the PIMS project was to allow a firm to obtain an
estimate of the average ROI of businesses which were similar to the business under
study. The regression model is a useful tool for determining the "predicted"
level of ROI given a profile of characteristics. However, the PIMS model has been
given other uses, particularly the determination of the impact of changes in one
of a business' explanatory variables on the ROI of that business [10]. In using
the model for this latter purpose, the firm would input data on the current level
of each of its characteristics, and the computer model would output the impact of
a change in each characteristic on the ROI of the business. Such print-outs,
termed Strategy Sensitivity Reports, permit management to "explore the implications of making fundamental changes in the strategy of a business, and the performance trade-offs that might be involved in the short and long run" [1, p. 28].

The effect on ROI of making a change in a variable is determined by the estimate
of the coefficient of that variable (plus the magnitude of the change). Quite
apart from the problem of simultaneous relationships, the accuracy of predictions
in the Strategy Sensitivity Report depends upon the degree to which coefficient
estimates obtained from cross-sectional data can be used to determine the impact

of changes which occur over time. That is, can we use a model estimated across businesses to infer the impact of a change within a business.

This problem was considered by Ed Kuh over 20 years ago in the article "The Validity of Cross-Sectionally Estimated Behavior Equations in Time Series Applications" [12], a title which succinctly describes the question confronting the use of PIMS models for time-oriented predictions. Kuh's approach was largely empirical in the sense that he compared parameter estimates from cross-section data with corresponding estimates from time-series data. In particular, he estimated an investment function which related investment to profit and capital stock and found that the "cross-section estimates of the profit coefficient are typically almost twice as large as the corresponding time-series estimates, while the capital stock coefficients are substantially smaller." Kuh explained the difference via a specification-bias argument and concluded that "we cannot estimate dynamic coefficients from cross-sections with any degree of confidence unless there is supporting time-series information." He goes on to state that estimates from cross-sections do serve useful purposes, but not in time-series applications. Hence, Kuh's empirical work indicates that the results in a Strategy Sensitivity Report should be considered biased and hence suspect.

Although Kuh's work indicated a bias in the coefficient estimates, it was the work of Dennis Aigner and Julian Simon [18], (Aigner and Simon [3]) which clearly defined the source of bias. The source of bias derives from the fact that factors which impact a firm's profits are dynamic in nature in that their impact can be spread over several years. Since models based upon data from a single time-period must ignore this dynamic nature of the world, they suffer from the "omitted variables" problem. The proof, which is sketched below in terms of an ROI model, is shown in Aigner and Simon [3] and the result is used in Simon and Aigner [3] to resolve some conflicts which evolved from Milton Friedman's Permanent-Income Hypothesis.

Suppose ROI is actually related to both the current and lagged values of a set of explanation variables by the following model

$$ROI = AX + BY + E, \qquad (1)$$

where X is a matrix of observations on the current levels of a set of explanatory variables; Y is a matrix of the lagged values of the same variables; A and B are vectors of parameters, and E is a random disturbance term. Suppose, however, that data are collected for one time-period, and the following model estimated:

$$ROI = aX + u, \qquad (2)$$

where a is a vector of coefficients and u is a disturbance term. The key question concerns the degree to which the estimate of a, termed $\hat{a}$, captures only the current effect of X or both the current and lagged effects of X. It could be argued that since Y is omitted in equation (2), we would like the parameter $\hat{a}$ to provide an estimate of A, and not the sum of A and B. However, if we are using the model to predict the total impact of a variable on ROI, we would want "$\hat{a}$" to measure A+B. The degree to which the estimate of "$\hat{a}$" measures A or A+B can be obtained by examining the expected value of a. It was shown by Aigner and Simon (1970) that the following relationship holds,

$$E(\hat{a}) = A + CB, \qquad (3)$$

where C is the vector of regression coefficients in the following model

$$Y = CX + V,$$

i.e., the regression of the omitted lagged variables on their current values. It appears from this case that $\hat{a}$ measures current impact when C = 0, or when explanatory variables have no correlation between current and lagged values. Further, â measures the sum of current and lagged effects when the variables have perfect correlation between current and lagged values.

The problem is more complex when the degree of autocorrelation differs among the explanatory variables. To see implications of the problem, consider a hypothetical situation in which there are only two explanatory variables, with each variable impacting ROI in the current period and in one lagged period. The appropriate model would be

$$ROI = a_1 X_t + a_2 X_{t-1} + b_1 Y_t + b_2 Y_{t-1} + U_t \tag{4}$$

where X and Y denote the two explanatory variables. However, if we only have cross-sectional data, we would have to estimate the model

$$ROI_i = C X_i + DY_i + e_i$$

where the subscript "i" denotes a unique business. If X and Y are uncorrelated, the expected value of the estimates of C is given by

$$E\left[\hat{C}\right] = a_1 + a_2\beta \tag{5}$$

where β is the regression slope of regressing X_{t-1} on X_t, (i.e., the slope in the model $X_t = \alpha + \beta X_{t-1}$). The parameter β is a measure of the autocorrelation in the explanatory variable X. As pointed out by Aigner and Simon [3], when we are considering yearly data, the variance of the explanatory variables is fairly constant over time, which allows us to reduce equation (5) to

$$E\left[\hat{C}\right] = a_1 + a_2 P_x, \tag{6}$$

where P_x, is first-order autocorrelation in the variable x. Similarly, the expected value of D is given by

$$E\left[\hat{D}\right] = b_1 + b_2 P_y, \tag{7}$$

where P_y, is the first-order autocorrelation in the variable Y.

From equations (6) and (7), it is clear that to understand the meaning of the estimate of the impact of an explanatory variable obtained from cross-sectional data, we must consider the time-series property of the variable itself. Consider three situations and the implications for the estimated parameters.

1. The explanatory variable is relatively stable over time, which means that autocorrelation in the X variable is very high, i.e., $P_x \cong 1.0$. In this case, the estimate of C captures the total impact of the variable X because $E\left[\hat{C}\right] \cong a_1 + a_2$.

2. The explanatory variable varies erratically from period to period, which means that $P_x \cong 0.0$. In this case, the cross-sectional regression only measures the current impact of the variable.

3. Increases in the explanatory variable are followed by decreases in the variable, which means that the explanatory variables exhibit negative autocorrelation. In such a situation, the cross-sectional estimate of the impact of the variable has no meaning and may indeed have the wrong sign.

Based upon these implications, it appears that the coefficients in the PIMS model may not provide an accurate estimate of the impact of a change in an explanatory variable on ROI. That is, the conclusions are sensitive to the autocorrelation properties of the various explanatory variables. The potential nature of these conclusions are given in the following table.

Autocorrelation Property of Explanatory Variable	Potential Conclusion of PIMS Model Based Upon Cross-Sectional Data Given Variable Is Important
Stable (Positive auto-correlation) Example: Capital Intensity	Very Important Variable Measures Total Impact
Fluctuates Erratically (Zero Autocorrelation) Example: Advertising	Under-stated Importance of Variable (Measure Only Current Impact)
Cyclical (Negative Autocorrelation) Example: Inventory	Uncertain Importance . Could indicate inaccurate direction if lagged effect is greater than current effect . Could indicate no relationship if current and lagged effect are about equal

If in equation (1), the variable X was highly autocorrelated but the variable Y exhibited very little autocorrelation, the cross-sectional regression model would yield parameter estimates which would tend to understate the impact of Y relative to X. When such a model is used for portfolio planning, it would lead to the selection of products and/or strategies which utilized the X variable as a strategic variable.

These problems - simultaneity and dynamic application of a static model - cause us to question the use of PIMS models for strategic purposes. However, the PIMS project has sufficient data to perhaps overcome both problems. The rich data-set should permit the formulation and estimation of simultaneous equation models. In fact, published work utilizing the PIMS data indicates that a good foundation is in place for such work. Buzzell, Gale, and Sultan [5] have developed a model of market share, Buzzell and Farris [6] have modelled marketing costs, and Reibstein and Farris [14] have studied the pricing decision.

The models can be made dynamic by adding time-series information to the cross-section of businesses. Since the PIMS project has been in operation since 1970, the data base should contain time-series of up to 10 years for some of the businesses. Techniques are available for combining or pooling these data which should be able to overcome the bias problem inherent in cross-sectional models.

CONCLUSION

Let us return at last to our perspective of the star gazer struggling to get meaning out of a configuration of business units in competitive space. As astrological systems the three portfolio models each have unique advantages and disadvantages. The Product Screen is the most flexible in that both the positions and the direction of the celestial bodies are defined by the managers. While this may lead to more consistency internally it also renders the system difficult to verify externally. The BCG model, in defining both the constellations (cash cows, heifers) and their meanings (milk cows, breed heifers), is somewhat more bucolic and primitive than, say, Ursa Major or Sagittarius (or even Business Position, for that matter). Its very simplicity, however, allows one to test the appropriateness of its precepts for the firm. The PIMS model, by contrast, is the most similar to early attempts to transform astrology into astronomy. The position of a firm is assumed to be related to its past position and velocity and influenced by the effect of other bodies in the heavens. Like the early attempts at astronomy, however, such analyses require more data and more careful specification of the relationships before we can be confident in their predictions.

REFERENCES

[1] Abell, Derek F. and John S. Hammond. Strategic Market Planning, Englewood Cliffs, New Jersey: Prentice-Hall, 1979.

[2] Abernathy, William J. and Kenneth Wayne. "Limits of the Learning Curve", Harvard Business Review, 52 (September, 1974), 109-119.

[3] Aigner, Dennis J. and Julian L. Simon. "A Specification Bias Interpretation of Cross-Section vs. Time Series Parameter Estimates", Western Economic Journal, June 1970, 144-61.

[4] Boston Consulting Group. Perspectives on Experience, Boston, 1972.

[5] Buzzell, Robert D., Bradley, T. Gale and Ralph G. M. Sultan. "Market Share - A Key to Profitability", Harvard Business Review, January-February 1975.

[6] Buzzell, Robert D. and Paul Farris, "Marketing Costs in Consumer Goods Industries", in Strategy + Structure = Performance: The Strategic Planning Imperative, Hans B. Thorelli (Ed.), Indiana University Press, 1977.

[7] Dhalla, Norman K. and Sonia Yuspeh. "Forget the Product Life Cycle Concept", Harvard Business Review (January-February 1976), 102-112.

[8] Elliott, J. Walter. "A Comparison of Models of Marketing Investment in the Firm", Review of Economics and Business, April 1971, pp. 53-70.

[9] Elliott, J. Walter. "Forecasting and Analysis of Corporate Financial Performance with An Econometric Model of the Firm", Journal of Financial and Quantitative Analysis, March 1972, pp. 1499-1525.

[10] Gale, Bradley T., Donald F. Heany, and Donald J. Swire. The PAR ROI Report: Explanation and Commentary, Strategic Planning Institute, January 1977.

[11] Johnston, J. Econometric Methods, 2nd Edition, McGraw-Hill, 1972.

[12] Kuh, E. "The Validity of Cross-Sectionally Estimated Behavior Equations in Time Series Applications", Econometrica, April 1959.

[13] Mueller, Dennis C. "The Firm Decision Process: An Econometric Investigation", Quarterly Journal of Economics, February 1967, pp. 58-87.

[14] Reibstein, David J. and Paul W. Farris. "Consistency in Relative Advertising and Relative Pricing Strategies: A Cross-Sectional Analysis of the PIMS Data", unpublished paper, Harvard Business School, March 1979.

[15] Schendel, Dan and G. Richard Patton. "Simultaneous Equation Models of Corporate Strategy", Paper No. 582, Institute for Research in The Behavioral, Economic, and Management Sciences, Purdue University, 1976.

[16] Schoeffler, Sidney. "Cross-Sectional Study of Strategy, Structure, and Performance: Aspects of the PIMS Program", in Strategy + Structure = Performance: The Strategic Planning Imperative, Hans B. Thorelli (Ed.), Indiana University Press, 1977.

[17] Sherer, F.M. (1980) Industrial Market Structure and Economic Performance, 2nd Ed. Chicago, Illinois: Rand McNally, 1980.

[18] Simon, Julian L. and Dennis J. Aigner. "Cross-Section and Time-Series Tests of the Permanent - Income Hypothesis", American Economic Review, June 1970, pp. 341-51.

[19]   Strategic Planning Institute. "Using PIMS As a Portfolio Planning Systems",
       Mimeo, 1979.

[20]   Tsurumi, Hiroki and Yositi Tsurumi. "An Econometric Model of A Japanese
       Pharmaceutical Company", in Readings in Managerial Economics, Kristian S.
       Palda (Ed.). Prentice-Hall, 1973.

AN OPTIMIZATION MODEL FOR CORPORATE FINANCIAL PLANNING[1]

William F. Hamilton

University of Pennsylvania
Philadelphia, Pennsylvania
U.S.A.

Michael A. Moses

Graduate School of Business
New York University
New York, New York
U.S.A.

Computer-based corporate models have generated considerable interest among management scientists and corporate planners in recent years. The number of operating corporate models is growing rapidly and represents virtually all types of industries.[11,17] Not surprisingly, the size and complexity of corporate-level planning problems have tended to favor the development of descriptive simulation models for evaluating selected planning alternatives. Perhaps the best known corporate simulations are those described by Brown [3] and Gershefski[10].

In contrast to the widespread use of corporate simulation models, few practical applications of corporate optimization models have been reported,[9] despite the distinct computational advantages offered by optimization methods where a large number of strategy alternatives and environmental conditions must be considered. Under such circumstances, simulation can require the evaluation of an excessive number of cases.

The mixed integer programming model presented in this paper operates in conjunction with a detailed corporate financial-accounting simulation model and as an integral part of the corporate planning process. A primary reason for developing this optimization model was the practical need to improve the efficiency with which alternative combinations of corporate strategies, financing mechanisms, and planning assumptions could be evaluated. The mixed integer formulation was designed to exploit the latest developments in integer-programming solution techniques and to permit realistic representation of discrete investment and financing opportunities.

Other attempts to apply mathematical-programming approaches to corporate financial planning fall into two general groups. First, a number of theoretical models have been conceptualized and discussed in the literature [1,5,18]; they typically imply input and computational requirements that preclude widespread practical application.[14] Second, there is a group of models solvable by standard linear programming techniques; they include a number of specialized applications--e.g., to operations planning,[8] short-term financing,[15] cash management,[13] and bank-asset management.[7] However, the simplifying assumptions required to obtain linear formulations limit the applicability of such models to more general financial-planning situations. Furthermore, only the discussions in references 7 and 8 give any indication of actual implementation.

The modeling approach described here can be applied in a wide range of planning contexts. It was developed with close management cooperation to ensure the appropriateness of the assumptions, the availability of required model inputs, and the ultimate implementation of results.

On the basis of early experience with a corporate simulation model, management established the following general specifications for the financial optimization model:

1. <u>Corporate scope</u>. The model should reflect the full range of financial

planning variables actually considered at the corporate level, including internal
capital budgeting, acquisition and divestment, debt creation and repayment, stock
issue and repurchase, and dividend payout.   A five- to ten-year planning horizon
consisting of one-year planning periods was considered adequate.

2. <u>Analytical requirements</u>. Explicit provision should be made for evaluating discrete investments and extensive parametric variations in model inputs.

3. <u>On-line operation</u>. Direct access to the model and data base should be
possible via remote terminals to allow its most effective use as a creative
planning tool.

4. <u>Input/output flexibility</u>. Alternative input and output options should be
provided to facilitate model implementation for standard and special planning
studies in both batch and interactive modes.

The corporate planning process under study is typical of those found in many
large, decentralized organizations. Over fifty wholly and partially owned subsidiaries with operations in many different countries submit their plans, or strategies, for annual corporate review in light of corporate goals, available funds,
and other opportunities. The corporate strategic plan is essentially a composite
of approved subsidiary strategies, selected financing programs, and corporate-
level strategies (e.g., portfolio investments and acquisitions). The most appropriate plan maximizes total corporate performance over the multiperiod planning
horizon without violating important financial, legal and operating constraints.

Several important issues arise in attempting to design a financial optimization
model in this context: (1) selecting an appropriate measure of corporate performance, (2) defining exogenous limits on performance, and (3) developing a model
structure consistent with established planning practices and perspectives.   In
each case, we gave primary consideration to the general applicability and effective implementation of the model, recognizing that any planning model, however
sophisticated, is of value only to the extent that it is actually used in the
planning process.

The primary corporate objective was defined by management as maximizing the value
of the corporation to its stockholders. Translating this into a more operational
objective function for planning purposes raises the problem of defining value and
the factors that affect it.   In the literature, the value of a corporation is
often taken to be the present value of expected future returns (dividends, income,
or cash flows), discounted at an 'appropriate' cost of capital rate. [5,14,18] In
practice, however, determination of an acceptable discount rate is a matter of
considerable debate.   Another approach is to maximize the value of stockholders'
equity during the final period of the planning horizon. This avoids the need to
determine a discount rate, but implies a willingness to sacrifice current income
in favor of a higher future value of stockholders' equity.[7] In the absence of
an acceptable explicit functional representation of market valuation, management
selected earnings per share (EPS) as the most reasonable surrogate measure of
corporate performance for the planning model.   Explicit representation of all
earnings opportunities and constraints on the time pattern of EPS in the model
ensures a realistic basis for evaluating planning strategies and financing programs. As indicated later, however, this implies a fractional objective function
to reflect the effects of stock issues and repurchases.   A simpler, but less
desirable, alternative is to use selective reruns of the model based on a simple
linear objective function, as suggested in reference 7.

The interactive, decision-aiding role of the corporate optimization model was
reflected in the use of exogenous limits for a number of widely used financial
ratios. No attempt was made to change the process by which these limits are set
by financial management, but explicit provision has been made for parametric
analysis to evaluate the effects of changes in the limits themselves.   This

permits use of the model to determine optimal values of the financial ratios. Given expected debt costs as a function of the corporation's debt/equity ratio, for example, relaxation of the debt/equity limit will allow comparison of the marginal returns with marginal debt costs. Future prices of common stock in the model are also determined exogenously by management. Attempts to project stock prices internally as a function of EPS and other variables would result in non-linearities that would make the mixed integer formulation computationally intractable. Instead, parameterization of stock-price projections is used to explore the implications of possible variations.

In order to reflect the incremental nature of the existing corporate-planning process, the model distinguishes between strategies that maintain the firm's momentum in existing lines of business and strategies that represent changes in the nature or level of present activities, a structure allowing proper representation of potential expansion and divestment strategies that involve discrete overhead costs. Of course, incorporation of these opportunities as incremental strategies in a realistic model is only possible by using recently developed integer-programming solution codes.

As in the financial planning studies we have referred to, no attempt has been made to introduce uncertainty into the model formally. However, constraints on values of traditional financial ratios and on minimum corporate income permit exploration of managerial risk preferences through parameterization and examination of the relevant dual evaluators. As Carleton[5] has noted, more formal treatment of uncertainty suggests an order-of-magnitude increase in model complexity, thus severely limiting practical application.

These subsidiaries and certain corporate groups may submit plans of two general types: momentum strategies, which reflect continuation of present activities in current lines of business; and development strategies, which reflect proposed changes in the nature or level of present activities.

There is a momentum strategy associated with each existing line of business. Although it is sometimes difficult to distinguish between strategy types, the incremental financial effects of all major shifts in the momentum business are described by development strategies. Included in this latter category are acquisitions, divestments, and market and product-line expansions. Strategy selection requires decisions of the go/no-go type, except where explicit provision is made for partial strategies.

Financing selected strategies may be arranged through a variety of fund sources at the corporate and subsidiary levels. Stock issues and both short- and long-term debt instruments must be considered. Short-term debt includes all financing whose duration is less than one year. Long-term debt may be arranged at the corporate level for internal allocation to selected strategies or at the subsidiary level for a particular strategy. In the latter case, the debt is referred to as 'tied financing', since its use is restricted to the strategy for which it is proposed.

Each section of the corporate optimization model and the corresponding notation will be introduced in turn. The primary planning variables represent strategies and fund sources. To simplify the discussion, all strategy variables are treated as zero/one integer variables--that is, only go/no-go strategy decisions are permitted.

THE OBJECTIVE FUNCTION

If we let E_t be total corporate earnings in period t and hold constant the number of shares s_0 of common stock outstanding at $t=0$, then the multiperiod objective function may be written simply as

$$\max \text{EPS} = \sum_{t=1}^{t=T} E_t / s_0, \tag{1}$$

where EPS is total corporate earnings per share over the T periods.

In practice, of course, it is vitally important that due consideration be given to expansions and contractions of the stock base s_0; certain acquisition or expansion strategies may involve new stock issues, and analysis of corporate-financing opportunities may dictate the sale or repurchase of corporate stock. This results in a fractional objective function that can be approximated by the linear form

$$\max \text{ EPS} = \Sigma_{t=1}^{t=T} \left| E_t/s_0 - \Sigma_i \overline{\text{EPS}} \Sigma_{p=t}^{p=T} [u_{ip}/(u_{ip}+s_0)]X_i \right.$$
$$\left. + (T-t)\ \overline{\text{EPS}}[1/(v_t+s_0)]S_i - (T-t)\ \overline{\text{EPS}}[1/(V_t*+s_0)]S_t* \right|, \tag{2}$$

where $X_i=0$, 1 indicates the rejection or acceptance, respectively, of strategy i, $\overline{\text{EPS}}$ is an estimate of the average earnings per share EPS, u_{it} is the number of new common shares to be issued for strategy i in period t, v_t, and v_t* are the maximum numbers of common shares that can be repurchased or sold in the market in period t, and S_t and S_t* are decision variables that indicate the numbers of shares of common stock repurchased or sold, respectively, in period t. The negative adjustment terms in (2) reflect dilution of EPS caused by expansion of the stock base, while the positive adjustment term reflects the effects of a reduction in the number of shares outstanding in period t due to treasury repurchases of outstanding common stock. Equation (2) was developed through successive expansion and linearization of terms in (1). Several iterations are typically required in solving a new problem before EPS = $\overline{\text{EPS}}$.

Corporate earnings E_t in any period t have the general form

earnings = [income (or loss) from strategies]-[financing costs].

Computation of E_t requires the following additional variables:

X_i* = 0, 1 indicates the rejection or acceptance, respectively, of the divestment of strategy i,

Y_{jp} = the dollar amount of long-term debt selected from source j starting in period p (this debt can be applied to any strategy i),

W_{ip} = the dollar amount of long-term debt tied to strategy i starting in period p (this debt may be utilized only if strategy i is accepted),

V_{kt} = the dollar amount of short-term debt from source k in period t,

P_p* = the number of shares of preferred stock issued in period p, and

R_{ipq} = the dollar amount of long-term debt from source j starting in period p and voluntarily repaid in period q>p.

Effective tax rates vary widely among subsidiary companies and financing may be arranged at both the corporate and company levels, resulting in the following terms:

.   <u>Income from strategies</u> (since all financing may be arranged at the corporate level, strategy income is computed after taxes but before interest):

$$\Sigma_i o_{it}[p_{it}(1-r_{it})+p'_{it}(1-r'_{it})]X_i + \Sigma o_{it}p*_{it}(1-r'_{it})X_i*, \tag{3}$$

where o_{it} is the fractional ownership associated with strategy i in period t, p_{it} and p'_{it} are the regular and capital gains incomes of strategy i in period t, r_{it} and r'_{it} are the effective income and capital-gains tax rates associated with strategy i in period t, and $p*_{it}$ is the capital-gains income from the divestment of strategy i in period t.

. Cost of long-term debt at corporate level (since strategy income is computed before interest, all interest payments must be adjusted for tax credit):

$$\Sigma_j \; \Sigma_{p=0}^{p=t} \; g_{jp}(1-r_{ct})[Y_{jp}-(t-p)h_{jp}Y_{jp}], \tag{4}$$

where j_{jp} is the interest rate associated with Y_{jp}, r_{ct} is the effective corporate income tax rate in period t, and h_{jp} is the fraction of Y_{jp} required as a constant payment to principal in each period.

. Cost of long-term debt tied to strategies (adjusted for tax credit):

$$\Sigma_i g_{i0}(1-r_{it})o_{it}[W_{i0}-th_{i0}W_{i0}]X_i$$
$$+\Sigma_i \; \Sigma_{p=1}^{p=t} g_{ip}(1-r_{it})o_{it}[W_{ip}-(t-p)h_{ip}W_{ip}], \tag{5}$$

where j_{ip} is the interest rate associated with W_{ip}, W_{i0} is the long-term debt outstanding at t=0, and h_{ip} is the fraction of Y_{ip} required as a constant payment to principal in each period.

. Cost of short-term corporate debt (adjusted for tax credit):

$$\Sigma_k e_{kt}(1-r_{ct})V_{kt}, \tag{6}$$

where e_{kt} is the interest rate associated with V_{kt}.

. Divident cost of preferred securities:

$$\Sigma_{p=0}^{p=t}b_p P_p\ast, \tag{7}$$

where b_p is the dividend rate (dollars/share) associated with $P_p\ast$.

. Credit from early corporate debt repayment:

$$\Sigma_j \; \Sigma_{p=0}^{p=t} \; \Sigma_{q=1}^{q=t}g_{jp}(1-r_{cq})R_{jpq}. \tag{8}$$

It is assumed in (3) and throughout this section that the divestment of a momentum strategy always takes place in t=1. Furthermore, only common stock is repurchased, and early repayment is allowed only for corporate-level debt exceeding a fixed schedule of mandatory repayments.

After combining terms (3) through (8), corporate earnings in period t become

E_t = (income from strategies) - (cost of corporate long-term debt) - (cost of long-term debt tied to strategies) - (cost of short-term debt) - (dividend cost of preferred securities) + (credit from early corporate-debt repayment).

GOAL/CONSTRAINTS

The distinction between an objective or goal and a constraint is often an arbitrary one. Most organizations have multiple objectives, any of which might be selected as the primary goal, while the others operate as constraints. Depending upon the particular analysis, the following three goal/constraints may be used in either role.

1. Stable growth in earnings per share. Management considers the pattern of growth in earnings per share to be an important determinant of investor confidence and, hence, of the market value of corporate stock. Where EPS_t is the earnings per share reported in period t, it was decided to limit fluctuations in EPS_t to

a specific range by using constraints of the form

$$\alpha_t^+ EPS_t \geq EPS_{t+1} \geq \alpha_t^- EPS_t, \qquad\qquad (t=1, \cdots, T)$$

where α_t^+ and α_t^- are fractions defining upper and lower limits on the period-to-period changes in earnings per share.

2. Return on assets. The return earned on assets is a common measure of corporate performance that may be treated as either an objective or a constraint. Return in this model is restricted to earnings from the sale of goods and services (E_t adjusted for earnings from capital gains). Where a_{it} is the incremental change in assets associated with strategy i occurring in period t and a_{i0} is the total assets of strategy i at the start of the planning period, return on assets in period t can be limited to some minimum value β_t by constraints of the form

$$E_t - \Sigma_i o_{it}(1-r'_{it}) \ (p'_{it}X_i + p^*_{it}X^*_{it}) - \beta_t [\Sigma_{p=0}^{p=t} \Sigma_i o_{pi} \alpha_{ip}] X_i \geq 0.$$

3. Return on equity. Return on total shareholders' equity is another useful measure of performance. As above, return is restricted to earnings from goods and services. The total equity Q_t in period t can be defined in terms of Q_0, the outstanding equity at t=0, the earnings E_t in period t and the following three factors:

. Dollar value of the common stock issues associated with strategies:

$$\Sigma_{p=1}^{p=t} \Sigma_i u_{ip} c_p x_i.$$

. Net sales of common and preferred stock:

$$\Sigma_{p=1}^{p=t} [c_p(S_p^*-S_p)+f_p P_p^*],$$

where c_t is the average price of common stock in period t and f_t is the average price of preferred stock in period t.

. Payment of common-stock dividends:

$$\Sigma_{p=1}^{p=t} \Sigma_{q=1}^{q=t} d_q(\Sigma_{ik} u_{ip} X_i + S_p^* - S_p + s_0),$$

where d_t is the dividend rate on common stock in period t.

Thus, total equity in period t is

$$Q_t = Q_0 + \Sigma_{p=1}^{p=t} E_p + \Sigma_{p=1}^{p=t} \Sigma_i u_{ip} c_p X_i + \Sigma_{p=1}^{p=t} [c_p(S_p^*-S_p)+f_p P_p^*]$$
$$- \Sigma_{p=1}^{p=t} \Sigma_{q=p}^{q=t} d_q(\Sigma_i u_{ip} X_i + S_p^* - S_p + s_0)].$$

Return on equity in period t can therefore be limited to some minimum value γ_t by constraints of the form

$$E_t - \Sigma_i o_{it}(1-r'_{it})(p'_{it}X_i + p^*_{it}X^*_{it}) - \gamma_t Q_t \geq 0.$$

CORPORATE CONSTRAINTS

A number of additional planning restrictions must be considered at the corporate level. These include the important flow-of-funds constraint, two constraints that enforce acceptable financial ratios, and others.

1. Funds flow. The funds allocated in any period will seldom balance the sum of funds generated internally plus those obtained from various funds sources. If provision is made for a cash balance at the end of period t, then the net change in cash balance during period t is the difference between the total inflow

and total outflow of funds. The inflow of funds is generated by:

. <u>Selected strategies</u>:

$$\Sigma_t z_{it} X_i,$$

where z_{it} is the cash generation (or demand) of strategy i in period t after taxes and interest from financing tied to this strategy.

. <u>Divestments</u>:

$$\Sigma_i (w_{i1} - W_{i0}) X_i^*,$$

where w_{i1} is the net cash received after taxes from sale of strategy i.

. <u>Equity sales</u>:

$$c_t S_t^* + f_t P_p^*.$$

. <u>Net debt proceeds</u>:

$$\Sigma_k e'_{kt} V_{it} + \Sigma_j g'_{jt} Y_{jt} + \Sigma_i g'_{it} W_{it},$$

where e'_{kt} is the fraction of short-term debt actually available for use, and g'_{it} is the same as e'_{kt}, but for long-term debt.

The outflow of funds, on the other hand, is distributed to:

. <u>Dividend payments</u>:

$$\Sigma_{p=1}^{p=t} \Sigma_i d_t [u_{ip} X_i + s_o + (S_p^* - S_p)].$$

. <u>Debt expenses</u>:

$$\Sigma_k V_{k(t-1)} + \Sigma_k [e_{kt}(1-r_{ct})] V_{kt} + \Sigma_{p=1}^{p=t} b_p P_p^* + \Sigma_j \Sigma_{p=1}^{p=t} \left| [g_{jp} Y_{jp}(1-r_{ct}) \right.$$
$$[1-(t-p)h_{jp}] - h_{jp} Y_{jp}] \left| + \Sigma_i \Sigma_{p=1}^{p=t} \right| [g_{ip} W_{ip}(1-r_{it})][1-(t-p)h_{ip}] - h_{ip} W_{ip}] \left| o_{it} \right.$$
$$+ \Sigma_i \left| g_{i0} h_{i0}(1-r_{it})[1-th_{i0}] X_i + th_{i0} g_{i0} X_i \right| o_{it}.$$

. <u>Debt retirement</u>:

$$\Sigma_j \Sigma_{p=1}^{p=t} [-1+(1-r_{ct})g_{jp}] R_{jpt} + \Sigma_{p=1}^{p=t} \Sigma_j \Sigma_{q=p}^{t-1} (1-r_{it}) R_{jpq}.$$

. <u>Stock repurchases</u>:

$$c_t S_t.$$

Combining these terms, the funds-flow constraint for period t can be written as:

(funds generated by selected strategies) + (funds generated by divestments)
+ (funds generated by equity sales) + (new debt proceeds)
- (funds required for dividend payments) - (funds required by stock repurchases)
- (funds required by debt retirements) - (funds required by stock repurchases)
$\geq$ (net increase in the cash balance required during period t).

2. <u>Interest coverage</u>. Certain financial ratios are commonly used as measures of operating performance and financial stability. Most corporations strive

to hold these ratios within 'acceptable' ranges to control operations, as well as to maintain a good image among shareholders and the financial community. One such measure, interest coverage, is defined here as the ratio of income from goods and services before interest and taxes to total interest costs in any period t. If L_t is the minimum acceptable value of the interest-coverage ratio, or the minimum number of times that interest expenses must be 'covered' by income from goods and services in period t, then this constraint takes the form

(income before interest and taxes) - L_t (total interest expense ≥ 0,

or

$$\Sigma_i o_{it} P_{it} X_i - L_t \{ \Sigma_j \Sigma_{p=0}^{p=t} g_{jp} [Y_{jp-(t-p)} h_{jp} Y_{jp}]$$

$$+ \Sigma_i g_{i0} [W_{i0} - th_{i0} W_{i0}] X_i$$

$$+ \Sigma_i \Sigma_{p=1}^{p=t} o_{it} g_{ip} W_{ip-(t-p)} h_{ip} W_{ip}] + \Sigma_k e_{kt} V_{kt}$$

$$= \Sigma_{p=0}^{p=t} \Sigma_{q=p}^{q=t} (\Sigma_j q_{jp} R_{jpq})\} > 0.$$

3. <u>Leverage ratio</u>. Another financial ratio is the ratio of long-term debt to the sum of long-term debt plus total equity; it provides another indication of financial stability. Letting H_t be the maximum acceptable value of the corporate leverage ratio in period t, we have

$$\Sigma_j \Sigma_{p=0}^{p=t} [Y_{jp-(t-p)} h_{jp} Y_{jp} - \Sigma_{q=p}^{q=t} R_{jpq}] + \Sigma_i g_{i0} (W_{i0} - W_{th} W_{i0}) X_i$$

$$+ \Sigma_i \Sigma_{p=1}^{p=t} g_{ip} W_{ip} [1-(t-p) h_{ip}] + H_t / H_{t-1} \leq 0.$$

4. <u>Short-term debt</u>. In order to limit the total amount of short-term debt undertaken in period t to an acceptable value N_t, management has imposed a set of constraints of the form

$$\Sigma_k V_{kt} \leq N_t.$$

5. <u>Additions to common stock</u>. An upper limit on the net increase in outstanding common stock s_t can be imposed as a matter of management policy by a set of constraints such as

$$\Sigma_i u_{it} X_i + S_t^* - S_t \leq s_t.$$

6. <u>Minimum corporate income</u>. Associated with each strategy i is an estimate of the minimum (or maximum loss) m_{it} possible in period t. Since strategy income is at best a point estimate, a very conservative method for reducing overall corporate risk is to require total minimum strategy income to be greater than the minimum allowable corporate income level I_t established by management for period t. The parameter m_{it} can also be a percentage of p_{it} that depends on the projected variability of the industry to which that strategy is related:

$$\Sigma_i m_{it} X_i \geq I_t.$$

GROUP CONSTRAINTS

Where subsidiary companies are organized into groups or division, management may wish to establish performance requirements or to place restrictions on certain aspects of group activity. Often, the rationales behind such constraints derive from funding, business-mix, or legal considerations.

1. <u>Business mix</u>. Groups or divisions are typically composed of companies with related product lines or business operations. It is common management policy to restrict the 'mix' of corporate activites in order to retain or promote a specified corporate character or to help minimize risk. One way to accomplish

this end is by limiting the total assets employed by any group g in period t:

$$\sum_{p=0}^{p=t} \sum_{i \in g} [a_{it}X_i - a^*_{it}X_t^*] \leq A_{gt}, \qquad \sum_{p=0}^{p=t} \sum_{i \in g} [a_{it}X_i - a^*_{it}X_t^*] \geq B_{gt},$$

where a_{it} and a^*_{it} are the increase and reduction in assets, respectively, associated with the adoption and divestment of strategy i in the period t, and A_{gt} and B_{gt} are the maximum and minimum limits on total assets employed by group g in period t.

2. <u>Strategy source/constraints.</u> A number of additional model constraints relate directly to the variables representing strategy and funds-source selection.

3. <u>Divestment.</u> The momentum strategy for each business line must be either accepted or divested, but not both. Thus, for all momentum strategies (ieM), $X_{i \in M} + X^*_{i \in M} = 1$.

4. <u>Development/momentum strategies.</u> Because selection of an incremental development strategy (i∈D) has meaning if and only if the corresponding momentum strategy (i∈M) is acepted, we require for each business line that $X_{i \in M} - X_{i \in D} \geq 0$ for all i.

5. <u>Tied financing.</u> The amount of tied financing that can be taken out in period p is limited to some maximum value λ_{ip} associated with each strategy i. In adition, the tied financing may only be used if the corresponding strategy is accepted Thus, we must required that $Y_{ip} - \lambda_{ip}X_i \leq 0$ for all i.

6. <u>Early debt repayment.</u> In allowing the voluntary repayment of outstanding corporate debt ahead of schedule, it is necessary to ensure that total repayments over the planning horizon do not exceed the amount of debt outstanding at the end of period T:

$$\sum_{q=1}^{q=t} R_{jpq} - Y_{jp}[1-(T-p)h_{jp}] \leq 0 \qquad \qquad \text{(all } j, p)$$

7. <u>Funds-source limits.</u> The funds drawn from any source j in period t may be limited to some range by constraints of the form $Y^+_{jt} \geq Y_{jt} \geq Y^-_{jt}$, where Y^+_{jt} and Y^-_{jt} are the upper and lower limits on the funds drawn from source j in period t.

MODEL EXTENSIONS

This basic model formulation can be extended to include consideration of these additional factors:

(a) A more precise objective-function approximation using yearly estimates of earnings per share $\overline{EPS}_t$, and outstanding stock s_t.

(b) Strategy divestments in any period.

(c) Postponement of strategy selection.

(d) A variety of preferred securities with allowance for repurchase.

(e) Variable debt-repayment schedules and conversion of debt to common stock.

(f) Additional constraints on group and company activities similar to those at the corporate level.

(g) Stock issues by subsidiary companies.

(h) Payment of subsidiary dividends to outside minority owners.

(i) More complex financial accounting relations.

(j) Enriched tax and depreciation considerations.

(k) More complex debt agreements (such as warrants and minimum borrowing thresholds).

IMPLEMENTATION

The model presented here is a simplified version of the strategic planning opti-mization model designed and implemented in a large multinational company. The following discussion of computational considerations and results is based on solution and implementation experience with the larger, more complex model.

Computational Considerations

In its present form, the model contains approximately 1000 variables and 750 con-straints, not including upper- and lower-bound constraints. There are over 200 zero/one variables, including both strategy variables and structural variables relating to definitions of subsidiary companies not described in the previous section. The remaining variables are continuous and represent the many alterna-tive sources of funds. Constraints similar to those described here are comple-mented with additional restrictions on groups and subsidiary companies.

Model Solution. Two aspects of the model cause most of the computational diffi-culties. First, the management requirement that strategy selection be treated as a go/no-go decision creates the need for mixed-integer-solution capabilities. An extensive survey of available codes revealed that a model of this size and struc-ture could be solved by most modern mixed integer programming algorithms (avail-able on CDC, IBM, and Univac systems). Use of zero-one round-off routines and other approaches were also considered, but were rejected in favor of available mixed integer codes. Maximization of earnings per share implies a mixed-integer fraction objective function, and therefore also poses some computational problems. Practical experience with large-scale fractional programming problems is quite limited, and it was therefore fortunate that a linear approximation of total EPS per share could be developed as shown in (2). This requires an estimate of average earnings per share, $\overline{EPS}$. This initial value $\overline{EPS}$ may be based on current projected corporate earnings for the planning horizon under consideration. Of course, $\overline{EPS}$ should equal the value computed for EPS in the subsequent model solu-tion, but this is seldom the case. Generally, the objective-function value com-puted in one solution provides a reasonable estimate of $\overline{EPS}$ for the next trial. Only a few iterations are generally required to reduce the difference between the two to an acceptable value. An extension of the initial model now being imple-mented is substitution of yearly EPS estimates for the single average-value $\overline{EPS}$.

Postoptimal analysis. One of the major reasons for management's decision to develop a corporate financial planning optimization model was the capability it offered to test the robustness of proposed solutions and to determine optimal reallocations of corporate resources in response to changes in the planning environment. Because of the complex functional relations used to compute the matrix coefficients from data inputs, and because about one-fourth of the model variables were restricted to values of either zero or one, standard linear programming sensitivity analyses and parametric routines are of limited use. An on-line system was therefore developed to facilitate post-optimal studies of the mixed integer solution. A simplified flow chart of this system is presented in Figure 1.

In the initial run, the data necessary for the optimization model are collected from the corporate financial, accounting, and management files. These data are then processed through the matrix generator, which computes appropriate model

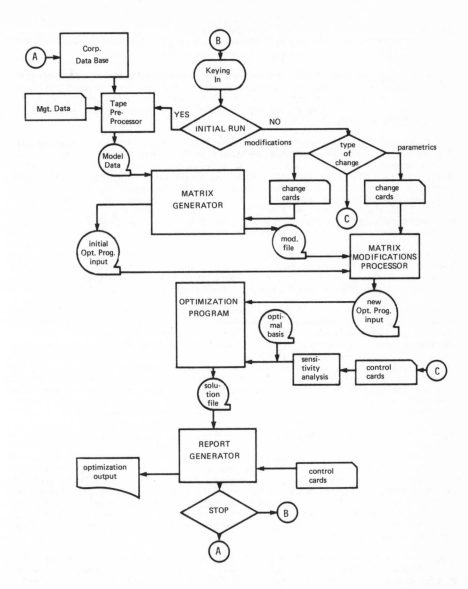

Figure 1. A simplified flow chart for the optimization system.

coefficients and structures the optimization model in a form required by the optimization program. The optimal basis is computed and saved for use in post-optimal analysis.

Following each run, the results are stored for processing by the report generator, which produced desired solution-output reports. Two levels of reports are currently available: the complete mixed integer optimal solution generated by the computer system, and a summary report tailored to management needs and designed for output via a remote terminal.

Sensitivity analysis determines the permissible changes in cost and right-hand side parameters that maintain the variables in the optimal basis. In a mixed-integer problem, the small variations in values of the basic variables caused by changes in the objective function (OBJ) and right-hand side (RHS) coefficients should be limited to the variables that take on continuous values. To ensure this, and yet exploit the power of available programming techniques, the strategy variables in the basis can be fixed at their optimal levels while values of the accepted fund-source variables change. Sensitivity analysis in this case only reflects the robustness of the accepted fund sources.

Additional postoptimization procedures were desired to determine the effects of changes in corporate data on the optimal solution. These effects are determined by the upper right branch of the flow chart in Figure 1. Two types of changes, "parametrics" and "matrix modifications," are illustrated.

Parametrics allow OBJ and RHS coefficients to vary over predefined ranges. An optimal solution is generated at each change in the basis caused by a change in one or more coefficients. Each new optimal solution is forced to the mixed integer optimum. One difficulty experienced in applying this procedure is that many of the corporate model coefficients have no clear financial or management interpretation. Each matrix element computed by the matrix generator may be a function of multiple data inputs. For instance, the coefficient of a single strategy variable in the earnings row may be a composite function of profits from goods and services, profits from capital gains, tax rates, tied financial costs, and others. A change in any of these may not only affect a number of OBJ coefficients, but also certain RHS coefficients. Thus, the effects of incremental changes in basic data inputs are often difficult to trace. The "modifications" option facilitates analyses of revisions in model structure and variations in specified elements of the financial, accounting, or management data bases by first processing the changes through the matrix generator, where appropriate revisions in matrix coefficients are computed. The changes are then merged with the optimization input file to produce an updated file for solution. Since most revisions are minor, the initial basis for modification runs is usually the final basis for the previous mixed integer optimal solution. The results of both para-metric and modification runs are available, through the report generator in either complete or abridged form.

Thus, this optimization system has all the power of the parametric and sensiti-vity-analysis routines found in most large-scale mathematical programming systems. It also provides capabilities that enable the planning staff to derive meaningful interpretations of changes in their data base and to perform certain additional postoptimal analyses of mixed-integer solutions with a minimum of effort.

Computational Experience

Like most integer programming routines, the computer code first solves for the optimal linear programming solution and then proceeds to the mixed integer optimum. A modified branch-and-bound search technique is employed to find the mixed integer solution. The density of the coefficient matrix is about 5 percent and the continuous solution usually requires about 10 central-processing-unit (CPU) minutes on a Univac 1108 computer system. In most runs, about ten strategies have been accepted at fractional levels. The remaining strategies were integer-valued.

The integer solution typically requires an additional 15-30 CPU minutes beyond the optimal continuous solution. Additional integer solutions initiated by the modification section of the optimization system usually required an additional minute using the previous optimal integer basis as the initial basis for the new problem. Both the continuous and the mixed integer solutions were validated using a corporate financial simulation to develop detailed financial statements for selected sets of strategies and fund sources.

An interesting characteristic of the mixed integer solution was that the strategies accepted were often quite different from those selected in the continuous solution. For example, two strategies that were accepted at levels of 0.89 and 0.03, respectively, in one continuous solution were accepted at levels of 0.0 and 1.0 in the final solution. Despite such shifts in variable values, however, the optimal objective-function value for the integer solution was generally within 3 percent of the continuous solution. Simply rounding off the continuous solution produced a much greater divergence in objective-function values.

Applications

Applications of the corporate optimization model to date fall naturally into two categories: (1) evaluation of subsidiary and corporate strategies and financing alternatives proposed in the annual planning cycles, and (2) special studies of investment and financing opportunities or problems that arise during the year. These span the full range of financial decisions made at the corporate level and have shown a number of interesting results in comparison with management intuition and the financial simulation model. Several such applications involving analyses of acquisitions, divestments, and financial-ratio limits are discussed briefly in this section to illustrate the practical value of an optimization model for corporate strategic planning.

Acquisition analysis. The model assists in deciding not only what to acquire, but also how it should be financed and when during the planning period it should be undertaken. In the annual planning cycle and in special studies, acquisition candidates are generally proposed to the model with a range of pooling (common-stock financing) and purchase (equity, debt, or cash financing) options. For example, a major subsidiary proposed several small pooling acquisitions that were accepted by the model, but only as cash purchases, in view of the low projected price of common stock and the unexpected availability of cash generated by divestments. In another case, the model recommended delay of two planned subsidiary acquisitions in favor of immediate seizure of a corporate-acquisition opportunity.

In another study of common-stock financing, three major acquisitions, each in excess of $100 million, were considered both individually and in combinations. Taken one at a time, acquisition A (the smallest) showed a positive contribution to EPS over the planning horizon, acquisition B resulted in slight dilution (reduction in EPS), and acquisition C (the biggest) caused significant dilution. Traditional acquisition evaluations would have recommended accepting A and rejecting the other two. When all three were submitted for evaluation, the optimization analysis suggested acceptance for both A and B and indicated that rejection of B would have reduced the optimal EPS value by an amount nearly twenty times the expected dilution effect. Further examination revealed that the funds-balance constraint became limiting in periods 3 and 4 when acquisition B was expected to contribute substantial cash flows. Since the debt/equity constraint was also limiting in these periods, rejection of acquisition B would have forced use of expensive equity financing to meet corporate cash requirements or curtailment of promising internal investments.

In addition to its application in evaluating proposed acquisitions, the model has

also been used effectively to select general profiles of desirable acquisition
candidates to guide the search for promising companies. This is accomplished by
presenting the model with alternative hypothetical acquisitions, each with different financial characteristics, and allowing it to evaluate these in the context
of other corporate opportunities.

Divestment analysis. Group executives assist the planning staff in assigning divestment values for all existing subsidiaries. This provides complete flexibility
in developing the optimal corporate plan. In contrast to previous planning, the
optimization model often chose to divest existing business lines (momentum strategies) in amounts up to 40 percent of the total momentum business. The most common
rationale was that divestments represented relatively inexpensive sources of funds
for investment in more productive alternatives. Because management was not
willing to accept the ambitious divestment programs generated by the model and
because the corporate staff could not possibly cope with more than a few divestments in any single planning period, constraints were added to limit the total
number of divestments in each period. By parameterizing the constraint limit, a
rank-ordered listing of divestment candidates was easily generated.

Evaluation of policy restrictions. Theoretical considerations and management
judgment combine to establish values for a number of policy parameters, including
the debt/equity ratio, interest-coverage ratio, return on assets, and dividend
payout. Extensive parametric analyses of these policy restrictions has allowed
management to evaluate the implications of the traditional financial rules of
thumb. In one study, for example, the high marginal cost associated with the
interest-coverage restriction and subsequent parametric analysis revealed that the
planned divestment of a subsidiary with no significant debt would prevent acceptance of a highly profitable, but debt-financed, expansion of an existing subsidiary. The result was an explicit determination of the trade-off between the
policy limit and EPS. This information led to a management decision to lower the
required interest coverage, subsequent completion of the planned divestment, and
acceptance of the expansion strategy.

In these and other applications, the optimization model has demonstrated great
power and flexiblity in evaluating planning alternatives and assumptions. It
should be noted, however, that approximations inherent in the formulation of such
a model may produce solutions that are not valid in a strict accounting sense. Of
course, this is not its primary purpose. Rather, it is to identify the combinations of alternative strategies and financing programs that best satisfy corporate
objectives and constraints. Once strategic plans have been selected, more detailed analysis can be conducted using a financial-accounting simulation model or
standard accounting procedures (12).

ACKNOWLEDGMENTS

We are grateful to James McSweeny of the International Utilities Corporation for
his significant contributions to the formulation and application of the corporate
model. We also wish to thank Douglas Moffit and Thomas Johnson, whose understanding and efforts made computer implementation of the model possible.

REFERENCES

[1] William J. Baumol and Richard E. Quandt, "Investment and Discount Rates Under Capital Rationing--A Programming Approach," Economic Journal. 75, 317-329 (1965).

[2] James B. Boulden and Elwood S. Buffa, "Corporate Models: On-Line, Real-Time Systems," Harvard Business Review 48, 65-83 (July-August 1970).

[3] David E. Brown, "The Xerox Planning Model," presented to the American Management Association Seminar on Corporate Financial Models and Management Decision Making (December 16-18, 1968).

[4] Willard T. Carleton, "Linear Programming and Capital Budgeting Models: A New Interpretation," Journal of Finance 25, 825-883 (1969).

[5] _____, "An Analytical Model for Long-Range Financial Planning," Journal of Finance 25, 291-315 (1970).

[6] A. Charnes, W. W. Cooper, and M. H. Miller, "Application of Linear Programming to Financial Budgeting and the Costing of Funds," Journal of Business, 32, 20-46 (1959); also reprinted in The Management of Corporate Capital, Ezra Solomon (ed.) pp. 229-255, The Free Press, New York, 1967.

[7] Kalman J. Cohen and Frederick S. Hammer, "Linear Programming and Optimal Bank-Asset Management Decisions, Journal of Finance 21, 147-168 (1967).

[8] Jared H. Dickens, "Linear Programming in Corporate Simulation," in Corporate Simulation Models, Albert N. Schrieber (ed.), pp. 292-314, University of Washington, Seattle, Washington, 1970.

[9] Gary W. Dickson, John J. Mauriel, and John C. Anderson, "Computer Assisted Planning Models: A Functional Analysis," in Corporate Simulation Models, Albert N. Schrieber (ed.), pp. 43-70, University of Washington, Seattle, Washington, 1970.

[10] George W. Gershefski, "Building a Corporate Financial Model," Harvard Business Review 47, 61-72 (July-August 1969).

[11] _____, "Corporate Models--The State of the Art," Management Science 16, B303-B312 (1970).

[12] William F. Hamilton and Michael A. Moses, "A Computer-Based Corporate Planning System," in Model and Computer-Based Corporate Planning, Cologne University Press, Cologne, Germany, 1973.

[13] Yair E. Ogler, "An Unequal-Period Model for Cash Management Decisions," Management Science 16, B77-B92 (1969).

[14] Alexander A. Robichek, Donald G. Oglivie, and John D. C. Roach, "Capital Budgeting: A Pragmatic Approach," Financial Executive, pp. 26-38, April 1965.

[15] _____, D. Teichroew, and J. M. Jones, "Optimal Short-Term Financing Decisions," Management Science 12, 1-36 (1965).

[16] David P. Rutenberg, "Maneuvering Liquid Assets in a Multi-National Company," Management Science 16, B671-B684 (1970).

[17] Albert N. Schrieber (ed.), <u>Corporate Simulation Models</u>, University of
      Washington, Seattle, Washington, 1970.

[18] H. Martin Weingartner, <u>Mathematical Programming and the Analysis of Capital
      Budgeting Problems</u>, Prentice-Hall, Englewood Cliffs, New Jersey, 1963.

AN OPTIMIZATION ALTERNATIVE
TO PORTFOLIO PLANNING MODELS

Malcolm B. Coate

Federal Trade Commission
Washington, D.C.
U.S.A.

INTRODUCTION

Portfolio models have been widely used to structure the strategic planning problems of the large diversified firm ([1], [12], [14]). These models share three
key assumptions: (1) the firm can be divided into business units operating in
different markets, (2) the business units that "dominate" their markets will earn
higher profits, (3) the firm faces some limitation on corporate investment funds
[5]. In each model, the goal of the firm is to attain a strong position in as
many markets as possible to generate current and future returns. The decision
variables are the strategies followed by the business units. Strategy is assumed
to be based on the unit's position in a portfolio matrix. The models conclude
by qualifying their solution with the requirement that the sum of the individual
strategies must meet the corporate level constraints. The portfolio model represents an interesting qualitative approach to planning but it doesn't allow the
firm to consider alternative investment levels within a strategy. This implies
the firm faces the difficult task of implicitly considering the potential lost
revenues in its other business units when defining each unit's strategy. This
trade off, between profitable opportunities in business units, has never been
completely incorporated in a quantitative model. The few optimization planning
models that exist either concentrate on the firm's financial decisions [10] or
follow the portfolio models by limiting the number of potential investment levels
to one or two in each unit [2].

This paper presents a planning optimization model that can solve for the strategy
and investment level in each of the firm's business units. We will start by discussing the Boston Consulting Group's (BCG) model [12] to illustrate the fundamental problem. Then we will define the strategy variables, parameters, and data
that are used in the model. Next the actual objective function and constraints
are discussed as a simplification of the underlying theoretical model. The potential uses of the model are illustrated with numerical examples and the optimal
strategies are compared to a basic portfolio model solution. The paper concludes
with a discussion of a few generalizations on the model, a brief summary of the
major characteristics of the model, and a comment on the potential for use of
optimization models in strategic planning.

THE STRATEGIC DECISION VARIABLES

To set the foundations for the choice of an optimal strategy, we will discuss the
operation of the BCG portfolio model. This model is the simplest portfolio model
because it uses a matrix defined by the relative market share and the market
growth rate of a unit to measure the potential investment opportunities in a
business. The other portfolio models use a large number of additional variables
to structure their matrices. Thus a discussion of the BCG model should capture
the essence of the portfolio methodology [5].

The BCG portfolio matrix is illustrated in Figure 1 with the BCG's title for each
type of unit in the appropriate box. Hedley notes "the first goal should be to

maintain position in the "cash cows" but to guard against the frequent temptation
to reinvest in them excessively [11,p.11]." Next the firm should invest in the
"stars" to consolidate their market share. Any surplus funds are invested in the
best "question marks" to acquire more market share. The firm invests in "stars"
and selected "question marks" in the hope that they will become "cash cows" when
their growth rate decreases. The "dog" and most of the "question mark" businesses
are managed to generate cash or divested from the portfolio because the BCG model
suggests they will never yield a future cash return [3]. In summary, the BCG
strategies attempt to allocate investment funds among the units of the portfolio
with the goal of generating present or future cash earnings. The BCG experience
curve [11] implies the returns are highest in the markets the firm dominates
(i.e., its relative market share is greater than 1). Thus the BCG notes "every
business and every product within a business must be pressed into a leadership
position or close to it, within a reasonable period, or it should be managed in a
manner to throw off cash on a near term basis [4]." Once a leadership position
has been attained, the unit can push for a better position or generate high
earnings due to its low costs. Therefore the BCG model implies every business in
the corporate portfolio should follow either a growth or cash strategy. It should
be possible to quantify the two plans by the growth rate and rate of return that
is expected to result from an individual strategy in a given unit [2]. The
magnitude of both variables depends on the unit's position in the portfolio matrix
and the expected strategies of the unit's competitors. For example, a unit in a
high growth industry will have a high potential growth rate. Also a unit with
high relative market share will have high potential earnings due to the advantages of its size. Figure 2 illustrates a hypothetical combination of growth and
return for the growth and cash strategies of a business.

In the growth strategy, the firm invests heavily in the business to increase its
assets. The growth plan also requires the firm to reduce price and/or raise
expenditures for advertising, research and development and product quality to
increase sales. Thus attracting additional sales will depress the measured rate
of return. Alternatively, the cash plan requires the firm to manage for earnings
and forego many investment opportunities so the growth rate is low. Thus both
strategies define specific investment levels for a business and do not explicitly
consider the availability of corporate funds.

The simple BCG portfolio model defines either the growth or cash strategy as
optimal for a business on the basis of the unit's position in the portfolio matrix
and the available investment funds. Given the expected values of growth and
return, the strategy choice can be quantified in a simple optimization model [2].
In many cases, one strategy is obviously superior to the other because the growth
rate is much higher while the rates or return are about equal or the return is
higher while the growth rates are about equal. Thus the firm has only one potential strategy in these units. For example, a growth plan for a "cash cow" business is inferior because it can offer only a slightly better growth rate at a
substantial cost in earnings. Other business units will have two strategies that
merit consideration.

The basic portfolio concept involves the re-allocation of investment funds from
low return uses in cash generating businesses to high return uses in growth
businesses. But the optimal search is limited to two strategies and investment
levels per unit so the re-allocation of investment funds between units is restricted. Thus a more general model is necessary to allow the firm to optimize
the return on its portfolio of businesses.

The number of investment choices available to each unit can be expanded by defining an additional strategy and constructing investment levels within each
strategy. First there is no reason why a firm cannot consider a strategy that
pursues both earnings and growth goals simultaneously. For example, a high share
"star" business may not need to follow a growth strategy but it also may not want
to risk losing share by following the cash strategy. Thus an intermediate strat-

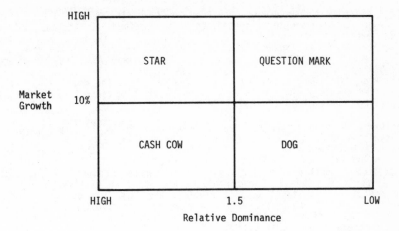

Figure 1.   The BCG Portfolio Matrix

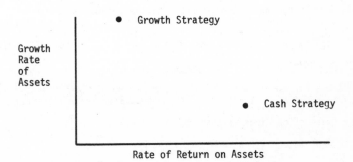

Figure 2.   Growth Rate and Rate of Return Combinations
for the Growth and Cash Strategies

egy that offers a higher growth rate than the cash strategy and a higher return that the growth plan should be considered. The intermediate strategy could offer a growth-earnings combination along line segment A of Figure 3 if the growth-earnings trade off is linear. But the BCG would suggest that the true growth-earnings relationship lies on a curve below line segment A.[1] They would argue a plan tailored to one goal can be more successful than a partial strategy so line segment A doesn't represent a realistic exchange. Thus the growth-earnings point of the mixed strategy would lie somewhere below the line connecting the results of the other two strategies.

In addition, the growth rate in Figure 2 implicitly limits the firm to one investment level per strategy. This restriction can also be relaxed by defining a set of discrete investments that support the chosen strategy of the business. We will define an initial return on assets based on the firm's initial assets and investment project. Additional projects attempt to further the goal of the unit and offer a specified return. These projects are based on existing assets. Thus acceptance of an investment project requires the firm to undertake all earlier projects. The model requires a yes/no decision on each investment project of each strategy. Thus a binary decision variable is defined for each investment project of each strategy of each unit as:

$$x_{jk}^i = 0 \text{ or } 1 \text{ for all } i,j,k$$

where

i refers to the business unit.

j refers to the strategy (growth, mixed, cash).

k refers to the individual investment plan of the strategy.

The investment project formulation recognizes the fact that most investments available to the firm are discrete projects. Thus the input data of the model can be directly linked to real opportunities and the optimal solution will define a set of projects to implement. This allows the firm to use the strategic planning model for long term capital budgeting. Of course the model will also specify an optimal strategy for each business unit in the corporate portfolio.

THE INTEGER PROGRAMMING OPTIMIZATION MODEL

The coefficients of the integer programming model are defined from the parameters and input data supplied by the firm. The parameters of the model are:

p   - the share of earnings retained by the firm.

m   - the debt to equity ratio of the firm.

h(t)   - the cost of debt capital to the firm at time t.

c(t)   - the cost of equity capital to the firm at time t.

d(t)   - the cost of capital to the firm at time t.

K   - the number of investment projects per strategy.

Ge   - the required growth rate in earnings per share.

Eq(t) - the number of share of stock outstanding at time t.

Ms(t) - the noncash expenses in period t (i.e. goodwill write off).

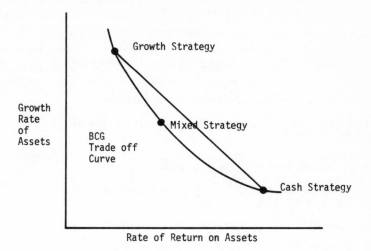

Figure 3.   The Growth - Earnings Combinations Available

to the Firm in a Business Unit

$Ca(t)$ - the exogenous cash requirements at time t.

$Ia_i(t)$ - the total value of assets employed by all firms in the i'th industry at time t.

$V^i(t)$ - the required share of industry assets held by the i'th business unit at time t.

L^i - the loss on the i'th unit's assets from divestment.

The firm must also supply input data for the results of the investment projects. These variables are defined as:

$r_{jk}^i(t)$ -the after tax return on assets in the i'th unit corresponding to the k'th investment plan of the j'th strategy at time t.

$I_{jk}^i(t)$ -the investment level in the i'th unit under the k'th investment plan of the j'th strategy at time t.

$A_j^i(0)$ -the initial assets held by the i'th unit (identical for all j).

δ^i - the depreciation rate of assets in the i'th unit.

$Z_{jk}^i(T)$ -the residual profit from the k'th investment plan of the j'th strategy in the i'th unit.

The results of an investment plan are based on the expected returns from the actual investment projects the plan represents. This is influenced by the overall strategy, the portfolio position of the unit, and the expected strategies of the firm's competitors. The accuracy of both the parameters and the input data is crucial to the usefulness of the optimal solution.

The actual integer programming model is defined by the choice of an objective function and a set of constraints. This decision must balance theoretical and operational questions to create a model that is both theoretically acceptable and operationally viable. The objective function is described first and then we discuss the constraints added to the problem by the specific objective function.

The theoretical goal of a profit maximizing firm is to optimize the present value of net after tax income[2] (income after capital costs and taxes) subject to the firm's overall production function.[3] When the firm is owned by a set of stockholders, the goal should be changed to reflect the individual's claims on the firm's income. But this is difficult because the use of an earnings per share formulation generates a nonlinear objective function that makes the solution to the optimization problem more difficult. Also, when considering changes in outstanding stock, the firm must incorporate the relationship with the cost of capital and allow for the earnings per share - stock value function. These problems were avoided by making stock outstanding and its price exogenous so a simple formulation of the objective function can be used.

The model can also be complicated by variable capital costs.[4] This would require the firm to choose the optimal debt-equity ratio and retention rate in the objective function subject to a nonlinear cash flow constraint. But this problem is eliminated if the debt to equity and retention variables are considered parameters. Thus the capital cost is simply the weighted average cost of equity and debt capital [16]. If a firm believes it will have more capital than it can profitably invest, it should incorporate a dividend variable in the objective function. This variable requires the firm to pay out the surplus retained earnings and reduce the total debt. Thus the firm is prevented from investing in a project with a return below the cost of capital. Since the portfolio model implicitly assumes capital rationing, we will not discuss this situation further.

Finally, the infinite time horizon in the theoretical model is very difficult to operationalize in practice. To avoid this problem, the firm must pick a planning horizon T and summarize the net liquidation value[5] of each unit in a residual term Z_{jk}^i. If this residual term is omitted, then the objective function would bias the investment choice against long run growth strategies. In conclusion, the firm is interested in maximizing the present value of net earnings over a fixed time period. The objective function sums the discounted potential income from each strategy in each unit.[6] It can be written as:

$$(1) \quad Y = \sum_{t=1}^{T} (\pi \sum_{s=1}^{t} (1/1 + d(s)) \sum_i \sum_j S_j^i(t)) + \sum_i \sum_j \sum_k Z_{jk}^i(T) x_{jk}^i$$

where $S_j^i(t)$ is the income generated by employing the j'th strategy in the i'th unit. This income is defined by summing the returns from the initial assets and all investments and subtracting the capital charges.

$$(2) \quad S_j^i(t) = r_{j1}^i(t) \quad (1-\delta^i) A_j^i(t-1) x_{j1}^i + \sum_k r_{jk}^i(t) I_{jk}^i(t) x_{jk}^i - d(t) A_j^i(t)$$

One can write the objective function solely in terms of parameters and decision variables by making the level of assets endogenous to the model. The capital accumulation equation defines current assets as a function of the depreciation rate, past assets, present investment, and the decision variables. This equation can be written as:

$$(3) \quad A_j^i(t) = (1 - \delta^i) A_j^i(t-1) x_{j1}^i + \sum_k I_{jk}^i(t) x_{jk}^i$$

solving the equation for $A_j^i(t)$ in terms of A_0 and the I_{jk}^i's gives:[7]

$$(4) \quad A_j^i(t) = (1 - \delta^i)^t A_0 x_{j1}^i + \sum_{s<t} (1 - \delta^i)^{t-s} \sum_k I_{jk}^i(s) x_{jk}^i$$

Finally, equations 3 and 4 are substituted into equation 2 to give:

$$(5) \quad S_j^i(t) = (r_{j1}^i(t) - d(t) (1 - \delta^i) [(1-\delta^i)^{t-1} A_0 x_{j1}^i$$

$$+ \sum_{s<t-1} (1-\delta^i)^{t-s-1} \sum_k I_{jk}^i(s) x_{jk}^i]$$

$$+ \sum_k (r_{jk}^i(t) - d(t)) I_{jk}^i(t) x_{jk}^i$$

The final definition of the income of a strategy depends solely on parameters and decision variables of the model.

Divestment is modeled with the final investment project of the cash strategy. A negative investment level for the project should be picked to make the asset equation (3) to equal to zero. The rate of return (r_{jk}^i) is defined such that the unit has no net return. Thus the choice of the divestment strategy will cancel out the earlier returns and investment projects and allow the firm to use the proceeds from the liquidation of the business in other units. These proceeds will be defined as the difference between initial assets of the unit and the potential loss or gain from the sale of the assets (L^i).

Acquisitions or new ventures are easily modeled by including additional decision variables in the objective function. The returns should be defined as if the unit was part of the portfolio but the initial investment project must include the purchase or start-up costs of the business. Then the model will consider both the initial investment decision and the strategy decision for the new unit.

The actual cash return generated by a business unit is the accounting profit. This adds the return on equity to the next profit to give:

$$(6) \quad B_j^i(t) = S_j^i(t) + c(t) \ (\tfrac{1}{1+m}) \ A_j^i(t)$$

The model can be adjusted to optimize accounting profit if all the investment projects cover the cost of capital and the available investment funds are limited. The optimization routine will incorporate the shadow cost of investment in the analysis and choose a set of projects that maximize potential returns for the given level of investment funds.[8] This model may be easier to operationalize because it uses accounting data but its usefulness as a capital budgeting tool can be limited by restriction that all projects considered must be profitable. This new objective function is:

$$(7) \quad Y = \sum_{t=1}^{T} \ \pi_{s=1}^{t} \ (1/1 + d(s)) \sum_i \sum_j B_j^i(t) \quad [9]$$

The residual profit term $z_{jk}^i(T)$ is deleted to keep the model simple. This basic model represents a useful starting point for a firm considering an optimization planning model. But to utilize the full power of the optimization model for both strategic planning and capital budgeting, the net income objective function should be used.

Both objective functions incorporate the assumptions imposed on the present value maximization model by the initial production function constraint. But the use of either of the objective functions requires a set of constraints to minimize the problems caused by the assumptions and another set to account for the interrelationships between the choice variables. The model includes constraints requiring a balance in cash flow, a minimum growth in earnings per share, a minimum growth in assets, and the appropriate selection of investment projects.

Cash Flow Constraint

The cash balance equation is required to incorporate the limit on investment funds. The exogenous cash variable $(Ca(t))$ determines the balance between cash generated by earnings and new debt and cash used by dividends and growth. The constraint incorporates the constant debt to equity and retention variables that justify the constant cost of capital. The equation implies the firm increases dividends and reduces debt to eliminate any residual funds due to the lumpiness of investment projects. Imposing the constraint over a few years allows the firm to shift the surplus funds from period to period, but does not allow the firm to retain the interest on the funds. The residual funds in the final period are paid out as special dividends. Thus the multiyear constraint will not be as tight as a set of single year constraints. The basic form of the equation is:

$$(8) \quad \sum_i \ \sum_j \ (B_j^i(t) + m/(1+m) \ NI_j^i(t) - NI_j^i(t) - (1-p) \ B_j^i(t)) \geq Ca_t$$

where

$$NI_j^i(t) = \sum_k \ (I_{jk}^i(t) \ x_{jk}^i) - \delta A_j^i(t-1) - L^i x_{3K}; \text{ the net investment in unit i}$$

and

$\sum_j B_j^i(t)$ - the cash available from the net income of unit i.

$\sum_j m/(1+m)\ NI_j^i(t)$ - the cash generated by new debt in unit i.

$\sum_j NI_j^i(t)$ - the cash required for net investment in unit i.

$\sum_j (1-p)\ B_j^i(t)$ - the cash allocated for dividends in unit i.

The addition term, L^i, represents the loss of assets if the i'th unit is liquidated. Also the accounting profit is used because it represents the cash available for dividends and net investment.

Growth in Earnings Per Share Constraint

The earnings per share equation is incorporated in the model to ensure some growth plans are accepted regardless of the objective function's potential preference for current returns. The constraint requires the firm to choose a minimum growth rate in earnings per share (G_e). The equation can be applied for each year or for a set of years if the firm wants to specify an average growth rate. The annual form of the constraint is:

$$(9)\quad \sum_i \sum_j B_j^i(t+1) - Ms(t+1)/Eq(t+1) \geq$$

$$(1+G_e) \sum_i \sum_j B_j^i(t) - Ms(t) / Eq(t)$$

Market Share of Assets Constraints

The asset share constraint is included to prevent the truncation of the objective function from forcing the firm to follow a myopic strategy in a given unit. The constraint can be used when the firm believes a given market share offers benefits that are not quantified in the objective function[10] or when the residual term is not used. The equation sets a floor on the growth rate of assets of each business unit by linking the unit's assets to the total assets employed in the market. If asset share is related to market share, then the firm can pick the units in which it desires to gain or hold share. The constraint can be imposed for each year, a set of years, or the entire planning period. The general form of the equation is:

$$(10)\quad \sum_j A_j^i(t)\ x_j^i \geq V^i(t)\ Ia^i(t)$$

Investment Project Choice Constraints

The final set of constraints accounts for the mutual exclusiveness of the strategies and the dependence of the projects. Equation 11 requires the firm to pick only one strategy per unit and equation 12 makes acceptance of the k'th project contingent on acceptance of the previous k-1 projects.

$$(11)\quad \sum_j x_{j1}^i = 1 \text{ for all } i$$

$$(12)\quad x_{jk-1}^i \geq x_{jk}^i \text{ for all } i,\ j \text{ and for } k=2\ \ldots\ldots\ K$$

The integer programming solution to this problem will give the optimal set of strategies and investment plans the firm should employ to maximize its return given the other goals of the firm as quantified in the constraints [18]. The coefficients of the model can be adjusted to estimate the effect of various changes in the assumptions and goals of the firm. Thus the integer programming model is a useful tool that can improve the firm's strategic planning decisions by incorporating trade offs between investment projects and analyzing the effects of changes in factors that affect the firm's return.

In the next section, the model is solved using hypothetical test data based on business portfolio concepts. The accounting profit objective function is used because it involves fewer initial calculations. Either model should highlight the potential differences between the general portfolio methodology and the optimization model.

An Example of the Model

A numerical example is presented in this section to illustrate possible uses of the portfolio optimization model. Computational limitations restrict the test to six business units; each with four or five investment choices. The firm is assumed to have a portfolio of two "star" units, two "question mark" units and two "cash cow" units. Also, two new venture plans are considered to show the model can be easily adapted for diversification analysis.

The basic data, defined in line with the general portfolio hypothesis, are given in Table 1. Five strategy choices are listed for the "star" and "question mark" business units and four for the "cash cow" units. Each variable incorporates the results of both its investment plan and the previous investment plans to minimize the number of constraints needed in the model.[11] Annual results are given for two four year periods in Table 1. The second period data imply the strategic position of each business unit changes during the planning period. The "star" units become "cash cows", the "cash cow" units become less profitable, and the "question mark" units can move toward the "star" category. Also the new ventures come into existence. These shifts allow the firm to incorporate some of the expected results of their strategies in the analysis. The form of the information differs slightly from the variables given in the discussion of the model. The rate of return on assets represents profit after interest expense and taxes and the investment levels are implicitly given as percentage growth rates in assets. Depreciation is incorporated in the net growth variable so the depreciation parameter is zero. The values of most of the other parameters are set to zero to simplify the analysis of a base case.[12] The few nonzero parameters are given at the bottom of Table 1.

The parameters and data were used to calculate the accounting profit objective function. Constraints for cash flow and growth in earnings per share were defined for each of the four year time periods. Also one market share equation and one investment choice constraint were specified for each business unit. Then a simple integer programming routine was used to solve for the optimal solution. Finally, some of the parameters of the model were adjusted and new solutions were generated.

Table 2 presents the results of the various solutions of the model. The optimal strategies generated by a portfolio model, using only the full cash and growth strategies (CH and GH), are given in Column 1.[13] The general solution to the optimization model is presented in Column 2. It suggests the firm sacrifice some growth in the "star" business units to finance full growth in the "question mark" units. The addition of a few investment levels increases the overall return to the firm because the allocation of investment funds is improved. But the firm may be concerned about the position of the "star" business. Using the asset share constraint, the firm can require a minimum level of growth in the "star" businesses. The solution to this problem is listed in Column 3. The growth in one "star" unit increases and the growth in the other decreases to the minimally acceptable level. The income falls slightly but the loss may be necessary to

Table 1

Data Used in the Test of the Model

Strategies	Results for		Years 1-4		Years 5-8	
	Return on Initial Investment	Net Growth in Assets	Return on Project	Additional Growth in Assets	Return on Initial Investment	Net Growth in Assets
Star 1	Assets = 200					
CL	9.2	4	0	0	10.2	3
CH	9.2	4	5.2	6	12.2	3
M	8.0	12	0	0	12.7	3
GL	7.2	13	0	0	13.2	3
GH	7.2	13	3.2	2	14.2	3
Star 2	Assets = 200					
CL	12.2	4	0	0	13.2	3
CH	12.2	4	8.2	6	15.2	3
M	11.0	12	0	0	15.7	3
GL	10.2	13	0	0	16.2	3
GH	10.2	13	6.2	2	17.2	3
Question Mark 1	Assets = 100					
CL	0	-100	0	0	0	0
CH	9.2	-3	0	0	4.2	-3
M	6.2	10	0	0	6.2	10
GL	4.2	14	0	0	7.7	14
GH	4.2	14	2.2	6	9.2	20
Question Mark 2	Assets = 100					
CL	0	-100	0	0	0	0
CH	9.2	-3	0	0	4.2	-3
M	6.2	12.5	0	0	6.2	12.5
GL	4.2	17	0	0	7.7	17
GH	4.2	17	2.2	8	9.2	25
Cash Cow 1	Assets = 200					
CL	17.2	-3	0	0	9.2	2
CH	17.2	-3	15.2	5	10.2	2
M	15.4	3	0	0	10.7	2
G	14.2	4	0	0	11.2	2
Cash Cow 2	Assets = 200					
CL	14.2	-2	0	0	6.2	2
CH	14.2	-2	12.2	5	7.2	2
M	12.4	4	0	0	7.7	2
G	11.2	5	0	0	8.2	2
New Venture	Assets = 100					
NV1	0	0	0	0	6.2	10
NV2	0	0	0	0	4.2	20

Parameters

h = .04	M = .25	K = 2	Ge = .06
p = .8	d = .04	T = 8	Eq(t) = 100

ensure a profitable future for both the "star" units. In each of the solutions, the firm accepts a new venture business unit.

The liquidation option is used in Column 4 when the firm requires a positive net cash flow of 200 units in each four year period. The loss on the liquidation (L^1) of "question mark 1" is increased to 20 units in Column 5 and 40 units in Column 6 and new optimal solutions are generated. In Column 6, the firm retains "question mark 1" and liquidates "question mark 2". This shows a divestment decision must look at both the potential earnings of a unit and the liquidation value of the unit.

Finally, Columns 7 and 8 imply the firm prefers cash strategies as the discount rate for the second period increases. A rate of 10 percent, used in Column 7, causes the firm to reduce the growth in "star 2" and "question mark 2". Column 8 presents results derived when the planning horizon is set at four years (i.e. an infinite discount rate in second period). It requires the firm to use the cash strategy for the "star" and "cash cow" business units and the mixed strategy for the "question marks". These results show the model favors cash strategies when the time horizon is shortened and the residual term is ignored.

The example was simplified because the available integer programming algorithm had strict limits on the number of variables and constraints. A firm that desired to operationalize the strategic planning model would need a better computer program. If the necessary computer programming expertise were available in-house, the company could devise their own computer program based on a published algorithm ([6], [8], [9]). Alternatively, a corporation could use one of the large scale integer programming algorithms commercially available (for example IBM's MPSX, Univac's SCICON, CDC's APEX, or UCC's UMPIRE). Hamilton and Moses [10] report these codes can solve a problem with 1000 variables and 750 constraints. Also, Forest, Hirst and Tomlin [7] report success with large problems using the UMPIRE program. Finally, a recent article by Sweeny and Murphy [15] should allow one to solve very large strategy choice problems by breaking the optimization problem into various subproblems. Thus the solution of a real portfolio optimization problem should be possible given enough time and effort.

The examples in this section show the additional strategies of the optimization model improve the ability of the firm to define optimal investment plans. The optimization model also offers a better framework to analyze acquisition and divestment decisions. Finally, the importance of the choice of the discount rate is illustrated.

Expansions of the Model

The financial side of the model could be improved by evaluating the effects of new equity issues on the optimal solution. This should allow the firm to estimate the investment opportunities foregone due to the lack of capital. Also, a particular run could be used to evaluate the effects of an acquisition financed by equity. Additional expansions along the lines of the Hamilton and Moses [10] paper are possible. The firm could differentiate between short and long term debt, common and preferred stock and stock sales and purchases. Finally, the firm could incorporate the rising cost of capital in the model and invest until this cost equals the marginal return.

The model could also be used to evaluate the risk of a set of strategies. The solution of the model under various scenarios (for the return rates) would allow the firm to investigate the robustness of the certainty equivalence solution. Alternatively, each strategy could be discounted for its degree of risk. This would give a risk adjusted optimal solution. Of course the definition of the risk adjusted discount rate would be difficult.

New variables could be added to the model to allow the firm to change a strategy

Table 2

Results of the Optimization Model

	1	2	3	4	5	6	7	8
Star 1	GH	CH	M	M	CH	CL	CH	CH
Star 2	GH	GL	M	CH	CH	CH	CH	CH
Question Mark 1	CH	GH	GH	CL*	CL*	GH	GH	M
Question Mark 2	GH	GH	GH	GH	GH	CL*	GL	M
Cash Cow 1	CH	CH	CH	CH	CH	CH	CH	CH
Cash Cow 2	CH	CH	CH	CH	CH	CH	CH	CH
New Venture	NV1	NV1	NV1	-	-	-	NV1	-
8-year income	1128	1137	1135	986	977	896	1058	963

1 Simple 2 Choice Portfolio Model

2 Base Run of Optimization Model

3 Asset Share requirement in "Stars"

4 Cash Requirement (Ca(t)) of 200 units per period

5 Same as 4 with loss of 20 on sale of "QM1"

6 Same as 4 with loss of 40 on sale of "QM1"

7 Discount results of 2nd 4 year period at 10 percent in the objective function

8 Delete results of 2nd 4 year period from objective function

*This strategy requires the divestment of the unit

during the planning period. This could be useful for a firm trying to plan for a major exogenous change. For example, the oil companies anticipated a large cash loss due to the windfall profits tax so they had to be prepared to change a few strategies. The possibility of changing strategies would also be useful for risk planning.

The ability to expand the model is another major advantage of an optimization model. In fact, any situation that can be quantified with a decision variable or a linear constraint can be considered with the integer programming model. Thus the portfolio optimization model can be directly applied to a broader set of problems than the portfolio matrix model.

CONCLUSIONS

This paper has presented an integer programming portfolio planning model that allows the firm to allocate investment funds between units to maximize the long run return. In the model the firm chooses individual investment levels within a strategy for each unit. Also the effect on the firm of an acquisition of a new unit or the divestment of an existing unit can be analyzed. The model can be solved to define the optimal strategies for variations in the time horizon, the discount rate, the cash flow constraint, growth in earnings per share and required assets. This type of analysis is more difficult in the usual portfolio model. Finally, the optimization model can be expanded to handle financial and risk analysis and changes in strategies easier than the simple portfolio models. Thus the optimization model represents an attractive alternative to ordinary portfolio analysis if reliable input data is available.

But one should note that seven years after the Hamilton and Moses paper [10], integer programming is rarely used for corporate strategy and investment decisions. We can offer a few reasons for integer programming's failure to gain acceptance. First, any optimization model imposes heavy demands on the corporate staff for reliable data since the firm must define a number of alternatives for each business unit in the corporate portfolio. Also, specific computer software is necessary to calculate the coefficients of the integer programming problem from the raw data. Changes in the time horizon or discount rate will force the firm to calculate a new integer programming problem. Both these problems suggest an optimization model requires a large input of corporate staff time. Given the structured problem, no algorithm is guaranteed to solve an integer program in a finite amount of computer time. Thus the firm can invest resources to overcome the first two problems but not get the desired results. Finally, attempts to implement optimization models may fail because of internal political problems [13].

Fortunately, many integer programming algorithms will allow the firm to salvage a partial solution if the model fails to converge. This partial solution can be analyzed and will probably prove to be acceptable. Also strong support from top management can overcome the various political problems [13]. Thus the integer programming model can be successfully applied to the firm's investment allocation problem if top management commits the necessary resources to the project. Since the optimal solution incorporates the implicit trade offs between investments in different units, it should at least be a very useful test of the strategic plan of any diversified company.

APPENDIX A

THE LONG RUN OBJECTIVE FUNCTION

The objective function of the firm can be formulated in terms of cash flows, net accounting profits,[1] or economic profits. Given an infinite time horizon, all the methods give identical results. If a finite horizon is used, a different salvage value has to be added to each objective function to keep them equivalent.

The three measures differ only in their treatment of capital costs. The cash flow formulation measures the net cash generated by the operation of the firm. Investment is incorporated as a negative cash flow so no depreciation or capital expenses are considered. This objective function also includes a positive payment for the salvage value of capital. The net accounting profit method capitalizes many tangible (plant and equipment. . .) and intangible (goodwill and patents) assets. But other assets such as advertising and research and development costs are expenses even though these expenditures are expected to yield positive returns in the future. Profit is calculated by subtracting depreciation and capital costs from the operating margin (net of the expensed assets) of the unit. The depreciation allowance must be based on the loss of asset value to the firm and not on an accounting convention. Finally, only the additional salvage value (above the net capital stock) is included in the objective function when the asset is sold or time horizon reached.

The economic profit function requires the firm to capitalize any expenditure that is expected to yield a future return. Then the imputed costs for depreciation and the use of capital are deducted from the operating margin to give the net profit. The gain or loss on the liquidation of an asset should be incorporated in the objective function when the asset is sold or the time horizon reached. The present value of the firm is calculated by discounting any of the objective functions with the cost of capital. Because each objective function is defined in a different manner, the individual terms should differ. Thus only economic profits are relevant as a short run performance measure.

The operational use of each method has its difficulties. The terminal value of a unit is very important in the cash flow model if it represents a large share of the return of the strategy. Unfortunately, the terminal value is difficult to estimate because it occurs at the end of the planning period. A large error in defining this value can lead to incorrect planning decisions by distorting the relative returns of the various plans. To avoid this problem, one would like to capitalize all the firm's assets and measure the economic profit in each period. This would allow the firm to incorporate the returns from a strategy in the model as they accrue. But the measurement of profit requires the firm to define a depreciation rate for each asset. This is a difficult task, especially for intangible assets. Incorrect estimates of the depreciation rates will cause a bias in the profit level of a strategy by affecting the depreciation and capital costs. Biased profit rates can lead to mistakes in defining the firm's optimal strategies. The net accounting profit formulation suffers from a mild case of both problems. Terminal values are required to account for non-capitalized assets and depreciation rates are needed for the capitalized assets. Thus any approach suffers from a few operational problems.

This paper uses net accounting profit because it corresponds closely to the regular accounting profit that is used in business. Also, one can hope the capitalization of many assets with easily determined depreciation rates (i.e., plant and equipment) will reduce the importance of the terminal value. This may allow the model to define the optimal strategy even if some error exists in the parameters.

APPENDIX B

OPTIMIZATION IN AN INFLATIONARY WORLD

The optimization model discussed in this paper, abstracts from the very real problem of inflation.[1] In an inflationary environment, assets measured at book value underestimate the value of the capital stock of the firm.[2] Thus the firm's total cost of capital is biased downward so the net accounting profit formulation of the model may not generate the optimal investment strategy. This implies management must either avoid the use of assets or include inflation adjusted assets in the model.

The cash flow optimization objective function initially avoids the need for assets. The firm simply estimates net cash flows from the different strategies and investment plans and discounts the cash returns with the inflation adjusted cost of capital. But the cash flow method also requires the firm to project a liquidation value for the end of the planning period. This requires some idea of the real value of the assets held by the firm at the time horizon. Also the value of assets in each period is required if the firm desires to maintain a constant real debt-equity ratio. Thus the firm must be able to define inflation adjusted assets to use an optimization model.

To project the value of the capital stock in any period, the firm must first define the real value of assets in the initial period. Then, for each year, capital appreciation should be incorporated in the asset variable. Also the investment project assets should be allowed to appreciate. This method allows the firm to model the nominal value of assets in each period. Once a consistent set of values are defined for assets, the firm can use any formulation of the objective function.

The accounting profit objective function can be implemented with all the data defined in terms of nominal dollars. The depreciation expense must be based on the inflated value of assets. Also the cost of capital must allow for the average appreciation of the firm's assets during the period. This implies a net cost of capital can be defined as:

$$ad_j^i(t) = d(t) - \bar{a}_j^i(t)$$

where

$d(t)$ = the inflation adjusted cost of capital

$\bar{a}_j^i(t)$ = the average appreciation of the assets existing at time $t-1$ for the i'th unit following the j'th strategy

The net accounting income for a representative unit can then be written as:

$$\sum_j S_j^i(t) = \sum_j \left((r_{j1}^i(t) - ad_j^i(t)) (1-\delta^i) (1+\bar{a}_j^i(t)) A_j^i(t-1) x_{j1}^i \right.$$

$$\left. + (r_{jk}^i(t) - d(t)) \sum_k I_{jk}^i x_{jk}^i \right)$$

Summing the income from each unit will give the firm's objective function.

A few minor adjustments in the constraints are also necessary. In the cash flow equation, the firm should be allowed to issue additional debt to keep the real debt-equity ratio constant.[3] The new debt should be related to the appreciation of the existing assets. Thus the following term is added to the cash flow constraint (equation 8) to represent the additional debt capacity:

$$m \; \bar{a}_j^i \; A_j^i(t-1) \; x_{j1}^i$$

The firm may also want to allow the required growth rate to vary with time if the expected inflation rate is not constant. Finally industry assets must be defined in future dollars to be compatible with the asset definition. These changes will allow the firm to adjust the model for inflation.

Operationally, it is important to note anticipated inflation offers the firm some tax advantages and disadvantages. First, depreciation for tax purposes is based on book value. This implies the firm must pay a higher effective tax rate in an inflationary period. Also, the cost basis for a liquidated asset is the net book value. Thus the firm will have to pay tax on the inflation incorporated in the value of the asset. On the other hand, interest expense is tax deductible even though the inflation premium represents the payment of principle. Thus the firm benefits from debt more in inflationary periods. All of these factors should be incorporated in the parameters for the after tax returns of a strategy.

Our optimization model, with all the input data defined in nominal terms, will allow the firm to define an optimal strategy. Alternatively the firm could define all the data in real terms and solve for the same optimal solution. We use the nominal formulation because it allows the firm to use the market cost of capital. Use of the real value formulation would require the firm to estimate the market inflation premium in addition to defining all the other parameters in real terms.

FOOTNOTES

[1]The BCG literature doesn't consider a mixed strategy so we conclude they consider it inferior.

[2]Three equivalent approaches to present value optimization are discussed in Appendix A.

[3]A firm value model should be used if risk is considered.

[4]Although the issued equity is fixed, the capital available to the firm and its cost can change with the debt-equity ratio and the retention rate.

[5]The net liquidation value is the difference between the liquidation value and the value of the capitalized assets.

[6]The adjustments in the model necessary to account for inflation are given in Appendix B.

[7]The decision variable $(x_{j1}^i)^{t-s}$ is removed from the summation term because it is extraneous.

[8]A slight error can be introduced if the shadow cost of funds varies over time.

[9]Accounting profit can also be written as:

$$B_j^i(t) = (r_{j1}^i(t) - h(t) \ (m/1 + m) \ (1-\delta^i)[(1-\delta^i)^{t-1}A_0 \ x_{j1}^i.$$

$$+ \sum_{s<t-1} (1-\delta^i)^{t-s-1} \sum_k I_{jk}^i(s) \ x_{jk}^i]$$

$$+ \sum_k (r_{jk}^i(t) - h(t) \ (m/1 + m)) \ I_{jk}^i(t) \ x_{jk}^i$$

[10]For example, shared experience with other units or future profit potential not captured in residual term.

[11]Therefore the decision variables are mutually exclusive.

[12]The following parameters are nonzero: h=.04, n=.25, K=2, Ge=.06, p=.8, d=.04, T=8 and Eq(t) = 100.

[13]This solution would be generated by the BCG.

APPENDIX A

[1]Net accounting profit is the difference between accounting book profit and imputed capital costs. We assume the firm uses the theoretically correct depreciation rates.

APPENDIX B

[1]The firm is assumed to be able to anticipate the inflation in the economy.

[2]For a capital budgeting approach to the inflation problem, see [17].

[3]Debt is defined in fixed dollar terms so it depreciates with inflation. Likewise monetary assets will also depreciate with inflation, but real assets will appreciate. Thus the firm's real debt-equity ratio will fall unless additional debt is issued.

REFERENCES

[1]   Allen, M. "Competitive Business Strategies", in Strategic Leadership: The Challenge to Chairmen, pp. 14-22. London McKinsey & Co., 1978.

[2]   Boston Consulting Group. "A Strategy Based Resource Allocation Model", BCG Report, 1972.

[3]   _____. "Cash Traps", BCG Perspectives, No. 102, 1972.

[4]   _____. "Pay Off on the Corporate Portfolio", BCG Perspectives, No. 195, 1976.

[5]   Coate, M. "The Boston Consulting Group's Strategic Portfolio Planning Model: An Economic Analysis", Unpublished Ph.D. Dissertation, Duke University, 1980.

[6]   Faaland, B. and Hillier F. "The Accelerated Bound and Scan Algorithm for Integer Programmng", Operations Research 23 (May-June 1975): 406-425.

[7]   Forrest, J. Hirst, J. and Tomlin, J. "Practical Solutions of Large Scale Mixed Integer Programming Problems with Umpire", Management Science 20 (1973): 736-773.

[8]   Garfinkel and Nembauser. Integer Programming. New York: John Wiley & Sons, 1972.

[9]   Gillett. Introduction to Operations Research, An Algorithmic Approach, New York: McGraw-Hill, 1976.

[10] Hamilton, W. and Moses, M. "An Optimization Model for Corporate Financial Planning", Operations Research 13 (May-June 1973): 677-692.

[11] Hedley, B. "A Fundamental Approach to Strategy Development", Long Range Planning 12 (December 1976): 2-11.

[12] _____. "Strategy and the Business Portfolio", Long Range Planning 10 (February 1977): 9-15.

[13] Naylor, T. "The Politics of Corporate Model Building", Planning Review (January, 1975).

[14] Patel, P. and Younger, M. "A Frame of Reference for Strategy Development", Long Range Planning 12 (April 1978), 6-12.

[15] Sweeney, D. and Murphy R. "A Method for Decomposition for Integer Programs", Operations Research 27 (November-December 1979): 1128-1141.

[16] Van Horne, J. Financial Management and Policy, Englewood Cliffs, NJ: Prentice Hall, Inc., 1977.

[17] _____. "A Note on Biases in Capital Budgeting Introduced by Inflation", Journal of Financial and Quantitative Analysis 6 (January 1971): 653-658.

[18] Weingartner, J. Mathematical Programming and the Analysis of Capital Budgeting Problems, Englewood Cliffs, NJ: Prentice Hill, Inc., 1963.

CAPITAL MARKET MODELS AND THEIR IMPLICATION
FOR STRATEGY FORMULATION

Michael R. Graham

Strategic Planning Associates
Washington, D.C.
U.S.A.

INTRODUCTION

Strategic planning tools took on quantitative significance with the application of financial economics to corporate and strategic business unit (SBU) problems. The application of the experience curve, growth share matrix, and the PIMS relations had a profound impact on the manner in which companies went about developing SBU strategies.

Evolution has taken place in the implementation of these tools over the past decade or so. The emergence of the cross-sectional experience curve concept has altered the cost benefit which is implied by the traditional experience curve approach. Plotting the experience curve for a company may indicate that a twenty-five percent reduction in cost is achieved with a doubling in cumulative value. However, smart follower strategies, technology transfer, and other effects make the reduction relative to another competitor, with half the cumulative value, only about five to ten percent in practice. Value-added share, the composite of the relative market shares at each value-added step, is often a better competitive measure than relative market share. Value-added leverage, linkage, and a host of other concepts have helped to make the implementation of these financial economic tools more relevant to what is actually occurring in the competitive arena.

In the past few years, capital market models have been evolving to the point where they now offer a sound linkage between corporate strategy and financial strategy formulation. Any capital markets model must be able to address the key question asked by top management: How do we create value for our shareholders? To get a handle on how this question can be answered the market to book equity ratio was chosen as a first cut measure of value creation and an empirical test of the key determinants of this ratio was performed. The market to book rato is a simple measure for value creation because it examines what the market is willing to pay for each dollar which has been reinvested on the shareholders. If the market to book ratio is greater than one, value has been created. If the market to book ratio is less than one, value has been destroyed.

At this point, it is worth addressing the issue of the validity of the use of book value. One argument is that many companies such as forest products and oil companies have meaningless book values because of the sale value of the assets on their books. It is true that the sale value of the land holdings of a timber company may be greater than the market value, let alone the book value, of the company. But the real issue is that as long as say a forest products company does not turn into a real estate venture company the market values the operating return of the company and hence its return on book equity. To take it to an extreme, if you were to look at market value to expected economic value the ratio would always be one. Market value to replacement cost, relative to return on replacement cost, has been examined, as well as the effects of LIFO/FIFO, and the expensing of significant marketing and research and development costs, yet the fact remains that the key insights can be gained from looking only at straight book equity.

Empirical Relation

The empirical work examined a number of relationships, and a good correlation was found by examining the market to book ratio versus the ratio of the return on equity to the required return on equity. Figure 1 shows a graph of this relationship for the forest products industry.

The Forest Products Industry Exhibits the General Relationship Between
Profitability and Market to Book Value

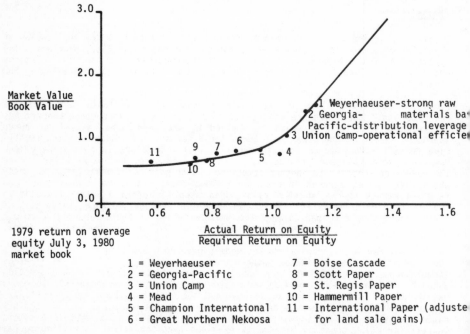

Market Value
Book Value

1979 return on average
equity July 3, 1980
market book

Actual Return on Equity
Required Return on Equity

1 = Weyerhaeuser   7 = Boise Cascade
2 = Georgia-Pacific   8 = Scott Paper
3 = Union Camp   9 = St. Regis Paper
4 = Mead   10 = Hammermill Paper
5 = Champion International   11 = International Paper (adjuste
6 = Great Northern Nekoosa   for land sale gains)

Figure 1

The general relationship is that above a return on equity to required return (defined as the profitability leverage) of one the market to book is a linear function of the profitability leverage. Below a profitability leverage of one the curve flattens out.

In order for this concept to have implications for strategy it is necessary for this relationship to hold over time as well as at one point in time. Figure 2 shows a ten-year time plot for Mead corporation. Following its significant portfolio clean-up of its "dog" businesses in 1975 Mead's profitability improved dramatically. Mead's market to book also moved up but it is clear that they are fighting up the shallow part of the valuation curve.

Mead Has Improved Its Market to Book Ratio 43% Since the Early Seventies

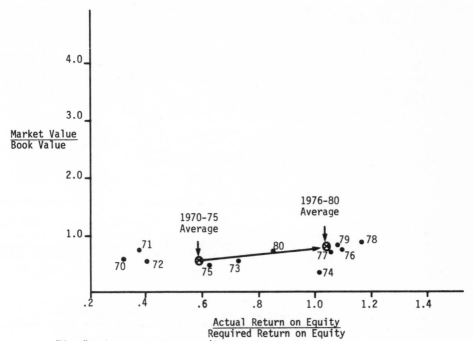

. "Year" return on average equity
. "Year"-end market to book ratio

Figure 2

By contrast, consider Union Camp's movement over the same ten years. Figure 3 shows how Union Camp's slight decline in profitability caused a precipitous drop in its market to book ratio. Union Camp was falling down the highly levered portion of the valuation curve during this period of time.

These examples help illustrate the general relation between market to book and the profitability leverage. The relation holds not only at a point in time but also over time; thus it has practical application in the quantifying of the change in the value associated with strategic change.

By plotting hundreds of companies in dozens of industries the second key determinant of market to book emerges. Figure 4 summarizes the results of the empirical study. When the profitability leverage is greater than one growth has a positive impact on market to book. The faster a company can grow and maintain a given superior profitability leverage, the more it will be rewarded by the market because of the compounding of that superior return. Conversely, a company making consistently poor investments will be penalized more the faster it grows. If a company is delivering exactly the required return on equity, growth has little impact. This explains why both Clorox and Bell Industries sell at a market to book of approximately one, even though Bell Industries is growing twice as fast as Clorox.

M.R. Graham

Union Camp's Profitability Has Slipped Since 1976 Resulting in a Deterioration of Its Market to Book Ratio

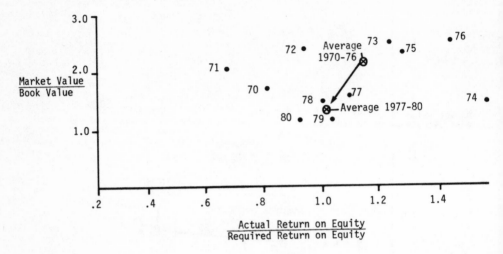

Figure 3

The Market Rewards Growth Only When ROE Eventually Exceeds the Cost of Equity; Otherwise Growth has a Neutral or Negative Impact on a Company's Value

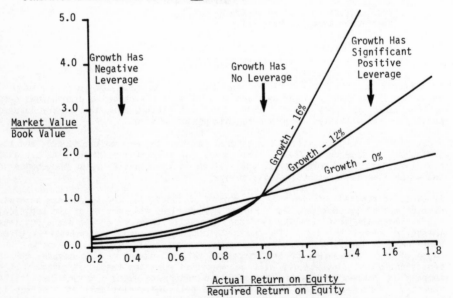

Figure 4

Theoretical Relation

The theoretical justification for this relationship is quite strong. Consider, for example, a simple one-stage, constant growth, free cash flow model of security pricing:

$$P_0 = \frac{FCF_1}{(1+k_e)} + \frac{FCF_1(1+g_{FCF})}{(1+k_e)^2} + \frac{FCF_1(1+g_{FCF})^2}{(1+k_e)^3} + \ldots = \frac{FCF_1}{k_e - g_{FCF}}$$

Where k_3 is the required return on equity, P_0 is the security price today, FCF is the free cash flow (dividend) next period, and g_{FCF} is the growth in free cash flow.

We could encompass more situations by expanding to a two or three-stage growth model but this will illustrate how the relationship is derived.

Using accounting relations we can derive an equation for the market to book ratio:

$$\left(\frac{M}{B}\right)_0 = \frac{ROE - g_{BV}}{k_e - g_{FCF}}$$

Where $(M/B)_0$ is the market to book ratio today, ROE is the return on (beginning of year) book equity, and g_{BV} is the growth in book equity value. In steady state, $g_{FCF} = g_{BV}$. Given constant growth and required return the linear relation becomes:

$$\left(\frac{M}{B}\right)_0 = \left(\frac{1}{1-\frac{g_{FCF}}{k_e}}\right)\left(\frac{ROE}{k_e}\right) + \left(\frac{-g_{BV}}{1-\frac{g_{FCF}}{k_e}}\right)$$

Empirically, this relation only holds true when the profitability leverage is greater than one. Below one companies are valued on (1) an improving investment mix, (2) free cash flow and the probability and timing of a takeover, or (3) free cash flow and the probability and timing of liquidation. Equations for these alternate states can be derived.

Business Valuation

As an outgrowth of the corporate valuation curve the implications for implicit business valuation can now be addressed. It is clear that a business which has negative free cash flow on a sustained basis will have a negative contribution to the corporate stock price. What isn't obvious is that if little or no information exists about an SBU, then that SBU can have a negative impact on the corporate stock price even if it has positive earnings. Consider the example in Figure 5: A company has two SBU's, each with a book value of $100 MM and growing at twelve percent.

From this example it is clear that low-return businesses are valued differently depending upon whether they are in a corporate portfolio or freestanding. This phenomenon is the driving force behind many of the asset redeployment moves by major corporations. If a company can get a stock price boost like Huffy received when they wrote off their lawnmower division or like Esmark received when they announced they were liquidating Swift and selling an underutilized asset then there is a powerful incentive to redeploy assets.

Figure 6 illustrates the difference between corporate valuation, the solid curve

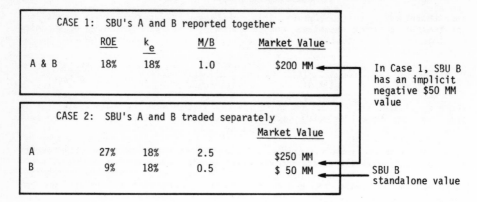

Figure 5

and business valuation, the dotted line extension. For an SBU, if it is not clear that management is going to take decisive steps and not fund an SBU whose long-term profitability leverage is below one, then that business will have a depressing impact on the corporate stock price.

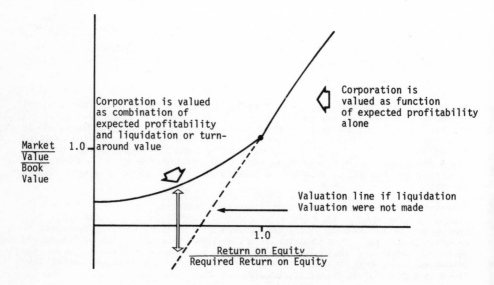

Figure 6

Three distinct zones of SBU valuation can be delineated. Value is created when the profitability leverage is above one; value is destroyed but there is a positive contribution to stock price if the profitability leverage is below one but yet the SBU can sustain its own growth, and value is completely destroyed and it has a negative contribution to stock price if it cannot sustain its own growth. Figure 7 identifies these three regions:

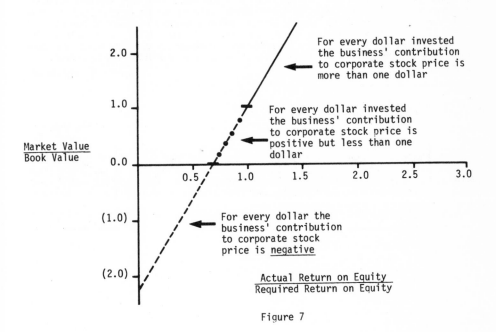

Figure 7

Corporate Strategy Implications

The implications for corporate strategy are threefold:

(1) Capital market required return on equity hurdles must be quantified in order to know how to evaluate which strategies will create value for the shareholders.

(2) Corporate strategy should identify and pursue all profitable growth strategies (profitability leverage greater than one). The valuation curves provide a framework for making the growth/profitability trade-off decisions. Comparing industry causes of profitability against the required return gives a strong indication of whether value will be created.

(3) The valuation curves can help to value strategic change. The trade-off between pursuing strategies which create value but disrupt the corporate culture can be

made easier if the amount of value created can be quantified. This valuation
framework will answer whether asset redeployment will pay off for a company or
not.

Financial Strategy Implications

Financial strategy addresses the options of how to balance corporate cash flow.
Given a set of profitable growth opportunities and operating characteristics the
two major balancing factors are debt policy and dividend policy. Debt policy
should be set so as to maximize the value to the equity shareholders. This is
achieved when the profitability leverage is a maximum. Return on equity increases
as more debt is used to lever up the returns. The return on equity tends to rise
less rapidly at high debt levels because of the rapid increase in the cost of
debt.   The required return on equity continues to rise rapidly with debt as the
financial risk of the free cash flow increases dramatically. Therefore, as shown
in Figure 8, there is a prudent limit at which the profitability leverage is a
maximum.

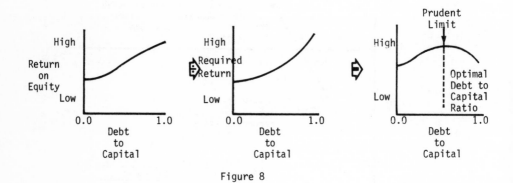

Figure 8

These relations can be determined and the value created by properly leveraging can
be quantified accordingly.

Dividend policy now becomes a fallout of the profitable growth strategies pursued
and the debt which can be prudently taken on. Institutional and clientele effects
on dividend policy may modify this straightforward policy in some cases.

Integrated Strategic Planning

Corporate strategy should identify all profitable growth opportunities available
and implement those strategies. Identifying profitable growth requires an understanding of the industry causes of profitability, industry key success factors,
corporate areas of distinct competence, competitive analysis, to name just a few
tests required to determine long-term profitability potential.

Financial strategy should limit the amount of shareholders equity required to fund
the corporate strategy.   Dividends, cash or share repurchase thus becomes the
fallout of the corporate and financial strategies.

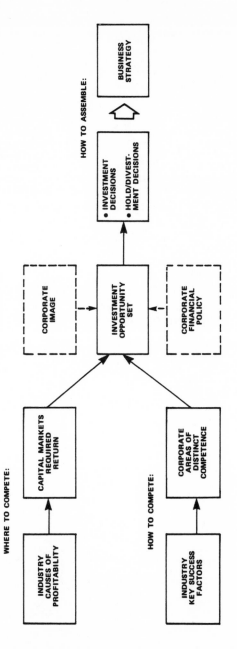

Figure 9

DECISION SUPPORT SYSTEMS FOR STRATEGIC PLANNING

THE ROLE OF DECISION SUPPORT SYSTEMS
IN CORPORATE STRATEGY

Michael S. Scott-Morton

Sloan School
Massachusetts Institute of Technology
Cambridge, Massachusetts
U.S.A.

The theme of this conference is the integration of economics and corporate planning models into corporate strategy. I have been asked to talk about computers
and their role in this whole process. To move directly to the subject of computers as it relates to this topic implies that everyone knows precisely what is
meant by these three terms, that is, economics, corporate planning models and
corporate strategy. The frequency with which people share common definitions of
these three terms is extremely low. This is not to say that each person does not
have their own definition of these three terms because, of course, they do.
However, given different backgrounds and the various ways in which one arrives at
this conjunction of fields makes it very unlikely that they will have a shared
definition of these three terms and the implications of computers for them.

Before getting to the primary theme, let me give you my view of the central one of
these three terms, that is, corporate strategy. I will not apologize for what
follows because I am hoping that you will all take it in the spirit in which it is
intended. I am not going to lay out a clear precise definition of the field of
corporate strategy as I am not as naive as to believe such a definition is possible at this point in time, and in any event there are others better qualified
than I to do such a monumental task. Rather, I am simply going to express my
biases so that what I have to say about the use of computers will perhaps make
more sense and be more useful, given there is an understanding of the perspective
with which I approach the field.

A very simplistic notion of corporate strategy for an organization contains the
following basic elements:

- An understanding of the organization's fundamental strengths and weaknesses, it's competition, and the forces that are acting in its environment.

- Having understood where the organization stands, there is then the task of
  forecasting the climate (the environment) that will be impacting the organization in the future.

- Following this understanding of the external forces there is then the task
  of deciding where the organization wants to position itself, some appropriate number of years in the future.

- Having identified this desired position there then becomes the task of
  identifying and selecting those strategies and programs for the corporation
  and its relevant business that are going to have to be implemented to
  achieve that end objective.

- There then is the task of monitoring and modifying the plans as time goes
  on.

Clearly, the steps implied in this brief statement of what corporate strategy must
consist of are overlapping, interactive, and involve a wide variety of substeps

and sub-analyses that must go on if a satisfactory conclusion is to be reached. It is also a generic view which does not take into account the particular characteristics of the kind of business, the size of business, and the goals that the business may have at this point in time.

Despite the fact this is a very simplified view of what corporate strategy consists of, it seems to me that it does include the basic elements. This definition of corporate strategy, albeit oversimplified, has been raised to emphasize the fact the corporate strategy really is a multi-faceted, complex subject. Having surveyed the ten or fifteen books which have come out in the last couple of years, one does not find in any one (see Bibliography) of them sufficiently clear view of what corporate strategy is all about, to leave one feeling as if we have yet got our hands around this complex topic.

An example of this semantic confusion may help to support the need for greater clarity. It is not uncommon in organizations when one is talking about strategy and the need for planning to have all the executives nod their heads and agree and say, "absolutely right, planning is a very important thing to do and it really is crucial for our organization, we believe in it." "However, unfortunately, in our firm, planning is not possible right now." "We believe in it and it is very important, but unfortunately in our particular organization we are in the midst of considerable technological change and there is a considerable shift in government regulation, our environment is very dynamic and we are just unable to plan!" It is not possible for them right now they say because as they look at the future and attempt to understand how the world is moving, they will turn out to be wrong. They have tried several times and failed to get anywhere close in their plan to what actually has occurred.

Now, of course, any professional in the field of planning understands the kind of response that has to be made to the managers in that organization. It is the simple one of explaining that planning is not forecasting and the two should never be confused! Put another way, one does not plan to be right, the plan is made so that one knows whether it has been achieved or not and can then analyze why. In planning, particularly strategic planning, one is not primarily in the business of trying to guess and forecast where the organization is going to end up five or ten years from now, but rather in understanding the forces that work in the world in which the organization operates and in making a decision about where one would like to be and in planning to achieve that objective in a rational way. It is true, of course, that no one will ever accomplish that rational purpose, and one should not be surprised to find the whole set of conditions and forces totally different two years from now. However, it is crucial to recognize where one is, and then to try to understand what forces and assumptions that led us astray and resulted in our not ending up in the place that had been planned. The insight gained from that analysis is a vital part of the input to the plan for the next time around. In short, planning is a dynamic process, not merely a product.

This oversimplified, generic view of strategic planning can be put in a diagramatic form. Figure 1 suggests that an early step in the processes of strategic planning must be to state one's goals and objectives for the organization and the major pieces of the organization in some explicit way, and to do that in light of the understanding of two things:

   - One's major internal strengths and weaknesses
   - The major external factors that surround the organization and impinge on it.

These two sets of factors constrain the organization and dictate what each relevant goal and objective ought to be. In short, an understanding of one's current position and the forces acting on one.

As is implied in Figure 2, a next step in strategic planning is to forecast what the major external environmental forces are likely to look like over some appro-

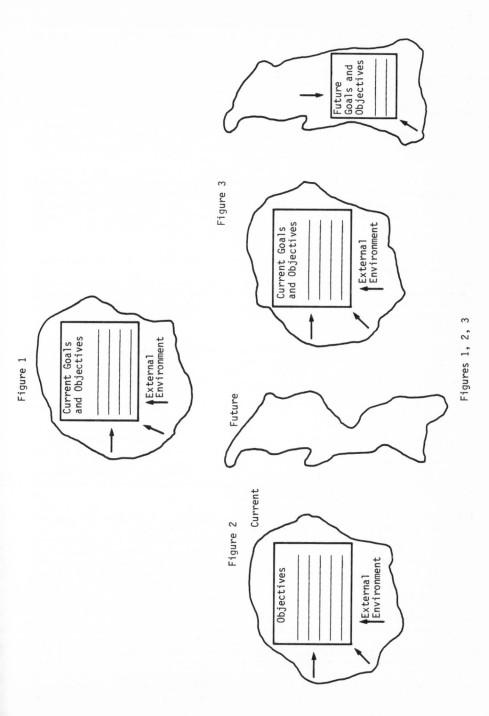

Figure 1

Figure 2

Figure 3

Figures 1, 2, 3

priate horizon. Let us say five years. Such a forecasting task is an important thing to do although, as is implied above, one is never correct in the estimates of what the future will bring.

Figure 3 suggests that having made one's best estimate of what the future will look like, one is then in a position to decide where one wants to position the organization in light of those forces and the shape of that future environment. In other words, this involves setting one's goals and objectives for some future point in time.

Figure 4 then identifies a view of one of the next steps that must take place. Given one is now at a certain position and wishes to get to another position there are certain alternative programs and strategic options that exist to move the organization from where it is now, to where they would like to be. Diagrammatically in this simple minded illustration there are three different alternatives that one might have developed. One strategy might be to buy market share, drive the competition out of business and then quietly proceed to make lots of money by raising prices! The other two lines represent other strategies. The options are as many and as creative as the managers who are putting the strategy in place in the organization.

Figure 5 suggests that having identified which strategy is likely to be the most effective, one then has to translate that into a series of programs over the years between where one is now and where one would like to be. These programs obviously include capital allocation, but in addition they involve the whole resource allocation process and the putting in place of strategic programs that will move the organization towards its strategic goal.

Figure 6 is the last step in the oversimplified view which suggests that having laid out the program and the milestones one then has to track at the end of each time period as to whether or not one has accomplished the objectives that were set. The analysis of why the objectives have not been met and understanding what caused one to fail to achieve one's original objectives, either an over-achievement or an under-achievement, is one of the most vital parts of strategic planning. In fact, it provides the input for restarting the whole process on the next cycle.

For almost any organization it is useful to look in 1980 at what one thought in 1975 that 1980 was going to look like on certain key dimensions such as: one's position in one's market, in one's productivity programs, in one's quality, to say nothing of one's cost picture and the major cost components. This contrast provides a level of insight and awareness which in many cases is truly staggering. Therein lies one key feature of strategic planning.

Let me repeat the point, that this simplistic six step process that has been laid out above does not represent the richness and complexity of corporate strategy. However, until we keep hammering at the question of definition and clarification then the subject will remain fuzzy and we will not get the kind of progress the field really ought to have. Anybody who looks at these steps and decides that in fact they have failed to capture the essence of strategic planning has a simple challenge. One should put in place something which is more robust and does a better job of capturing the essence of strategy.

It is interesting, for example, that when one goes back and looks at the history of practice and writing in the field of strategic planning over the last twenty years, one observes some clear changes in the way the field is viewed. The shifts, I suspect, occur for two reasons. One is the fact that our knowledge and ability to articulate the essence of strategy is improving markedly over time. The second reason is that the planning needs of organizations change. I am sure that each person looks at the first fifteen years differently, but it is instructive to go over it and construct one's own view of the major waves of thought that have

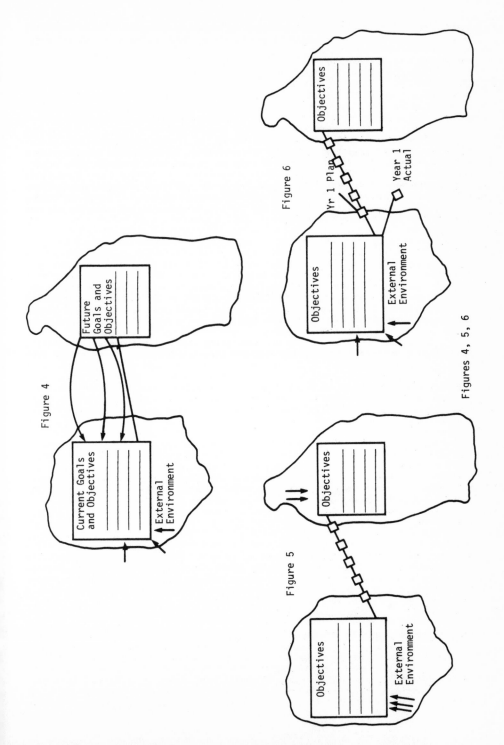

Figure 4

Figure 5

Figure 6

Figures 4, 5, 6

taken place in the field of planning over these years. The most obvious point is, of course, that the term 'planning' has gradually given way to the term 'strategy' and that the two have now come, at least in many people's minds, to mean two quite different things. However, let me leave this semantic question behind and just look at one view of the previous fifteen years.

As the next figure (7) suggests, one can identify six different waves that have occurred. The first was back in the 1958 to 1965 time period and has been going in some firms ever since. This is the "functional long-range planning" point of view. This was perhaps most ably raised in George Steiner's book, Top Management Planning, which was, to my knowledge at least, the first clear call for organizations to look out over time and plan in a sensible, explicit way. At the time I thought the book was absolutely first rate and contained a number of new ideas. The content of what Steiner was asking for was less innovative, largely dollar, budget kind of items, mostly to do with expenses. There are organizations today who have what is predominantly a functional planning approach, although that seems to be insufficient by itself in light of the kind of world we are in today and the kind of understanding we now have about the field of strategy.

The second visible trend was the 1964 to 1968 period in which there was a big push for a 'bottom-up' approach. At the time perhaps most vigorously espoused by Stanford Research Institute. A great many American and foreign firms used their methodology and their forms and procedures with some success. The essence of that whole activity was again, largely dollars of expense, but this time adding the capital requirements element to it. However, basically their approach was asking the organization to come up with their plans at the lowest level of the firm and then those came filtering up towards the top and eventually were packaged and delivered to the Board as the suggested corporate plan. The environment in which this all got started was the go-go period of the '60's when there was a lot more money than there were ideas, so the approach had a great deal of merit at the time it was first raised.

The next wave that seems to be visible was from 1968 onwards, which was McInsey's pronouncements exemplified in the book by Wilson and Tooms, called Improved Profits Through Integrated Planning and Control. Crudely put, one could argue that this book suggested that the way to do good strategic planning was a top-down process which involved a chief executive officer saying, here is the direction we are going to go, and the remainder of the organization spent their time filling in the details of how that should best take place. If their book is read carefully and one talks to companies that were involved with this approach at that point in time, it is clear that the content also shifted slightly and not only were there the regular dollar items of expense and the regular capital budgeting kinds of things, but also coming into play, for perhaps the first time, were a number of non-dollar items, critical success factors. Things such as market share, product quality and the like.

The reaction to these two approaches, that is to say bottom-up and top-down, was a natural evolution to top-down guidance, bottom-up planning. This has been perhaps most clearly stated in the book by Vancil and Lorange. In this book they really focus entirely on process and not on the question of what the content of the planning is all about. Judging from the reviews of the book and its sales they seem to have captured a pervasive view of current practice.

The next visible move was not so much a focus on the question of process, but rather people began to pay more attention to the 'strategic content' of what was done in the planning activities. This is where the first use of the words strategic planning began to be more widespread and were pushed vigorously and in my opinion very well, by the Boston Consulting Group. Their work with GE and the understanding that GE brought to that process has been very helpful for American business and their approach is by now, too common to comment on. However, the combination of the experience curve, the focus on competition and the

ACTIVE TIME PERIOD	FOCUS	CONTENT
1958 - 68 on Functional Planning	. Emphasis on plans by function . George Steiner, Top Management Planning	$ budget items
1964 - 68 on Bottom-up Planning	. Emphasis on plans being created by the lowest level organizational units Stanford Research Institute, The Corporate Development Plan	$ Expense & Capital items
1968 on Top-Down Planning	. Senior Management specifies precise direction, organization fills in the details . Wilson, S.R. and Toombs, J.O., Improving Profits Through Integrated Planning and Control	$ Expense, Capital & non-dollar items
1970 on Top-Down Guidance, Bottom-up Planning	. Emphasis on iteration between levels in the organization and the focus on the situational context . Vancil and Lorange, Strategic Planning Systems	Heavy emphasis on process
1973 on Strategic Content	. Emphasis on key analytical concepts . Henderson, On Corporate Strategy	Experience Curve, market position & lifecycle
1979 on Integrated Strategy	. Stresses financial market expectations; strategic content; industrial economics planning process; strategic program implementation	Includes much of the above together with Finance (CAMP) and Economics (I.O.)

Figure 7

One Historical Perspective on Planning

emphasis on looking outside the organization is powerful and noticeably changed the way strategic planning was thought about in American organizations.

More recently we have to come to what I think is perhaps going to turn out to be the next stage in this process, what I would call 'integrated strategy', for lack of a better term. This approach accepts the insights that have come from the 'strategic content' view of strategic planning and goes beyond those to add the powerful new insights from finance, as represented by modern portfolio theory and the capital asset pricing model. In addition, this approach adds economics as represented by the resuscitated field of industrial organizations. Michael Porter's book Competitive Strategy, ably represents the best of current thinking in this area.

So, what one calls 'integrated strategy' adds some powerful insights to the arsenal of those who wish to think strategically. Equally important, this approach also focuses attention on the process by which planning is carried out in an organization, the tools which can be used and the means by which an organization can implement and monitor its strategic programs. In short, the field of strategic planning has reached a new plateau, at least among the very best practitioners, that is impressive in its degree of power. Whether this power will be sufficient to bring American industry back to the level of supremacy it once enjoyed is still an open question, but it is certainly true that there are enormously more powerful approaches being taken now than was the case five years ago.

Now let us go back to the theme of the conference, integrating economics and corporate planning models into corporate strategy. One way in which this might be abstracted or generalized is to say that the conference theme deals with the subject of bringing logic and analysis to a fuzzy topic! Corporate strategy is a fuzzy topic and when we say economics and corporate simulation models, we are using them as two examples of logic and analytical power. Those who come from a background of finance would surely argue that theirs is an equally relevant topic, and I am going to argue, coming from a background of computers, that it is also one such topic. In talking about computers here, I would like to focus on just one particular kind of way in which computers can be used.

Computers have been used to support planning for a long time. In fact, they have been used to support planning over the last fifteen years. This use has been in what I would call, the traditional data processing and operations research style. I have listed in the accompanying figure (figure 8) the three principle ways in which I have seen computers being used in organizations over the last few years in pursuance of the organization's attempts to improve the way in which they do planning. It seems to me that all of these various ways in which the computer has been used so far can be useful. Used intelligently these existing types of application of computers each provide a different and effective kind of support to planning. The field, obviously, still suffers from the overselling by the narrowminded enthusiasts who believe that some particular optimization technique will solve the world's planning problems, or that some particular planning language will suddenly make all of an organization's planning problems magically disappear, but used intelligently in the furtherance of a sensible view of corporate strategy all these traditional ways can be extremely useful to any organization.

I would like now, however, to raise an additional way in which a number of firms are beginning to use computers which I think is equally interesting as the traditional ones. This approach is in its infancy in planning applications, although a great many U.S. corporations use it in other areas. This approach has been termed a decision support systems (D.S.S.) approach to strategic planning and it is different in subtle, but important, ways from the traditional use of computers implied in Figure 8. The primary emphasis, of course, is on the notion of supporting decision makers, not replacing them. It takes, as a given, that the process of strategy and strategic planning is necessarily fuzzy, somewhat ill-defined and in Herbert Simon's terms, 'semi-structured'. There are

I.   INFORMATION UTILITY - ACCESS TO DATA BASES

        - EXTERNAL:

                        PRIVATE: Neilson; Dun and Bradstreet, Lockheed's Dialogue,
                                  D.R.I., etc.

                        PUBLIC: Census Bureau; S.E.C., etc.

        - INTERNAL: Performance data by responsibilty center; Key Variables data

II.   MODELS - MACRO AND MICRO

        MACRO - NATIONAL ECONOMY - e.g. D.R.I.; CHASE

                        INDUSTRY MODELS - e.g. Forrester

        MICRO - COMPANY MODELS   - Specific purpose, e.g. cash forecasting

        In both cases:

            - Simulation or Optimization

            - Tailored model or General Language

            - Econometrics or System Dynamics

III.   DATA MANAGEMENT

            CLERICAL SUPPORT

            Adding, Printing, Dissemination

Figure 8

Computers in Planning - Current Practice

books[2] on the general D.S.S. approach, so it will not be developed further here. However, the key concept can be shown by using an analogy. In thinking about the subject of structured versus semi-structured problems and about the question of support for a manager versus replacing the human being, let me try to draw an analogy with the field of games. If one thinks about the game Tic-Tac-Toe, and is asked the question is this game structured or unstructured, one can immediately respond that it is, of course, structured. That is to say one can get the computer to play a perfect game of Tic-Tac-Toe, indeed it is sufficiently simple that two humans who understand the logic of Tic-Tac-Toe can play a thoroughly boring set of games because nobody ever wins. Now this issue of what is structured and what is unstructured is a little tricky because when a five year old is playing another five year old at this game, it becomes a very painful, tears, smiles, kind of situation. For them they understand the structure at one level, which is to say that the three crosses win or three zeroes win, but they do not understand the deep structure that lets them know where to put the X or the O in order to make sure that they had the best chance of getting three in a row or stopping the other person getting three in a row. So the issue of what is structured is very much a function of one's understanding at a given moment in time and as that understanding improves then clearly some of those tasks that we previously thought of as being unstructured turn out to be structured. The use of E.O.Q. formulas for inventory control would be one simple-minded business example which we are all familiar with.

To continue the analogy, if one turns from Tic-Tac-Toe to Chess and asks the question, is this a structured or unstructured game, then things become somewhat less clear. It is clearly structured because there is a board and a finite number of moves and the rules are unambiguous. Yet there are also Grand Masters and ordinary human beings! Thus it is unstructured to some degree.

Imagine a hypothetical problem where I am forced to play Chess with a mediocre opponent and I happen to be a good Chess player myself. Becoming frustrated with the mediocre quality of my opponent's play I issue a contract to my data processing department and ask them to replace my opponent with a Chess playing program that will play good Chess. They work hard and using Herbert Simon's heuristics and other techniques that have been developed they manage to come up with, for example, a micro-computer based Chess playing program such as the ones that many people bought last Christmas. An example would be Boris, which sells for around $390 and plays Chess at six different levels of expertise. Pleased with the results of my data processing department's work, I then proceed to play Chess against Boris. After a while at level one, I realize that I can beat Boris because there are certain patterns of play which Boris is quite unable to recognize. For example, let us say if one moves one's bishop five places diagonally to the right Boris becomes hopelessly confused.

Having discovered that Boris is too easy to beat at level one, I move to level two and so on up to level six. But at level six after a while it becomes clear that Boris has major errors in logic and after a while all that I can do is to discover how many errors in logic Boris makes when I play. So rather than play Chess, I am now in a position of merely discovering blind spots in Boris' program. Parenthetically this is all made far worse by the fact that Boris takes anywhere up to two days to respond to one move at this stage of technology development! In any event, I have become disillusioned with Boris' abilities and I throw Boris away and proceed to fire my data processsing department who failed in their assignment of replacing my opponent with a Chess playing program.

If instead I had given my computer department an assignment of helping my human opponent to play better Chess, that is to support my Chess playing opponent rather than replace my Chess playing opponent, they would have had a subtly, but importantly, different assignment.

To provide a Chess playing support system, for example, one could break the game into three obvious pieces. The beginning, the middle, and the ending game. At the beginning game they could have decided to provide just access to information, pure information retrieval, data base, kind of support system. In the data base let us say, were the first four opening moves of every famous Grand Master who ever played the game. By inquiring of the data base, my opponent might be able to find four or five opening moves which would so fool me that my opponent had won the game almost before it began. No models, nothing fancy, just a straight forward access to relevant information for my opponent.

There is an equally simple solution at the 'end game'. Where one could provide support in an algorithmic way. That is if we have just two men left on the board it becomes possible to work out the optimal solution and my support system would be able to tell me exactly what I should do in order to beat my opponent, or at least show as strongly as I possibly could against my opponent.

In the middle game, which is where things become very difficult for computers, is where we have to go back to the heuristics that Herbert Simon and others have developed. In this mode, I could take the rules of thumb that Boris is using and simply ask the system for some help, where upon I would be presented with a list of two or three different moves that I could possibly make, and I, as the human player would take a look at those three alternatives and decide which one I liked best. Now there is no guarantee that the three moves I had suggested to me are the best three moves, or in fact, the one that I had picked will be the best of the three that I have been given. Nonetheless I have been given some support and am using some judgement about what I am going to play next. Alternatively, I could have thought of an idea, for example, move my knight from one square to another square, give that alternative to the system and have it come back with its assessment of whether that is a good or a bad move. The system may come back and say fine, go ahead and do that, and then it turns out when I make the move it is checkmate in two moves! Or, alternatively it can come back and say that this move looks like its going to have the following implications, implications I have not seen. In no case is it telling me what to do and in no case is it guaranteeing me any kind of good move, it is simply using the best judgement that it has been given and providing me with some help.

Now these three types of support: the beginning game, pure information retrieval; and the end game, pure algorithms; and a simulation, what if, for the middle game are examples of three separate kinds of decision support systems. In some business settings, the decision support system could have just involved one of those three types of support and in other situations the decision support system will involve all three kinds of support.

Decision support systems incorporating these kinds of ideas are in active use in a great many American corporations. A bibliography and details of some examples of these are given in the publications that I referred to earlier, but in all cases they have had a powerful impact upon the way a particular key decision has been made by the managers or humans involved in making that particular decision. This use of decision support systems is not better than traditional use of computers in the data processing sense, but it is different. I am merely suggesting that in addition to all the traditional ways in which computers have been used to support planning, and strategic planning in particular, we also might consider the use of computers in a decision support systems mode. At least some corporations are doing exactly this right now. Such a mode is not necessarily better than the ways we have been using computers but it is certainly different.

In order to decide which aspects of this complicated, poorly understood and somewhat fuzzy problem of corporate strategy are worth supporting it becomes necessary to be very clear, by what is meant by corporate strategy in any given organization at any one point in time.

In the attached figure (Figure 9), I have diagrammed a somewhat more realistic

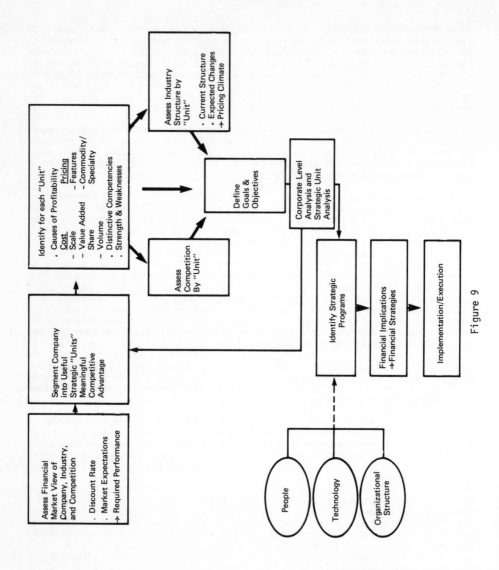

Figure 9

(than in Figure 6) view of the steps involved in strategic planning. These nine steps are self-explanatory at the level of generality which we are talking here, but it is quite clear that beneath each of these steps lie whole sets of analyses and logic flow that must take place if the step is to be done successfully. What is exciting right now is to see the level of solid theory and conceptual structure that lies underneath these steps and to be part of the emerging, evolving view.[2] For the moment, let us assume that these steps are self-explanatory and that one would accept the fact that this is at least a reasonable representation of what strategic planning is all about. I assume that it is self evident that the nature of the various steps is quite different. This in turn means that the way in which computers can be used in these various steps is quite different.

I will not belabor the obvious point of where the traditional uses of computer come into play in these steps. These kinds of uses are familiar to most organizations and will not be discussed further here, except to say that there is a lot of hard work yet to be done to make these traditional uses much more effective than they have been in the past. Although there is a lot of progress yet to be made in the traditional uses of computers in planning, it is worth recognizing the new roles and ways in which decision support systems can be applied to these various steps.

Let me just take two illustrations. A perfectly obvious one would be to take something like a standard portfolio bubble chart where the circle sizes are proportionate to sales or profit and imagine how much more effective analyzing business portfolios or corporate portfolios would be in interactive mode where one could put up the portfolio on a visual display screen and then watch how it looks dynamically over time as the portfolio changes over the planning horizon. This provides a sense of which way businesses are moving and how they are shrinking and growing in relation to the other pieces of their portfolio.

If one then takes a powerful extension of this original, simple, basic idea and plots on the axis some notion of the return required and the growth that is implicit if the organization is to attain sustainable steady state performance one could produce a portfolio diagram somewhat as follows (see Figure 10). Looking at how the resulting performance and overall business fit changes as a result of changing business plans provides an interesting perspective quite beyond what is normally done at senior management levels presently. I have watched this being done with chief executives in several situations recently and have been pleasantly surprised at the degree of awareness and insight that such an approach has created.

At a more mechanical level one can, as a planner, do a 'reasonableness' check on a division's plans through the interactive graphical use of an "expected profit" corridor and related statistical data bases. It can be fascinating to see in a given company which kinds of businesses fall out of the expected corridor of performance and then to try to understand what it is about the programs that will put them back in the expected corridor. In short, using decision support systems to provide for flexibility in strategy planning is a fascinating opportunity.

What makes all this different, from the things that have been talked about over the years about the way scenarios can be tested, and the way gaming can be done, is two things. On the one hand we have a very much more flexible technology in the form of graphical display devices driven by human interfaces which are genuinely natural to use. These are easy words to say, but they make an enormous difference to the acceptability and useability of this kind of technology. In addition to this we have had an extraordinary increase in the conceptual robustness of the various analyses and logical tests which ought to be run if a strategic plan is to be put together in a convincing way. I recognize that these are just words and it is hard to provide in this forum enough detail of exactly what I am saying on a topic which is still evolving.

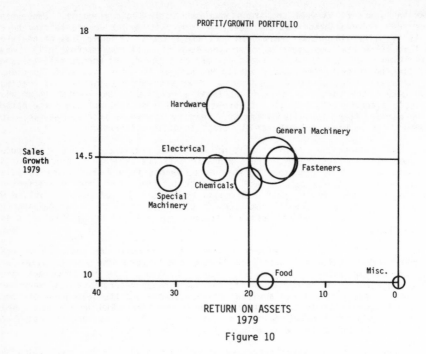

Figure 10

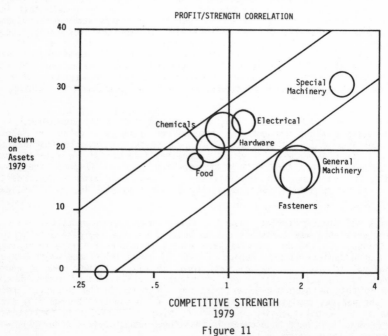

Figure 11

In addition, I would be the first to acknowledge that I am a prejudiced observer. I come from a background of the use of computers and work in the development of the decision support system ideas and so I obviously believe that these are particularly useful. I am spending this year on a leave of absence from MIT with a strategic planning consulting firm who has made it their business to develop some structure and robust conceptual frameworks that can be used to produce significantly useful results. The idea that decision support systems can be applied successfully to strategy is something that they have assumed all along is necessary if the planning department and the consulting firms are to be as productive as they ought to be in helping to develop strategies for companies. So there is no doubt that I am prejudiced and I recognize that what I have said should be discounted in light of my strong prejudices. But I would fall back on my original points, which are two.

The first is that one ought to have a clear view in one's own mind as to what strategy consists of and at the same time to be aware of where that falls in the historical evolution of planning, more recently strategic planning, in the history of U.S. organizations.

Secondly, it is important to recognize the enormous change in our conceptual understanding and the technology that is available to us. There are quite different ways of analyzing and executing strategy as well as the related use of computers now than was true as recently as five years ago. The combination of our evolving understanding and the evolving technology leads to a very exciting time. Whether this paper has provided that flavor and a structure in which to think about these changes is unfortunately a different question, but I do hope that it is clear that this field is going through an interesting stage and, at the very least, requires careful watching.

FOOTNOTES

[1]See for example Keen, P.G.W. and Scott-Morton, M.S. Decision Support Systems, An Organization View, Addison Wesley, 1978.

[2]See for example, Lewis, W.W. Strategic Planning - Theory and Practice, Strategic Planning Associates, Watergate 600, Washington, D.C. 20037.

REFERENCES

[1]   Abell, Derek, F. & John S. Hammond. Strategic Market Planning Problems & Analytical Approach, Prentice-Hall, Englewood Cliffs, NJ, 1979.

[2]   Andrews, Kenneth. The Concept of Corporate Strategy. Richard D. Irwin, Homewood, IL, 1980.

[3]   Anshoff, H.I. & R.P. Derlerk & R.L. Hayes. From Strategic Planning to Strategic Management. John Wiley & Sons, New York, 1976.

[4]   Henderson, Bruce. Henderson on Corporate Strategy. Abt Books, Cambridge, MA, 1979.

[5]   Hofer, Charles W., and Dan Schendel. Strategy Formulation: Analytical Concepts. West Publishing Company, St. Paul, MN, 1978.

[6]   Huff, Sid L. & Michael S. Scott-Morton. "The Impact of Computers on Planning and Decision Making," Man-Computer Research, Academic Press, Limited, London, 1979.

[7]   Keen, Peter G.W. and Michael S. Scott-Morton. Decisions Support Systems: An Organizational Perspective, Addison-Wesley, Reading, MA, 1978.

[8]   Lewis, Walker. Planning By Exception. Strategic Planning Associates, Washington, D.C., 1977.

[9]   Lorange, Peter and Richard Vancil. Strategic Plannng Systems, Prentice-Hall, Englewood Cliffs, NJ, 1977.

[10] Porter, Michael E. Competitive Strategy. The Free Press, MacMillan Publishing Co., New York, 1980.

[11] Quinn, James B. Strategies for Change, Logical Incrementalism, Richard D. Irwin, Homewood, IL, 1980.

[12] Rothschild, William E. Putting It Altogether - A Guide to Strategic Thinking, AMACOM - American Management Association, 1976.

[13]   Strategic Alternatives, Selection, Development and Implementation, AMACOM - American Management Association, 1979.

[14] Steiner, George & John Miner. Management Policy and Strategy. MacMillan Publishing Company, New York, 1977.

[15] Steiner, George. Top Management Planning. MacMillan and Company, New York, 1969.

[16] Stewart, Robert F. & Marion D. Doseher. The Corporate Development Plan, Report Numbers 183, Stanford Research Institute, Menlo Park, 1963.

[17] Wilson, S.H. & J.D. Tombs. Improving Profits Through Integrated Planning and Control. Prentice Hall, Englewood Cliffs, NJ, 1968.

SYSTEMATIC STRATEGIC PLANNING: A COMPREHENSIVE AID FOR BANK MANAGEMENT

Kalman J. Cohen

Fuqua School of Business
Duke University
Durham, North Carolina
U.S.A.

Hugh B. Wellons

International Business Machines
Corporation
Research Triangle Park, North Carolina
U.S.A.

INTRODUCTION

The first question that must be asked when designing any system is: "What is its purpose?" Any system which does not have a specific role in the management process is very likely a waste of effort. The combination of systems which we propose can act as a comprehensive aid to bank management. Does this mean that our system will run a bank? Of course not. Our system does satisfy some very basic needs, however, and could aid management in running a bank more effectively and efficiently.

The major steps of the management process are formulation of corporate goals, analysis of the environment, quantification of goals, disaggregation into divisional objectives, selection and implementation of strategy, and process evaluation and adjustment [Cohen and Cyert (1973)]. Upper level management must first set its long range goals and then disaggregate them into medium and short run goals. These goals must be further disaggregated into divisional objectives, each division manager stating what the capabilities of his division are. Strategies need to be developed at all levels, combined, and then related to the economic forecasts to determine their validity. The proper set of strategies should be implemented, and alternative plans made for the several contingencies that are envisioned for the economy. Periodically the strategies must be checked for accuracy and usefulness. The problem is that the economy is almost impossible to forecast accurately. The interrelationships between the economy and the various activities of a bank are very complex, and the information needed to deal with these problems could easily overload any set of managers.

The computer aided bank planning system is designed to be a management aid -- a very complicated and complete management information system. Just like the typewriter, the telephone, and later the copier, a computerized system is just another tool which, when designed and used properly, can greatly enhance the effectiveness of managers [Cohen (1969)]. It is an inefficient use of managers' time to have to go continually through the many calculations required to find the impacts that different strategies and changes in the economy might have on the bank's profit and safety. Many of these calculations that managers now perform can be done more quickly and more accurately on a computer, thus giving management more time to spend on important long term plans and strategy.

Thus the comparative economic advantage of computer systems should be obvious. Of course no such system dealing with the policies and interrelations of the bank can work without the continual support and help of management itself. To be successful, a management science approach must have both "firing line" executives and management science analysts involved in the development and implementation of the models [see Cohen (1969)]. This is important. For any bank model to be effective, the bank managers must indicate exactly what the relationships are and what is needed, and the computer analysts must be sufficiently involved in the management process at the bank to know how it works. This is true for both the original design and the improvements which will follow. The better each group

(managers and analysts) understands what is done by the other, the easier it
will be to eliminate errors from the model and make its operations more comprehensive!

In Section II we briefly describe two methods currently being used in bank dynamic balance sheet management and strategic planning--simulation and linear
programming--and then explore some of their strengths and weaknessess. We propose
in Section III a system that can help bank management do a more effective job of
planning; this combines the best features of simulation and linear programming,
together with an MIS system. Our concluding remarks are presented in Section
IV.

ALTERNATIVES

A. Simulation

A simulation model in its most basic form takes a set of given input values and
relationships and calculates the output values which they imply. A bank financial
statement simulation model [see, e.g., Robinson (1973)] is composed of equations
which represent the quantitative relationships that exist among the several
variables that are relevant to the bank's operations. Given a set of predicted
future values for the input variables, the model will produce quantitative predictions for the financial statement items. Different management decisions obviously
can affect the values that should be attributed to some of these variables (such
as mortgage loans, CD amounts, etc.). In knowing exactly what effect certain
decisions will have on these variables, management can run the model with different values for the input variables (which represent the corresponding management
decision set), obtain the relevant outputs (profit, cash flows, overall balance
sheet figures, or whatever), and thus evaluate different sets of decisions.

A one-period simulation model is not, however, sufficient for use in the real
world. Short run decisions can have medium and long run effects. Thus a useful
simulation model must not only deal with the simultaneous relationships among the
different divisions of the bank, but it must deal with the sequential relationships across time periods as well. This can be done by a staging of decision
sets, where long run goals are translated into short run objectives, and the model
is used to test both the viability of these objectives and the plans for meeting
them [Derwa (1972)].

It is clear, of course, that neither goals nor plans can be chosen optimally
without considering the relevant environment. A stable economy nullifies this
problem, but a dynamic economy which changes rapidly complicates the model's
design. The economy in which we now work is almost impossible to predict accurately, and it is a fact of life that choosing a strategy specifically to meet our
expectations of how the economy will move could result in disaster if the economy
took an unexpected turn. One way of dealing with the problem is to use multiple
economic scenarios and also do risk analysis. A set of several economic scenarios
which represent various possible directions of the economy can be placed in memory
and adjusted periodically to keep it current. On every run probabilities can be
associated with each scenario, and an "expected" scenario can be developed. This
allows management to see what effect a policy could have on the bank in each
scenario [Royer (1975)]. Risk analysis could be done fairly easily with this
information, and management would then be supplied with a probability distribution
of possible outcomes [Carter and Cohen (1967)]. It is conceivable that a project
could have a high expected profit, and still have a 30% chance of losing money.
Such a project almost certainly would be too risky for a bank. A good model must
supply this type of information. Management needs not only financial statements,
ancial statements, but also an analysis of risks, an ability to call up the
initial status of the bank, the structure of the overall plan and an analysis
of the past performance of the system.

B. Linear Programming

Linear programming is a completely different approach for developing optimal bank management decisions [see, e.g., Cohen and Hammer (1967, 1972) and Cohen (1972)]. While simulation involves creating final values for each of the alternative sets of decisions and then comparing the implications of those values, linear programming derives the optimal values of the decision variables directly from the information given. The objective function, which maximizes the appropriate goal (for example, a function of net income, assets, or deposits), is determined by management and quantified in terms of the decision variables that affect it. Constraints are also quantified and must cover all the relevant risks, limits, expectations, and policies that might affect the answers. Through an algorithm based on matrix algebra, the program maximizes the appropriate objective function according to the relationships with which it has been supplied, and in so doing also provides values for the decision variables of the model. Linear programming also supplies dual variables which represent the effect on the objective function of changing the value of some decision variable or constraint. Sensitivity analysis is much easier and more accurate because these dual variables supply quantitative data for a check of objective function sensitivities.

Deterministic linear programming is the simplest and most common type of linear programming. It optimizes under the assumption that the future is known with certainty. Since it ignores uncertainty, it may be used most appropriately when limited to short term decisions. In the short term when there is little risk of major change, this technique can supply an adequate method for optimizing with respect to a single period horizon, but it would then not properly deal with the long term implications of these short term decisions. Because a deterministic LP model ignores the uncertainty associated with the distant future, it can supply only "best guess" answers to longer term decisions, or decisions over multiperiod planning horizons, unless it is used in an artful manner employing sensitivity analysis and multiple runs based on alternative forecasts. But when skillfully used in this manner, deterministic LP models can provide useful insights to management.

An LP technique which is conceptually more sound for dealing with long term decisions is multistage stochastic programming with recourse (an extension of two-stage programming under uncertainty [Cohen and Thore (1970), Booth (1972), and Aghili, Cramer, and Thompson (1975)]). This method explicitly incorporates probability distribution of future parameters (e.g., future deposit levels, loan demand, etc.) which cannot be known now with certainty. It recognizes that present decisions will constrain future courses of action, and it explicitly models these relationships. It utilizes the fact that information accrues with the passage of time, so that a parameter which is now uncertain because it pertains to the future later will be known with certainty when "the future" has become "the past." The "stages" in multistage stochastic programming with recourse are synonymous with "decision periods" (e.g., the first stage may be for the coming quarter, the second stage should stretch only to where the future events are still relatively certain, and successive stages should decrease in certainty accordingly).

One possible approach to developing a multistage stochastic programming model with recourse for use in bank dynamic balance sheet management is discussed in Cohen and Rutenberg (1971). Essentially how such a model might be formulated is that for each period after the first, several possible economic scenarios with their associated probabilities are developed. For example, a three stage model with five scenarios will have 25 possible third stage occurrences, five each for the five second stage scenarios. This could be complicated further by developing specific possible third stage scenarios for each second stage scenario to represent a more realistic picture of what might really happen. Vectors describing the decision set for the first period, and for each possible scenario of the second period, third period, and any later periods must be developed. There are many methods that can be used to solve such a multistage stochastic problem (decomposition and dual methods, for example), but we will not go into the mathematical techniques here. There are also other procedures (such as the use of longitudinal scenarios spanning many time periods, as illustrated in Figure 1) for representing the uncertainties associated with the future which result in models of smaller size.

FIGURE 1

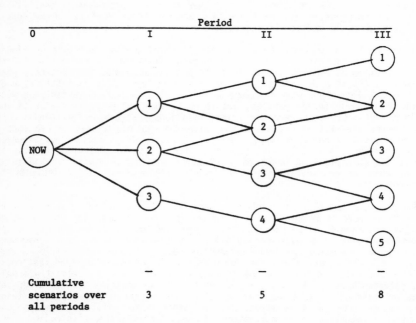

| | Period | | |
| 0 | I | II | III |

| Cumulative scenarios over all periods | 3 | 5 | 8 |

We must stress the value of the dual evaluators supplied by any LP model. These dual evaluators supply important sensitivity information. They indicate the opportunity costs of learning in one period that the wrong plans were previously made. This information can be vital in a dynamic world.

C.   A Comparison

   1.   Simulation--Advantages and Disadvantages. One important advantage of any mathematical model, including a simulation model, is that it forces management to organize and quantify the relevant relationships, look at the interaction between short and long run problems, and disaggregate the solution into smaller stages. A good simulation model could be designed and never used, and management would still benefit from it just by going through the stages of developing the model.

Another major advantage of simulation is that it frees management to improve strategic performance. Even upper level management spends much of its time doing rudimentary work -- verifying mathematical relationships, checking figures, etc. This is a waste of very expensive talent. In strategic planning much time is spent discussing the future and approximating its effect on the bank's (or business firm's) performance. If the relevant relationships are properly developed in the simulation model, then the model can do these needed calculations much faster and more accurately than management. This will free management to deal more effectively with planning and strategy, thus improving management performance.

Since simulation is conceptually very simple, it will be easier for management to understand and accept than an optimization routine. When properly designed by the various levels of management, a simulation model follows essentially the same steps as management in arriving at the forecasted statements. Few managers have trouble identifying with a model that is "trained" to think as they do. This may also make it easier to implement, as management will usually cooperate in its development. Because it so closely follows the process used by managers themselves, its design is not too complicated.

Simulation, like any mathematical model, can be cumbersome at first. It requires a substantial commitment of both time and money by upper level management to succeed as a comprehensive aid to management. Design, evaluation, and improvements must be guided by middle and upper level management for the model to operate correctly. And even with this commitment, it will take time to eliminate the inconsistencies in the model. No model runs perfectly the first, or even the tenth, time. Improvements are always possible. Management must be patient and recognize the benefits derived from the proper design and operation of a good model that serves as an aid to management.

The major weakness in the simulation method, as opposed to the LP approach, is that it does not optimize. Simulation greatly aids the comparison of alternatives, which is basically what is needed for good strategic planning. The problem is that for any given economic scenario there might be hundreds of alternative decision sets to compare. The time required to find an optimal or near optimal plan to suit bank goals, especially if there are several possible economic scenarios to consider, is more than any manager has available. Management would not have time to compare optimal strategies for each alternative scenario and would not be making efficient use of available information and insights. Strategic planning, while improved, would not be as good as it could be.

2. Linear Programming -- Advantages And Disadvantages. Linear programming, like simulation, is rather cumbersome at first. We feel that this disadvantage is unavoidable but more than compensated by the improved performance resulting from proper use of the model. But the problem of implementing the system correctly is further complicated in the case of linear programming by its appearance as a "black box" to many managers. Linear programming does not operate in the same manner as most managers. Because it is conceptually complex, it may be hard for bank executives to understand and trust. The system cannot be used optimally if management does not understand it well enough to initiate needed improvements and feel comfortable relying on its results. This, however, need not be a problem if executives from all relevant departments are integrally involved in the system design from beginning to end.

Linear programming complicates the organization of the model because all relationships must be in strict LP form. The objective function, which reflects the goal to be optimized, must be expressed as a linear function of the decision variables. Relevant restrictions are incorporated in the constraints (also linear functions of the decision variables). Since most businessmen do not naturally think in this manner, they may have trouble communicating the proper relationships to the management scientists. Linear programming also places heavy reliance on the accuracy of predictions. While the emphasis in simulation is to change some numbers and try again, the emphasis in linear programming is often conceived to be to design the model correctly and arrive at a conclusion. The simpler LP models assume perfect certainty, but now multistage stochastic programming with recourse is a proven optimization technique. We feel that this, along with the multiple run approach to using LP models, negates an unrealistic over-reliance on the accuracy of the model formulation and its input data.

One advantage to linear programming is that it can essentially be run like a simulation model. The model can be run many times, adjusting the parameters to represent different perceived relationships and expectations. Any counterintuitive result can be easily checked by referring to the constraints to which it relates. These will show you the relationships that resulted in any value that appears to be logically inconsistent. The problem may be shown to rest in the model or in the manager's lack of understanding of the complete interrelationships involved. Either way, the difficulty can easily be resolved.

Linear programming, like simulation, forces the executives in charge to organize and quantify the problem, look for the interaction between short and long run decisions, and disaggregate any problem into time stages and levels of action. Linear programming, however, unlike simulation, may force management to think in unnatural ways. For an LP model to be fine tuned, constraints must be categorized into those that are controllable, those that are uncontrollable, and those in between. Goals and objectives must be clearly stated, and recognition should be made of the different risks associated with each constraint. These changes in the planning formulation necessitate a more optimizing (and less satisfying) look at the strategic picture. This has to help.

The most obvious advantage of linear programming is that it does, of course, optimize. Multiple run comparisons are still easily facilitated, but LP models always optimize subject to their framework and information. This might allow an easier, if not more clearly understood, look at the implication of various policy decisions within the different possible future economic scenarios.

THE SYSTEM

It should now be obvious that simulation and linear programming complement each other very well. For every weak point in one, there is a strength in the other. Linear programming is fairly complicated and may take longer to show beneficial results, while simulation is easy for management to accept and use. Designing the LP model forces executives to think in an "optimizing" manner, but this adjustment can be eased by first having them help design a simulation routine. During the design of the original simulation model management scientists will get a better idea of what raw data will be required from the management information system for a linear programming model. And most of all, the major weakness of simulation is covered by linear programming's optimization characteristic, just as a major flaw in linear programming can be eliminated by a design which allows the LP model to be used to simulate. Clearly a combination of these methodologies would be beneficial. What remains is to design that combination in the way which will best aid the bank planning process.

In developing a conceptual framework for a systematic aid to bank management, one should first consider the objectives of such a system. The system needs to supply bank management with the information they need to make better strategic decisions. It needs to be understandable and must be designed by both the on-line managers and the management scientists to be effective. It must be implementable in phases, so the bank can adjust gradually and so all the needed information will be available. Finally, it must be easily evaluated, so the needed adjustments can be periodically made.

There have been previous attempts at combining simulation and linear programming in a corporate management system. The one which seems to be the most applicable to bank management was developed by Hamilton and Moses and implemented at International Utilities Corporation (now IU International Corporation) [Hamilton and Moses (1974)]. Basically this system is a large mathematical model which maximizes corporate performance (profits) over a multiperiod planning horizon by selecting appropriate operating, acquisition, and financing strategies. This system feeds relevant data into an optimization subsystem which maximizes corporate performance, and into a simulation subsystem which consolidates past strategies and relationships. These both supply data to the report generators which produce predicted results and financial statements. All of this is supported by a management information subsystem which is divided into strategic planning units. An econometric model supplies the feasible economic scenarios and the risk analysis subsystem evaluates the effect of certain areas on the firm's overall risk. This system is interactive and can be run whenever needed.

We see no reason why a similar system, with several changes which we will suggest would not benefit a bank's strategic planning process. We will describe our proposed system in the order in which it should be implemented. This should clarify the relationships between the various parts of the system, and also show why we have organized it in this manner.

A. MIS and Simulation

The most important part of any planning and control system is the information library. If all that management gets out of a system is an understanding of which data are really important, then they will still benefit. The problem is that it is hard to know what is needed until the system (simulation, LP, or just reporting) is designed. Likewise, it is difficult to design that system properly without knowing what data are available. That is why we combine the development of the management information subsystem and the simulation subsystem. The two are dependent on each other for proper design [McSweeney (1972)].

The first step in developing any management information system is deciding what information is needed. For a comprehensive strategic planning system such as this, management must supply all the relationships which affect the overall plan, and all the information that these relationships require. That does not mean that each individual loan and deposit will become an integral part of the system. On the contrary, this would create an information overload. The basic purpose of the MIS portion of this systematic strategic planning approach is to take the relevant information supplied by the bank's data processing systems and compact this into concise, clear amounts and ratios which are easily read, easily understood, and easily applied to a strategic approach. The purpose is not really to supply more information per se, but rather to limit the information flow to what is really relevant to the problem at hand. This can be done in several ways, but we feel that one particular approach best fits the present system in most banks.

Most large banks are presently divided into profit centers which run rather independently according to the requirements and goals set by bank management. These profit centers divide the planning, operational, and   reporting responsibilities. Whether the bank is organized geographically, or according to different functional areas (i.e., consumer loans, commercial loans, investments, etc.), or by a combination of both, does not matter. What matters is that the bank is used to operating and reporting in this manner. It would be foolish to try to change a properly functioning organization merely to facilitate design of the planning system. What we propose is to design simulation capabilities and discover what data are needed for strategic planning in each of the profit centers. There will, of course, have to be some standardization.

Central management will first have to design the flows for the overall strategic planning model, discovering how the separate areas interact and finding what specific information they will need from each profit center. A search into past reporting methods should give them an idea of what data can be supplied, and using this to estimate information constraints, they should be able to come up with a rough draft for the overall simulation model. This rough draft should give them a good idea of specific information needs. Once the profit center head knows what information is needed--both for reporting purposes and for the simulation model-- he, along with management scientists, could design a suitable system.

1. Management Information Subsystem. The MIS should be designed and implemented as soon as bank management has designed the simulation system well enough to know approximately what is needed. The simulation subsystem should be designed to represent a broad view of bank operations (as opposed to a detailed view which may include every type of bank action), and so the information needed for this should give management a good idea of what information is relevant to bank strategic planning. So, before the simulation or optimization portions of this system become operable, the MIS section will already aid bank management to plan properly for the future. But for it to do this, it must have certain capabilities. We will now discuss what capabilities this subsystem will require to be able to interact effectively with the already existing data system and the bank strategic planning process.

Any information system, to be effective, must be able to gather needed information and organize it into readable, accessible form. For strategic planning this information must also be reduced into concise, workable data. Some data, important for day to day operations, may need to be ignored or suitably aggregated when used in the planning process. Information overload is a major pitfall in strategic planning, and it can be avoided by taking pains to eliminate unnecessary data from the system. This elimination process will continue through data. Some data, important for day to day operations, may need to be ignored or suitably aggregated when used in the planning process. Information overload is a major pitfall in strategic planning, and it can be avoided by taking pains to eliminate unnecessary data from the system. This elimination process will continue through the evolution of the system. Just as new developments often demonstrate the need for new information, changes will also render some data no longer relevant. This must be constantly checked and adjusted, so the management information subsystem can best act as the bridge between day-to-day management decisions and strategic planning.

Once data have been reduced and somewhat organized, they must be properly catalogued according to their type, their impact, and their interrelations with other data. Interrelationships may even be kept in flow chart form, if this seems best. This cataloguing procedure could easily be done concurrently with the simulation system design, and may even aid this design. Much more than just aiding the system design and easing the chore of connecting these systems properly, this cataloguing will greatly enhance system adjustment and understanding. Later if system performance becomes unacceptable and certain relationships are thought no longer to hold, it will be easy to find exactly what the assumptions of the system are and how they can be properly adjusted. Also, it is likely that at some time a result will seem counterintuitive, and management will need to look at the underlying relationships to see if the result is correct.

This subsystem must, of course, store data about past results, past model inputs and their resulting predictions, past relationships, and past management opinions. This will serve as a reference for comparison of past and present performance. It will aid management in discovering what types of design changes improved or impaired performance. Such historical data will, of course, aid in the development of improved predictive models and they will aid management in discerning the risks of certain proposals.

It is important that the MIS subsystem contain relevant economic information. It should be obvious that the state of the economy will have a direct impact on any bank, and so predictions about the general economy and specific areas (such as interest rates, industrial production, housing starts, etc.) are vital for a future-oriented plan. The executives and analysts must decide exactly what economic information is needed and find a source for it. They may decide to use an already existing econometric model, a self-designed model, in-house economists, or a combination of all three. What is important is that they find a reasonable method for predicting the economy. For the system we propose, it is necessary to formulate possible economic scenarios for the different stages of the future and their probabilities of occurrence.

The variables within each economic scenario can also be described in terms of a (joint) probability distribution if risk analysis is desired. We feel, however, that risk analysis should be kept at a minimum. Trying to determine the probability distribution of every parameter in the system could be infeasible. Similar benefits can be derived, however, from accurately judging the relationships between bank operations and the economy, and then setting up rough probability distributions of how the economy is expected to move. An "expected" economy could easily be estimated from this and tests could be done on the simulation model to determine the effects of unexpected developments. This will probably be done later, however, when the bank is effectively using a deterministic model and is ready to progress.

    2. Deterministic Simulation. The initial simulation portion of the model will be deterministic rather than stochastic. Compared to the MIS subsystem, the simulation model will be harder to develop in any organization as complex as a large bank, since many of the relationships among the various divisions cannot be accurately quantified. But this is what is required. It will be hard for the management within each profit center to quantify how different changes within the division affect performance. For example, the people in the small business loan division will find it difficult to estimate how a rise in interest rates will affect volume, and in turn how this will affect administration requirements. But this volume will also be altered by such things as overall availability of funds, present and perceived future opportunities, etc.; and it will move, probably, in the opposite direction of the deposit accounts (assuming that most firms, when they need money, will reduce their cash and marketable securities before borrowing from banks). Thus the major parameters of this model will be affected by four types of relationships: relationships involving items within the division; relationships within the bank system that cross profit center lines; measurable effects from occurrences external to the bank; and, of course, random fluctuations which are impossible to predict. All of these, except the last, must be estimated with some degree of accuracy in the computer model, so that this simulation routine can easily interact with data from the MIS subsystem.

At first, the bank may want to develop a simulation model for the division which it thinks could receive the largest benefit for the least effort. This division's management must be involved in designing the division's simulation model for it to provide the needed information to central management. The experience gained from this first division should prove useful in the next profit center, and then the next, etc., until eventually a comprehensive system has been designed. This comprehensive system could be evaluated using past data and past economic predictions and testing its ability to simulate subsequent developments. No one can ever expect 100% accuracy, but adjustments should be made until it has proven itself able to reflect the fundamental relationships that are influencing the bank. Once the simulation subsystem seems to be adjusted, it can be added to the management information subsystem already on line. Both of these, of course, will have to be monitored and adjusted from time to time over the rest of their lives.

    3. Stochastic Simulation. After management has adjusted to a deterministic simulation model and found it useful, it will probably want to advance to a stochastic simulation model with the multiple scenarios already being supplied by the economics group. Where before management was restricted to planning for a single economic scenario, this extended model will allow management to consider

the impact of different economic scenarios on the various possible strategies.

This will work in the following manner. Management and the economists will decide what the lengths of the decision periods and the planning horizon should be (such as quarterly periods over a three year horizon), and the economics group will supply the MIS subsystem with possible scenarios for each period along with an associated probability distribution. After multiple scenarios have been developed management will be able to simulate the possible outcomes of their decisions, recognizing the uncertainty in the economy. Not only will they see the impacts of their projected decisions if the economy moves as expected, but they can readily estimate the adverse effects over future periods if the economy moves unexpectedly. This could be invaluable for a risk-averse bank.

B. Linear Programming

The combination simulation-management information system which we have just described should be a great help to the strategic planning process. It will allow management easily to attain needed information and should indicate the probable results of any decisions. Simulation, basically a repetitive approach, still has the weaknesses which we have mentioned above in Section II.C.1. We feel that the model can be further improved by an optimization routine. There are many implementation problems related to developing an LP model, which we have already mentioned in Section II.C.2. These problems can be reduced if management is integrally involved in the development of the model, if management already has experience with an operating simulation model, and if the first prototype model is fairly simple. Therefore it seems desirable at this stage to add a deterministic LP model to the simulation, thereby easing both the design and the implementation. We will now discuss a possible design for this deterministic LP model.

1. Deterministic Linear Programming. An LP model, to be truly effective, must not only improve the planning system but be easily incorporated into the old system as well. We feel that the easiest way to achieve both of these goals is to design the LP to optimize decisions within each possible set of scenarios. What we mean by this can best be shown by the following example. If management is planning in three periods--say six months, one year, and three years--and there are three possible economic scenarios in the first period, five cumulative scenarios in the second period, and eight cumulative scenarios in the third period, the possibilities may look like the pathways in Figure 1. So, in effect, there are eight total possible pathways in the economy allowed for over the next three years. Previously management has been trying various policies and objectives (involving deposit amounts, new loans, etc.) to see what the effect of these are. Suppose, however, that the management policies are included as constraints in an LP model, that relevant input data reflect forecasts based on a specific economic scenario, and that the appropriate relationships are maintained in the model. Then this LP model should be able to produce optimal values for the many decision variables (such as investment securities, CDs, etc.) for each scenario, and these values can be fed back into the simulation model to see their period by period effect on the bank's financial statements. Management can, of course, adjust these figures by changing the policy constraints and varying questionable relationships to approximate better the best alternatives and their likely effects. This will quickly supply "optimal" values which can only be found in simulation by trial and error, and so should speed and improve strategy formulation.

2. Multistage Stochastic Programming with Recourse. Bank management may be perfectly satisfied with a deterministic LP like the one we have discussed. If, however, they feel a need for further improvement, they should next install a multistage stochastic programming with recourse model. As we have mentioned in Section II.B, this basically considers the relationship between first and later stage events. In other words, because it makes the decisions within each stage interactively, it considers the effects of a decision made for a single stage on all the subsequent stages. Almost every decision made today imposes restrictions

on tomorrow's alternatives. This multistage programming technique explicitly considers the costs of being surprised in a later time period by an unexpected economic event.

The advantages of this technique are numerous. Because it optimizes over all the scenarios, it saves management the trouble of checking each scenario separately. It is designed explicitly to deal with the relationships and restrictions involved between the different stages, and so saves the bank from having continually to adjust the model to deal with this. It can be designed to print out both optimal decisions and the effect of these decisions if certain less expected scenarios occur. Thus management can quickly see the possible variances caused by uncertainty in the economy as well as the estimated variances caused by design and information error. If because of some fault in the forecasting system, or some unexpected turn of events, the economy moves differently than predicted, management can readily determine what effect this may have on the performance of the chosen decision set.

We would not claim, however, that this model is infallible. Multiple runs are still necessary, and this design, perhaps as much or more than the others, cannot act correctly without proper management interaction. Management will always want to look at the possible effects of different strategies and policy mixes, and so will have to adjust the model parameters to check these. Some relationships built into the model will always be questionable, so management will need to change these to compare results. This model does not and cannot automate management. It simply allows the bank to look at many of the things it has always looked at, but in more detail. Where before many of these problems could only be viewed qualitatively, this model, if properly designed, will allow them to be viewed quantitatively; thus management can have a more realistic picture of what can be expected. Finally, because this model can be made to interact with the simulation and management information subsystem, it can present conclusions in an easily understandable and familiar form.

CONCLUSION

This paper has examined the systematic aids available for bank strategic planning. Our purpose was to explore how a computer can best be used to facilitate this process and improve the results of strategic planning. We indicated that the order in which the system is designed and implemented is almost as important to the success of the system as the details of the models, so we have presented our system component by component, in the order we feel is appropriate for implementation. This implementation procedure will depend a great deal on management. It is possible that, for example, a particularly enlightened management will be able to go straight from the stochastic simulation to the multistage stochastic programming with recourse model (although we feel that the deterministic linear programming model has value in its own right), or that a bank will want to stop somewhere along the way, feeling that the system already meets its needs. The system we have described may take years to develop and implement. This slow process, however, should reduce many of the costs and problems associated with management acceptance, user education, model design, and system separation that often accompany the formulation of any new computer based system.

As can be seen in Figure 2, our system is large, but rather simple in design. The hub is the management information subsystem, which stores all the data, includes economic predictions, and interacts with all the other system components. The simulation subsystem contains both deterministic and stochastic simulation capabilities. It allows management to investigate possible occurrences and plans and to see how they may affect the bank. It has the capability of producing estimates of financial statements and other information that management deems important. Interacting closely with this is the linear programming subsystem which contains both deterministic and multistage stochastic models. This optimizes the decision variables within given restrictions. Within broad policy guidelines, this subsystem will present precise plans and goals which may optimize performance, and will show the risks involved. These various components effectively complement each other. Both simulation and linear programming rely completely on the information supplied them. Linear programming optimizes, supplying exact quantities to be attained for best performance and dual evaluators to facilitate sensitivity analysis. Simulation can use these data to demonstrate the expected effect on the bank from these plans in several economic conditions. Their combination supplies management with a comprehensive quantitative tool to deal better with real world problems in an analytical, accurate, and forwardlooking manner.

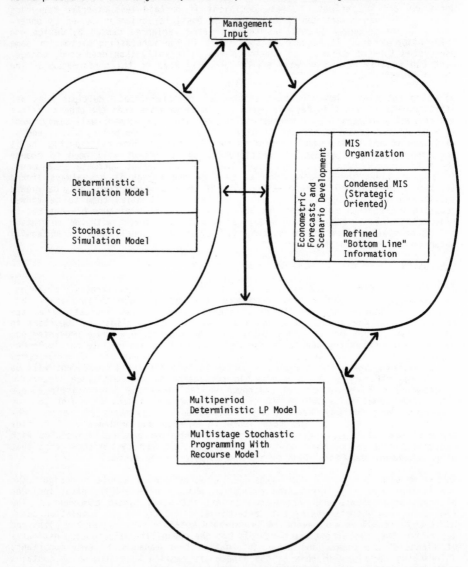

Figure 2

REFERENCES

[1] * Aghili, P., Cramer, R. H., and Thompson, H. E., "Small Bank Balance Sheet Management: Applying Two-Stage Programming Models," Journal of Bank Research, Vol. 5, No. 4 (Winter 1975), pp. 246-256.

[2]   Booth, G. G., "Programming Bank Portfolios under Uncertainty: An Extension," Journal of Bank Research, Vol. 2, No. 4 (Winter 1972), pp. 28-40.

[3] * Carter, E. E. and Cohen, K. J., "The Use of Simulation in Selecting Branch Banks," Industrial Management Review, Vol. 8, No. 2 (Spring 1967), pp. 55-69.

[4] * Cohen, K. J., "A Realistic Approach to Implementing Management Science," Magazine of Bank Administration, Vol. 45, No. 9 (September 1969), pp. 28-31 and 64.

[5] * Cohen, K. J., "Dynamic Balance Sheet Management: A Management Science Approach," Journal of Bank Research, Vol. 2, No. 4 (Winter 1972), pp. 9-19.

[6]   Cohen, K. J. and Cyert, R. M., "Strategy: Formulation, Implementation, and Monitoring," Journal of Business, Vol. 46, No. 3 (July 1973), pp. 349-367.

[7]   Cohen, K. J. and Hammer, F. S., "Linear Programming and Optimal Bank Asset Management Decisions," Journal of Finance, Vol. 22, No. 2 (May 1967), pp. 147-165.

[8] * Cohen, K. J. and Hammer, F. S., "Linear Programming Models for Optimal Bank Dynamic Balance Sheet Management," in Mathematical Methods in Investment and Finance, edited by Giorgio P. Szego and Karl Shell, North Holland Publishing Company, Amsterdam and American Elsevier Publishing Company, Inc., New York, 1972, pp. 377-413.

[9] * Cohen, K. J. and Rutenberg, D. P., "Toward a Comprehensive Framework for Bank Financial Planning," Journal of Bank Research, Vol. 1, No. 4 (Winter 1971), pp. 41-57.

[10] Cohen, K. J. and Thore, S., "Programming Bank Portfolios under Uncertainty," Journal of Bank Research, Vol. 1, No. 1 (Spring 1970), pp. 42-61.

[11] * Derwa, L., "Computer Models: Aids to Management at Societe Generale de Banque," Journal of Bank Research, Vol. 3, No. 2 (Summer 1972), pp. 84-94.

[12] Hamilton, W. F. and Moses, M. A., "A Computer-based Corporate Planning System," Management Science, Vol. 21, No. 2 (October 1974), pp. 148-159.

[13] McSweeney, J. J., "Strategic Management Systems," Proceedings Fourth Annual Conference, The Society for Management Information Systems, Montreal, Canada, September 7-8, 1972, pp. 87-111.

[14] * Robinson, R. S., "BANKMOD: An Interactive Simulation Aid for Bank Financial Planning," Journal of Bank Research, Vol. 4, No. 3 (Autumn 1973), pp. 212-224.

[15] * Royer, M. H., "Simulation at Banque de Bruxelles," Journal of Bank Research, Vol. 5, No. 4 (Winter, 1975), pp. 237-245.

* The nine items marked with asterisks are reprinted in Cohen, K. J. and Gibson, S. E., editors, Management Science in Banking, Warren, Gorham & Lamont, Inc., Boston, 1978.

THE ROLE OF ECONOMETRIC MODELS
IN STRATEGIC PLANNING

Thomas H. Naylor

Department of Economics
Duke University
Durham, North Carolina
U.S.A.

As recently as 1970, the number of companies using econometric models was extremely small (probably less than 100). Today if one considers the clients of Chase
Econometrics, DRI, and Wharton, one can conservatively estimate the number of
companies using econometric models to be somewhere between 750 and 1,000. In
March of 1980 we mailed a ten-page, in depth, questionnaire to 1691 corporate
members of the National Association of Business Economists. There were a total of
268 responses (15.8% of the sample) of which 234 were usable.

Of those companies which responded to our survey 66.5% indicated they are using
econometric models, 4.9% are developing an econometric model, 4.9% are planning to
develop such a model, and 23.7% have no plans whatsoever to develop an econometric
model.

The purpose of this paper is to summarize some of the findings of this survey of
users of econometric models. Specifically, we shall be concerned with answers to
the following questions. What has been the experience of corporations with the
use of econometric models over the past decade? How were the models developed?
What types of models are being used? What types of computational tools are
required? What can be said about the track record of the models? What impact
have econometric service bureaus had on the use of econometrics? What does the
future hold for corporate econometric modeling?

ECONOMETRIC MODELING EXPERIENCE

Ninety-two percent of the respondents are members of NABE. As corporate economists, we were interested in their attitudes towards econometric modeling. Their
responses appear in Table 1 below.

Table 1. Attitude of Corporate Economists Towards the
Use of Econometric Models

Attitude	Percentage
Very Interested	57.5%
Somewhat Interested	31.1%
Indifferent	6.2%
Not at all Interested	5.2%
	100.0%

We also asked the respondents to give their opinion of senior management's attitude towards econometrics. The top management responses in Table 2 are in sharp
contrast to those of the corporate economists.

127

Table 2.   Attitudes of Senior Management Towards the
Use of Econometric Models

Attitude	Percentage
Very Interested	19.0%
Somewhat Interested	41.4%
Indifferent	27.3%
Not at all Interested	12.3%
	100.0%

Since over three-fourths of the respondents are either using, developing, or
planning to develop econometric models, it is not surprising that nearly 90%
of them expressed an interest in econometric models. On the other hand, it is
safe to say that we still have a long way to go before top management is ready
to embrace econometrics. However, it was somewhat surprising to find that the
top management of over 60% of the companies who responded were thought to be
interested in econometric modeling.

Tables 3 and 4 shed some light on how econometric models are being used in American corporations. Not surprisingly, Table 3 shows that marketing is the activity
that has been modeled most often. Table 4 shows some of the more important applications of econometric modeling.

Table 3.   Activities Which have Been Modeled with Econometrics

Activity	Percentage
Marketing	43.8%
Finance	41.1%
Corporate	31.5%
Production	17.1%
Manpower	11.0%

Table 4.   Applications of Econometric Models

Application	Percentage
Long Term Forecasts	75.2%
Financial Forecasts	58.6%
Industry Forecasts	56.7%
Sales Forecasts	52.9%
Strategic Planning	51.6%
Budgeting	37.6%
Profit Planning	31.8%
Balance Sheet Projections	31.2%
Marketing Planning	31.2%
Cash Flow Analysis	30.6%
Cost/Price Projections	29.3%
Capital Budgeting	21.0%

Table 4. Applications of Econometric Models
(Continued)

Application	Percentage
Market Share Analysis	19.7%
Risk Analysis	17.2%
Supply Forecasts	17.2%
Merger-Acquisition Analysis	8.3%
New Venture Analysis	8.3%

That corporate economists are the principal users of corporate econometric models (Table 5) comes as no surprise. What was surprising to learn was that the Chief Executive Officer is among the users of the output data from econometric models in 58.7% of the companies in our sample. Table 5 gives some indication as to the more important users of the output generated by econometric models.

Table 5. Users of Output Data from Corporate Econometric Models

User	Percentage
Corporate Economist	63.9%
Chief Executive Officer	58.7%
Vice President of Finance	55.5%
Controller	41.9%
Marketing Analyst	40.6%
Chairman of the Board	40.0%
Financial Analyst	36.8%
Vice President of Marketing	36.1%
Treasurer	27.7%
Board Member	22.6%
Vice President of Production	19.4%
Production Analyst	16.8%
Management Science	13.5%

MODEL DEVELOPMENT

Next we turn our attention to the development of corporate econometric models. Table 6 indicates the department that is primarily responsible for the development of the econometric model. Of those models included in our sample, 55.4% were developed entirely in-house without any outside assistance whatsoever, 34.5% were developed in-house with some outside assistance, and 21.6% were purchased from an outside vendor.

Table 6. Department Primarily Responsible for Model Development

Department	Percentage
Corporate Economics	50.3%
Corporate Planning	40.5%
Marketing	11.8%
Operations Research	11.1%
Management Science	7.8%

The price range to develop those econometric models which were either purchased from outside vendors or were developed with outside assistance varied from a low of $2,000 to a high of $250,000. The average cost to develop such a model was $45,532.

The econometric model in our sample with the earliest start date was initiated in 1962. The mean date for the initiation of model development was the second quarter of 1975. The average elapsed time before the model was used by management was 8 1/2 months but the elapsed time ranged from one month to three years. The mean completion date was the first quarter of 1976. Although many companies began developing and using econometric models as recently as 1980, the average company in our sample has around four years of experience with econometric modeling.

This average time horizon for which forecasts have been generated by econometric models turned out to be 7.7 years. However, some companies are using their econometric models to produce forecasts for as long as 25 years out into the future.

For those companies which use their models to do simulation experiments the average cost to generate a single scenario forecast for one year was $268. The average cost of a single scenario forecast for five years out was $334.

Nature of the Model

Although a wide variety of different types of econometric models, estimation techniques, and solution techniques are being used, it is possible to generalize and say that the majority of the existing models are relatively simple in nature and do not incorporate a high degree of sophistication. Table 7 indicates that single-equation recursive models are much more popular than simultaneous-equation models. This is not surprising since the former are much easier to specify and estimate than the latter. Although 27.2% of the models were single equation models, some had as many as 2,500 equations. The average number of equations was 158.

Table 7.   Type of Model

Model Type	Percentage
Multiple-Equation Recursive	47.1%
Single-Equation	27.2%
Simultaneous Linear	20.6%
Simultaneous Non-Linear	14.7%

As for the time frame employed by the models, 56.3% were quarterly models, 38.4% were yearly models, and 15.2% were monthly models. (The fact that these percentages do not add up to one hundred is indicative of the fact that some models serve as quarterly and annual models.)

Ordinary least-squares is by far the most widely used econometric estimating technique. Ordinary least-squares was the choice of 86.6% companies in our sample and two-stage least-squares was a distant second with 22.7%. More exotic econometric estimation techniques such as full information maximum likelihood and three-stage least-squares were hardly mentioned at all by the respondents to our questionnaire. Table 8 indicates the extent to which several more specialized techniques are used by corporate economists.

Finally, nearly 90% of the econometric models included in our survey use national macroeconomic variables as input variables. Therein lies the rationale underlying the fact that 90% of the firms in our sample subscribe to some type of econometric service bureau which provides macroeconomic data and forecasts.

Table 8.   Other Econometric Techniques

Technique	Percentage
Almon Lags	57.8%
Cochrane-Orcutt Correction	37.3%
Hildreath-Lu Correction	34.9%
Koyck Lags	32.5%
Higher Order Autocorrelation Correction	25.3%

From a computational standpoint, 69.2% of the models were developed with the aid of an outside computer service bureau. On the other hand, 44.8% were built using the company's in-house computer. Nearly 75% of the models were developed using a computer in an interactive, conversational mode. Forty-seven percent were developed in batch mode on a computer and 11% were actually developed using a hand calculator. With the advent of higher level planning and modeling languages to facilitate the estimation, solution, and validation of econometric models, it was very surprising to find that FORTRAN was the most widely used computer language (Table 9) for econometric modeling. Of the seven languages used most extensively for corporate econometric modeling three are general purpose scientific languages - FORTRAN, APL, and PL/1. EPS, XSIM, EMPIRE, and SIMPLAN are special purpose planning and modeling systems.

Table 9.   Computer Languages Employed

Language (Vendor)	Percentage
FORTRAN (IBM)	35.0%
EPS (DRI)	33.3%
XSIM (IDC)	13.0%
APL (IBM)	8.1%
PL/1 (IBM)	5.7%
EMPIRE (ADR)	4.9%
SIMPLAN (SSI)	4.1%
SAS (SAS)	3.3%

Econometric Service Bureaus

As we indicated previously nearly 90% of the companies which responded to our survey subscribe to an econometric service bureau. Table 10 shows a breakdown of the various service bureaus which are used most by corporations to support their econometric modeling activities.

Table 10.   Econometric Service Bureaus

Bureau	Percentage
DRI	68.3%
Chase Econometrics	32.4%
Wharton	17.6%
Merrill Lynch	9.9%
General Electric	7.0%

Of those firms who subscribe to an econometric service bureau, 59.6% receive only
the printed forecasts from the bureau, 38.2% are able to read data interactively
from the bureau's central computer, and 33.8% actually have their corporate
econometric model linked directly to the service bureau's macroeconomic database
and forecasts. Table 11 attempts to identify the principal reasons why companies
use econometric service bureaus and Table 12 indicates how these service bureaus
are actually used. It is interesting to note in Table 11 that the degree of
interest expressed in the databases offered by these bureaus is almost equal to
the level of interest in their national macroeconomic forecasting model. This
can, in part, be explained by the poor forecasting track records of most macroeconometric models in the United States.

Table 11. Principal Interest in Econometric Service Bureaus

Interest	Percentage
National Macroeconomic Model	64.8%
Access to Database	63.4%
Industry Models	25.4%
State or Regional Models	12.7%

Table 12. Use of Econometric Service Bureaus

Uses	Percentage
Drive Corporate Model	61.8%
Check on other Forecasts	47.9%
Report to Management	46.5%
Information for Division Offices	24.3%

Three questions were included in our survey dealing with features offered by
econometric service bureaus (Table 13), benefits derived from the use of their
services (Table 14) and shortcomings associated with their use (Table 15).

Table 13. Features Provided by Econometric Service Bureaus

Feature	Percentage
Accurate Data	73.2%
Frequent Database Updates	70.4%
Consistent Forecasts	62.0%
Ease of Use	55.6%
Consulting Support	47.2%
Disaggregate Data	45.8%
Documentation	38.7%
Comprehensible Models	38.0%
Flexibility	34.5%
Manipulable Models	33.8%
Economical Computer Charges	12.7%

Table 14. Benefits of Econometric Service Bureaus

Benefit	Percentage
More Timely Information	66.9%
Ability to Explore Alternative Scenarios	55.6%
Reduced Personnel Time	53.5%
Greater Understanding of National Economy	52.8%
Ability to Test Own Assumptions	42.3%
Access to Consultants	35.9%
More Accurate Forecasts	33.1%
Cost Savings	19.0%

Table 15. Shortcomings of Econometric Service Bureaus

Shortcomings	Percentage
Computing Costs too High	46.6%
Subscription Cost too High	44.3%
Inaccurate Forecasts	37.4%
Incomprehensible Model	13.7%
Data not Disaggregated	12.2%
Poorly Documented	11.5%
Database Inefficiencies	10.7%
Not User-Oriented	9.9%
Inappropriate Output Variables	8.4%
Insufficient Technical Support	7.6%
Inflexibility	7.6%
No Shortcomings	7.6%
Too Much Computer Time	6.9%
Difficult to Interpret	5.3%
Not Manipulable	3.1%
System too Technical	3.1%
Inconvenient Access	1.5%

Several items are noteworthy in Tables 13-15. First, in Table 13, the two most important features of econometric service bureaus are both database related. Second, in Table 14, forecasting accuracy is the seventh most important benefit of econometric service bureaus. Third, in Table 15 it was not surprising to find that high computer charges and subscription fees are considered to be the major limitations of econometric service bureaus given the importance attached to economical computer charges and cost savings in Tables 13 and 14 respectively. Fourth, inaccurate forecasts ranked third behind high computer costs and subscription fees among the shortcomings of econometric service bureaus in Table 15.

In summary, users of econometric service bureaus seem to purchase these services primarily for the databases, consulting, and the ability to examine alternative economic scenarios. They continue to use these service bureaus in spite of their dissatisfaction with the forecasting accuracy of their macroeconometric models and industry forecasting models and the charges incurred for these services.

OBSTACLES TO THE USE OF ECONOMETRIC MODELS

To gain some insight into some of the major obstacles to the use of econometric models in corporations we included a question in our survey dealing with this topic. Table 16 contains the results.

Table 16.   Obstacles to the Use of Econometric Models

Obstacle	Percentage
Management Bias Against Econometric Models	34.4%
Lack of Understanding of Econometric Models	34.4%
Insufficient Staff Time to Develop Models	32.3%
Insufficient In-House Expertise	30.0%
Insufficient Data	14.4%
Insufficient Financial Resources	12.2%
Insufficient Computer Power	6.7%

CHARACTERISTICS OF RESPONDENTS

Finally, we were interested in knowing something about the type of people who actually responded to our questionnaire. Table 17 demonstrates that for the most part the respondents are affiliated with quite large companies. Only 25% of the responses were from companies with sales less than or equal to $500 million. As can be seen from Table 18 most of the respondents were either the user or the builder of the corporate econometric model. In some cases they played a dual role as both model user and model builder. Table 19 indicates memberships held in professional organizations by the respondents.

Table 17.   Company Size in Millions of Dollars of Sales

Sales	Percentage
Less than $50 Million	5.3%
$50 Million - $100 Million	2.9%
$100 Million - $250 Million	9.2%
$250 Million - $500 Million	7.7%
$500 Million - $1 Billion	11.1%
Greater than $1 Billion	63.8%
	100.0%

Table 18.   Relationship of Respondents to the Econometric Model

Respondent	Percentage
User	66.3%
Builder	59.9%
Sponsor	30.2%
Programmer	8.7%

Table 19.   Professional Membership of Respondent

Professional Organization	Percentage
National Association of Business Economists	92.2%
American Economic Association	45.8%
American Statistical Association	20.8%
North American Society for Corporate Planning	15.1%
Planning Executives Institute	8.9%
The Institute of Management Sciences	6.8%
Operations Research Society	5.7%

CONCLUSIONS

Advocates of econometric modeling will no doubt be pleased with some of the results presented in this paper. Believers in econometric models will note that the senior management of 60% of the companies in the survey were interested in econometric models and that the C.E.O. is among the users of the results of these models in 58.7% of the companies sampled. They will also take solace in the long list of econometric applications and benefits derived from econometric service bureaus.

On the other hand, critics of econometric models will revel in the statistics which showed that the top management of nearly forty percent of the companies in the sample are either indifferent towards or not at all interested in econometric modeling. They will also point out the results which express strong dissatisfaction with forecasting accuracy, computer costs, and subscription fees of econometric service bureaus.

Our purpose in conducting this survey of users of econometric models was neither to make the case for econometric models nor against them, but rather to try to ascertain to what extent they are actually being used, how they are used, and how they are regarded by corporate economists and top management.

We believe that corporate econometric modeling may be at a critical turning point. The 1980 recession will provide an acid test of the commitment of corporations to econometrics. The real question will be whether corporations will continue to use these tools when confronted with the combination of internal budgeting pressures created by the recession and the poor track record of econometric service bureaus in forecasting the economy of the United States. Will econometric models prove to be effective planning tools during a period of economic stress? Only time will tell.

SOME WAYS TO BRIDGE MANAGEMENT'S CONFIDENCE GAP
IN CORPORATE PLANNING MODELS

Albert N. Schrieber

School of Business
University of Washington
Seattle, Washington
U.S.A.

A corporate planning model is a statement about the future. It defines a strategy and suggests the likely consequences of the strategy. Let us look briefly at the concept of "strategy", and then at the concept of "consequences".

Strategy formulation begins by examining three areas of constraints. The first constraint is the history and past trends that are pertinent to the business at hand. The second constraint involves the external environment, such as government regulations, technological change, and the strength of competitors. The third constraint involves the internal milieu of the organization, such as the attitudes and personal values of key managers. These constraints broadly define the limiting borders of the strategy.

The next step involves the topics that comprise the functional elements of the strategy that are treated in the following sequence:

1. Goals or objectives of the organizations
2. Products or services
3. Customers or clients
4. Production and operations
5. Finances
6. Organizational structure
7. Control system
8. Reappraisal procedures

From the assumptions and decisions made about the eight functional elements it is then possible to identify the probable consequences of alternative possibilities (scenarios), and the opportunities and risks of these alternatives. From the analysis procedure just described, the new strategy is evolved covering:

1. Long term plans - five to ten years or longer
2. Intermediate plans - two or three to five years
3. Short term plans - one or two years ahead

For a manufacturer the consequences of the strategy will first be defined in terms of potential sales to customers, or the claims of clients. From this the process of satisfying customers and clients can be defined in physical terms that measure work force, material requirements, facilities, energy, waste products, etc. Finally, these physical terms will be translated into the common language of business - money terms - to provide pro-forma financial statements of a balance sheet, profit and loss statement, cash flow statement, source and application statement, and the return on investment statement.

The planning process I have described to develop an organizational strategy is becoming increasingly important and also more difficult due to:

1. The internationalization of business that requires more variables to be taken into consideration.

2. Improved communications and travel that have shortened lead times for every activity and stimulated greater competition. As a result, most managers feel that they are in the same condition as the white rabbit in Alice in Wonderland who every time he looked at his watch could only say "I'm late, I'm late, I'm late."

The inputs to the process involve some facts and figures that can be determined with reasonable accuracy. For example, one question might be "What is the potential for the geriatric market in the year 2000, 20 years from now?" All the people in that market (say 55 years and older) are now 35 years or older, and we know how many there are from census figures. Applying reasonable values from life cycle table, the development of a forecast for the geriatric market in the year 2000 is not too difficult to determine.

But, does a company want to focus on the market segment? Perhaps there is fear that too many competitors will also be seeking that market! Perhaps the government itself will provide and control that market through social security, nationalized health plans, etc. The problem of what the geriatric market in the year 2000 means to a specific organization is a judgmental decision that will be based as much on intuition ("gut feel" if you will) as on the hard facts that are available on the size of the market.

Where do corporate planning models fit into this picture? Such models are based on the intuition, experience, wisdom, knowledge, gut feel, luck or what have you of the executives who translate their assumptions and feelings into the decisions that drive the corporate planning models. The models, then, take these inputs, and by careful definition of process relationships and money flows, expressed by algorithms and parameters, provide the consequences. Some models can be very simple and can be based on a few rules of thumb that can be worked out on the back of an envelope. But for almost all large business organizations the models for them are exceedingly complex and require tedious and usually inaccurate hand calculations to evaluate or else the clerical work can be handled by a computer program.

To anyone acquainted with the power of the computer, it is only logical to go that route. Unless the top level decisions are made arbitrarily or capriciously (as exemplified by some of the actions taken by the late Howard Hughes), the establishment of a complex corporate plan by any other method than a rigorous computerized model would seem to many professional practitioners to be inept and irresponsible, and yet - we are all aware that many top level managers have limited confidence in such complex computerized corporate planning models - or worse yet are positively opposed to them, and such proposed projects are stillborn in their organizations. How can such confidence gaps be bridged?

The powerful simulation tools now available to us by way of the computer permit the evaluation of strategic assumptions and the establishment of expected consequences in greater or lesser detail as the circumstances require. Better yet, these simulation tools can quickly respond to "what if" questions, and thus explore a territory of ideas that can lead to a perceived optimal solution. How can managers be helped to make better use of these tools?

Let us examine the way some senior executives view their decision making problems regarding computerized simulation models.

In 1966, I spoke with Mr. X, then the managing director of a very large international company located in southern Europe, but with distribution activities in more than 125 countries and with manufacturing facilities in more than 30 countries. One of his major tasks was to evaluate and decide on proposals for capital equipment investments. He was troubled by the increasing numbers of proposals from his manufacturing plants and distribution centers requesting new or updated computer installations, each involving large sums of money. He found it extremely difficult to evaluate the proposals in spite of a one-week special course he had taken in New York sponsored by IBM to acquaint senior executives with basic principles of computer use and applications. At that time computers were primarily used as a clerical tool for routine record keeping, but already there were many proposals for the development of simulation models directed toward improving decision making at the top level. Mr. X had already been disappointed many times that computerized results had failed to live up to the promised expectations. At that point he was primarily concerned about the heavy investment in hardware and made the comment that buying computers was like getting powered forging hammers to crack nuts.

Last summer I discussed the same problem with Mr. Y, the head of a very large industrial manufacturing company in England. He was agonizing over a seven million dollar request for new computer facilities that had been awaiting his decision for more than six months. In spite of many meetings and explanations with the computer experts, he found it extremely difficult to evaluate the cost/benefit ratio from the proposal. The new equipment would not only assist the overloaded daily chores of record keeping, but they also promised to provide new capabilities of preparing simulation models for improving decision making at many executive levels. At the same time, Mr. Y had many other capital budget proposals that were competing with the computer request, all of which in total far exceeded the available funds. In contrast to Mr. X, Mr. Y was worried more about the software than the hardware. He felt that the seven million dollar budget request was only the tip of the camel's nose into the tent, and that the subsequent cost of preparing software, and implementing all the changes that would result, would involve expenditures far exceeding the current proposals. He already had experienced programs that had ended up costing five to ten times as much as the original estimates. He still questioned whether the proliferation of computerized activity was for real benefit, or was a fad to keep up with the current managerial style.

Mr. Z was the chief corporate planning officer in 1968 when I visited with him to discuss simulation models. His organization was one of the most technically advanced companies in the world with major manufacturing facilities throughout the United States, and with a worldwide market. His industry was involved with rapid technological change that required quick evaluation of new product and process directions. As a result, he was very anxious to speed up the four week lead time required to evaluate a major proposal regarding its interaction with all of the company's activities. He wanted the ability to rapidly collect the essential data needed to make a fast evaluation of alternatives, and then to maintain an effective tracking progress method on an up-to-date basis in order to compare current results with the annual corporate plan. His proposal was to put remote terminals in the offices of key executives at the various plants and provide them with a standardized corporate planning model located on the headquarters computer system, and directly connected by leased communication lines to each plant. The plan was that each plant manager and his subordinates could test out numerous alternatives regarding product line and operation on a standardized simulation model. After exploring various "what if" choices, they would then submit their optimum plan to the headquarters. At the headquarters the various plans could then be quickly consolidated, and reevaluated with another set of "what if" questions that would bring the various plant proposals into harmony on an overall corporate basis within the limited constraints of available funds, facilities and available work force. After 18 months of experimental use, he found that almost no executives were using the terminals in their offices. A few had hired special assistants to become acquainted with the use of the computer terminal and the simulation programs. This merely added additional overhead, when it was intended that the executive alone could sit at the terminal and in a few minutes obtain the answers he required on the VDU screen. At that time, it was decided that the concept was ahead of its time, and that managers were not ready to operate in this fashion. Although the project failed in terms of its grandiose total plan, a great deal was learned about the usefulness and power, and also the limitations, of computerized simulation models for corporate planning. As a result, the experiment was carefully evaluated and documented, the report was tied with a red ribbon and filed for reexamination in another seven years. At the headquarters work continued on the development of corporate simulation planning using computers. In 1970 Mr. Z reported his experience in a paper entitled "Simulation and Irritation" at a symposium on computer simulation models held at the University of Washington in Seattle.

Last month I contacted Mr. Z to find out how he now felt about his simulation experience of twelve years ago. He had now changed positions from his earlier staff planning role to a line position as the operating head of a major unit of the company. He was still enthusiastic about the concept of computerized corporate planning models and felt that his company was now ready for more extensive development in this direction. The new generations of computer hardware, the new software techniques, and the better understanding of computers by executives seemed to now provide a better environment for the implementation of computerized corporate simulation models. Nevertheless, he felt that many of the irritations of twelve years ago were still present and had to be carefully addressed if further progress was to be achieved.

I realize that my sample of three executives does not represent a comprehensive statistical survey. Nevertheless, I believe the insights of a few wise individuals may be worth a great deal more than a mashed-up statistical sample of a large number of executives, many of whom may be ill informed, and all of whom have difficulty in conveying their precise conclusions on a standardized questionnaire.

How can we respond to the comments of Mr's X, Y and Z, even though they have identified the "management gap" in very general terms? We can first note that these executives become irritated with computers and simulation techniques when the results fail to possess the characteristics which were expected or which created undesireable aspects that were not expected. What these executives seem to want are simulation models that are responsive to their needs in terms of providing desireable information at reasonable cost and within reasonable time limits. In addition, the results need to inspire confidence to permit practical use of the simulation output.

The irritations about responsiveness include the following complaints:

1. Computerized corporate simulation models take a long time to build, often three to four times as long as promised.

2. Changes and improvements also take a long time to incorporate into the program.

3. Often the data needed for the simulation is not readily available, and the collection of the data becomes a major operation in itself before the simulation can be used.

The lack of confidence in using the results of a simulation are often caused by some of the following problems:

1. The model never seems to be quite done or quite right, but the promise is made that it will soon be completed and correct. The end point never seems to arrive.

2. The problem to be solved has to go through complex translation from the concepts and ideas in the executive's mind into a complete new framework and ends up in unintelligible computer language. Do these strange algorithms of the computer program really represent the original problem that was in the executive's mind?

3. The computer model is difficult to explain in terms that are understand-

able to the executive. System analysts and programmers too often fall back on technical jargon to justify their activities. The executive is really not interested in "computerese", but wants to know "what have you really done to help me with my problem".

4. The real world and the problems to be simulated change faster than the model can be changed to update it for solving the current problems.

5. It is extremely difficult to define the probable range of errors in the output and the degree of limitation for its practical use.

Whether the professional systems designer accepts these irritations regarding responsiveness and confidence or not, they are in the executive's mind and form the basis of the management gap. If the professional simulation designer is to bridge this management gap, it is necessary to face up to it and devise a way to help the executive overcome the irritation and fears generated by the "black box" computer, the unintelligible computer languages and the poor experiences with results that have fallen far short of expectations.

May I now suggest an even dozen ideas that may be helpful in bridging the management gap.

1. INVOLVEMENT

Managers must be involved in the design of computerized corporate simulation models. The design involves three basic elements:

a. Defining the required input
b. Manipulating and transforming the input
c. Printing or displaying the output

The manager does not need to participate in the transformation process. That is the technical job of the systems analyst and programmer. The executive may contribute to the input of required data, but normally this is a minor role. The major task of the executive is to carefully define the required outputs. I cannot overemphasize the importance of first preparing in complete detail the content and appearance of the desired output. Even minor changes in the output, after the total program has been prepared, can cause consternation, delays, and excessive costs to incorporate such changes.

2. DOCUMENTATION

No matter how carefully advanced preparation has been made, it is inevitable that changes will be required in the program. To make such changes quickly and economically, it is imperative that careful documentation be created as the original program is prepared. On large simulation models it may take months or even years to complete the program. Usually the work is done by bright young persons who are highly susceptible to promotions and transfers to other activities. If the concepts of the programming are in their heads, rather than on paper, the transfer of such persons creates enormous difficulties for those who follow to complete the program and carry on the work. In developing the program, there is a tremendous excitement to get on with the job and produce some results. This excitement stimulates the temptation to take shortcuts and save time. Such shortcuts often involve setting aside the task of documentation on the assumption that it will be done after the programming is complete. This can be a fatal strategy. The subtleties of the design and program are usually forgotten or overlooked unless they are immediately documented as the design evolves. With this proper documentation the task of future changes, particularly by new people brought into the project, can be greatly simplified and speeded up.

3. FLEXIBILITY

In developing the simulation program, the designer must anticipate possible changes that require flexibility in the design of the program itself. Here the executive must again be called up to suggest possible changes that may be required in the output. For example, is it possible that a new corporate division may be established that must be included in the overall corporate plan? How large a product line must be allowed for? Should inflation rates be allowed for, and to what extent? Given such speculative choices, many executives will create a "wish list" of possibilities that may unreasonably complicate the design and its cost and time of development. As a result, a reasonable balance must be reached by intelligent negotiation between the program designer and the executive who will use the output. Each situation will require its own judgment.

4. DESIGN BY SMALL MODULES

To make a simulation program easily understood and easily changed, it is desireable that it be prepared in small modules that may require many subroutines that hook into a main program. The smaller the subroutine the easier it is to debug and change each one. It is also suggested that complex looping operations in the program be minimized. This often involves limiting the use of "IF" statements. Care must be taken that programmers do not become too enamored with program elegance and the objective of reducing computer process time. With early generation computers the reduction of process time was a very important factor. But with the modern generation computers this has become far less of a problem. As a result, it may be better to have independent tracks in the computer program for each logical alternative in order to provide easy understanding and simpler methods of making changes when required. An example of this occurred in the development of a program I use in my simulation called TOPEXEC involving the programing of notes receivable and notes payable. We designed the computer program so that all ten types of notes were processed through the same computer segment with many IF statements to adjust for different characteristics of payment periods, interest rates, discounts, regular and irregular periodic repayments, etc. Later, we discovered an error in the program resulting from very unusual conditions for a specific type of note. When we went to make the correction, we had to make adjustments for all the other types of notes. It was extraordinarily difficult to understand the problem, let alone make the corrections. If each type of note had been designed independently with its own algorithm, the computer program would have been much longer, but each segment would have been much simpler to understand and debug and change. In the end, it now is clear that the less elegant design would have been far better. The disease of oversophisticated design is one that too often affects our best and smartest programmers.

5. COST/BENEFIT ANALYSIS

When the designer goes about his task of developing the simulation program, there will inevitably be new ideas that arise to expand the program with more and better information or to add features that will result in savings at some future date. If these additions, which were not originally contemplated in the project, add significantly to the cost and time of development, the designer may find this to be a contribution to the irritation and frustration of the management who usually are more interested in immediate results than "pie in the sky" in the future. The designer must constantly keep in mind that it is necessary to make a contribution that produces a favorable cost/benefit relationship. If this does not occur, funds may be chopped off, or the next phase of the project will not be allocated the funds that are required. Thus, the designer must be able to justify what is being done and provide some evidence that the work will pay for itself. The frequency with which the designer must prove the justification of program design will depend on the tolerance level of the manager. This justification may be required every few months, but certainly at least once every six months. In this respect, the designer must be a salesperson who has to continually resell the product.

6. DATA

Careful consideration must be given to the amount and method of collecting the input data required to produce the desired output result. It is extremely frustrating to a manager to be in possession of an elegant simulation model, but one that lacks the necessary input data to drive it. The recreation of historical data that was not properly recorded at the time of its occurrence becomes a very costly and difficult operation. Anticipating the proper data base requirements becomes essential to successful design. If this is properly done, the data can often be collected as it occurs at very low cost compared to that of later collection. The designer must anticipate this problem.

Care must also be given to the output side by which the data is presented. Large detailed output, some people call it a "paper slinkey", can be extremely frustrating to managers. Top executives are usually extremely busy and overworked and want information presented to them in quick capsule form. Hence, the output should first be presented in the most abbreviated summary form that is possible, with backup detail that can be called upon if required by the top executive to satisfy the summary results. I have found it is best to conceal the detailed supporting evidence until it is really required. Otherwise, the top executive is overwhelmed and says silently, "Do I have to go through that mess to understand what's going on?"

7. ESTIMATING TIME AND COST

Designers must learn how to improve the task of estimating the time and cost of development of the program. It is not uncommon that the actual costs turn out to be five to ten times as much as the original estimate. If the rest of a business operated this way it would soon be bankrupt. One must appreciate that this is a very difficult task. Good estimating comes from experience. We can liken the task of estimating to the use of improvement curves in manufacturing. At the beginning improvement curve costs are very high, but rapidly decrease as experience and understanding permit improvements to be made. The design and development of simulation programs are usually at the high end of the improvement curve. It is far better to overestimate the time and cost of development (unless this kills the project) than to fail to meet the estimate and cause irritation and frustration in top level management.

8. CLOSURE

No simulation program is really ever complete. I am intimately acquainted with the problem, because I have been developing my TOPEXEC program for twenty-four years, and I still have things that I want to add and change. There are always new ideas, new computer hardware, new computer languages and techniques, new remote terminal equipment, changing cost relationships that open new design possibilities, and a host of other exciting and attractive opportunities for program improvement and development. The designer must be realistic about striking a balance between closure and future development. At some point the program and documentation must be completed so that it is useful. Instruction manuals must go out to users, and the results of the project must provide some usefulness. The designer must look at this problem in advance and develop a strategy for dealing with new models or marks of the program that will incorporate these new ideas and opportunities for enlargement and improvement.

9. SYNCHRONIZATION

Many, if not most, senior executives of today went through educational development and early experience on the job before computers were in common use. They probably have a very limited understanding of the technical features of how a computer operates, and probably have an unexpressed fear of the black box monster that they can neither understand nor control. In contrast, the college graduates of today all have exposure to computer technology and can program in at least one language. Even in the elementary school children are now being taught to be as comfortable with using a computer as they are with using pencil and paper. Future generations of executives will be quite at home with the computer. This is not the case today with older executives.

Senior executives have a hard time keeping up with the new developments and opportunities in the computer field. They tend to spend their time dealing with problems; and computers create problems for them to face at high cost, time delays, errors, debugging problems, and other frustrations and irritations. As a result, they tend to overlook the accomplishment and value that the computer activities produce.

The older executives are often very knowledgeable and comfortable with their personal system of planning that does not involve computers but gives them a high degree of control and visibility of the process. When the planning activity is transferred to computerized simulation programs they lose this control and visibility which is taken over by the bright young people applying new techniques and procedures. This problem is a major contribution to the management gap.

Designers of computer programs must be sympathetic to this problem and maintain open lines of communication with top executives to bring them along with understanding, appreciation and confidence in the new techniques. This requires real skill in communicating at the level that top executives understand. It is a delicate psychological problem that is often very difficult for the technical specialist to understand and effectively deal with.

10. OVERSELLING

There is great danger in overselling simulation models by implying greater results and accuracy than are really possible. Just because the computer program can print a financial figure in values of millions of dollars and carry these numbers out to two decimal places for the cents does not imply that such accuracy is justified. Perhaps we need to limit the output from simulation programs to rounding all the answers to three and no more than four significant figures, and thus imply limited accuracy. One must continuously keep in mind that all simulation programs are driven by the original estimates and assumptions that inevitably are only rough approximations of the future. It is inevitable that all simulation programs will be wrong when the forecasts are compared to the actual results that will occur in the future. Designers must maintain a degree of humility with reference to what they promise they can accomplish.

11. PACKAGED MODELS

It is not necessary for each organization to develop its own corporate planning models. Many consulting firms and computer service organizations have developed generalized computer models and computer languages that can be readily adapted to the needs of a specific organization. These programs are tested and can quickly be put to use. Although the cost of purchasing or leasing such programs may at first seem high, they are usually highly economical compared to the cost of developing an inhouse planning model.

An example of such a planning model is SIMPLAN (developed by Social Systems, Inc., Chapel Hill, North Carolina) which uses five integrated subsystems to deal with planning, management information, corporate modeling, forecasting, and econometric modeling. Many other planning models have been developed, and new and improved designs are constantly becoming available. It does take some effort, time and skill to locate the right packaged model that best fits a specific situation.

Often the biggest hurdle to overcome in making efficient and effective use of a packaged model is the resistance that develops internally (sometimes called the NIH factor - "not invested here"). For some, the opportunity and challenge of creatively developing a new computerized corporate planning model for their organization becomes so attractive and exciting that they have great difficulty in exercising the necessary unbiased judgement required in evaluating a "make or buy" decision regarding such models. In fact, some organizations have used the opportunity of developing computer corporate planning models to entice skilled analysts and programmers to join their company, and thus become available for other projects. Hence, modeling opportunities, involving inhouse developments or adapting packaged models, can become a recruiting tool in the current period of shortage of skilled computer practitioners.

12. MANAGEMENT GAMES

I have found that one of the effective ways to bridge the management gap is to expose executives to management games. I have been using a computerized management game for more than 20 years in undergraduate, graduate and executive development programs, and have found it to be the most effective teaching technique I know. It brings together the elements of top level corporate strategy formulation, the translation of physical activities into financial terms, the uncertainties of dealing with external environment, and the power of the computer to quickly and efficiently process the data to produce understandable and useable output. All of this can be done in an environment of excitement, great interest and pleasure. But like sex, however, it must be experienced to be understood.

The use of management games to bridge the management gap involves a group of executives divided into teams, each team representing the top level decision making group of an organization, all of whom are competing in a given market with similar products. Each group establishes a series of strategic decisions for their organization, and these decisions are the input to a computerized corporate simulation program that simulates the external environment and the internal structure to produce a set of output documents that replicate the typical financial statements used by executives - profit and loss statement, balance sheet, etc. The output for each team is analyzed by its group and becomes the basis for decision making for the next period. By an iterative set of plays that move through time the executives can experience in a few hours of exposure the effect of years of corporate experience.

The driving force of the simulation is its competitive aspect. Decision makers like to be winners and they have fun playing the game. The design of the management game, however, is very important. If the design produces trivial results, then the executives might just as well play the game of monopoly, or bridge, or other competitive amusement games that have little educational value. On the other hand, if the management game is highly realistic, using the typical tools involved in corporate strategy formulation, and the results are realistic and believeable, then the educational value can be tremendous. I have been constantly told by participants that playing an effective management game is one of the greatest educational experiences they have had.

For the executive, a management game illustrates how a computer can rapidly transform input data into output results. By using remote terminals for input of the decisions by the executives themselves, there is a "hands on" learning process that takes place in an environment that does not injure the dignity of the executives. For many technical executives with specialized training it is a wonderful opportunity to get acquainted and comfortable with accounting and financial terminology and analysis. Since the management game involves an artifical company, there is a tendency to take risks and experiment with new ideas that could never be tested in their own real organization. The minds and imagination of the participants are stretched to become more creative with greater understanding. There is also a greater appreciation of the complex interrelationships and interactions that occur between the various elements in an organization, including the personal relations of the participants within their own team.

For the computer program designers who participate as members of the team, they learn how managers think and what are the elements of corporate strategy formulation. As they are exposed to how the decision inputs are transformed by the computer program into the output results they learn about the rigidities and unrealities that may be produced by their programs. Designers develop new respect for the judgment, insights, assumptions, and uncertainties that executives face in their decision making tasks. I have often heard it said that it is easier for managers to learn about technical aspects of computing than it is for computer technicians to understand what the managerial decision processs is all about. The management game can be of great help to computer designers with this problem.

13. CATERING TO THE CLIENT

The last point I want to suggest is the need for the simulation designer to understand the problem from the manager's point of view. The manager is the customer, or client, and is the one who pays the bills that makes the simulation project a reality. Hence, it is necessary to cater to both the manager's overt needs and also to subtle feelings. The fears, irritations, frustrations, and disappointments many have experienced with simulations programs have conditioned their attitudes toward such projects and are as important an element of the project as the opportunities and potential attributed to simulation techniques.

* * * * * * *

Computerized corporate simulation models are a powerful tool for management. To the extent that a management gap exists in making effective use of these tools, it is the responsibility of the designer and technical practitioner to help ovecome this gap. Organizations that do not learn or use simulation techniques will find their competitors will use them. Those who succeed with this powerful tool will have a higher probability of winning in the competitive market place. If so, we all have a powerful incentive to close the management gap.

ECONOMICS:
THE LANGUAGE OF STRATEGIC PLANNING

ECONOMICS FOR CORPORATE STRATEGY:
FROM SUBSTANTIVE RATIONALITY TO PROCEDURAL RATIONALITY

Richard M. Burton

Fuqua School of Business
Duke University
Durham, North Carolina
U.S.A.

INTRODUCTION

Does economic theory have anything relevant to say about corporate strategy? Our intuition tells us there must be some connection. Yet, a first level review and comparison of the economics of the firm, as it is taught, and many corporate planning models reveal very little apparent connection. But there is a connection--a fundamental and basic one. To demonstrate the relation, we look at the fundamental characteristics of both models. There is a clear influence of the substantive theory in economics on the substantive theory for corporate planning and strategy.

The more important issue is whether economics offers guidance for procedural rationality in corporate strategy. The conjecture is that economists have a lot to offer, but they have not taken up these more difficult issues of procedural rationality and organization. As Simon suggests economists "will have to devote major energy to building a theory of procedural rationality to complement existing theories of substantive rationality."

This paper begins with a review of the classical economic theory of the firm to suggest a related substantive theory for substantive rationality for corporate planning and strategy. A procedural rationality for corporate planning is yet to be fully developed. However, there is a beginning which borrows from existing literature and relies heavily upon the economic reasoning from substantive economics.

THE RECEIVED ECONOMIC THEORY OF THE FIRM*

The economic model of the firm includes three basic elements: the input (factor) markets, the output (product) markets, and the production function which states the technological relation between inputs and outputs. With these elements, and under the assumption of a goal of profit maximization, one can derive the well known marginality conditions:

(1) Any output (product) is produced at a quantity such that its marginal revenue equals its marginal cost.

(2) Any input (factor) is employed at a level such that its marginal (revenue) product equals its unit cost.

(3) Any two inputs are employed in relative quantities such that the ratios of their marginal physical product to unit cost are equal.

The first principle states the optimal scale of operations, or how much to produce. The second condition gives a similar relation for the inputs; namely the

---

*The next few sections on economics and a substantive theory for corporate planning are adopted from Burton and Naylor (1980).

optimal level of input usage. The third principle states a condition of optimal balance between inputs for efficiency in production.

Embedded in this analysis are a number of important assumptions about modeling and efficiency. These issues are implicit:

(1) The outputs (goods and services) and inputs are known and specified. That is, we are given the total set of products and inputs (and their prices) that the firm can consider. It seems to be an innocent assumption. But the consequences are important. By definition, we have eliminated any prospect and method for search of new opportunities. That is, the theory tells us how to choose among a known set of opportunities, but is mute on how to generate new opportunities.

(2) The input (factor) and output (product) markets are given and known. These markets can vary from perfect competition to pure monopolies, but it is assumed at the start that the market characteristics are known. This assumption defines the firm's relevant environment at zero cost to the firm.

(3) The production function is known and given. Two issues are evident here--one conceptual and the other computational. First, the production function assumes that one has described the efficient technological relation between outputs and inputs, e.g. if we can produce one automobile with 500 lb of steel, 50 lb of leather, 100 hours of labour, etc., then it is not possible to build the same car with, say, less labour. This is the efficient technology. The result is that the economic principles for the firm cannot detect productive inefficiency, and consequently cannot guide us to find waste. Secondly, the classroom production function is usually a two product-two factor illustration with appropriate mathematical properties so that one can employ the calculus[1] to derive results. But real world firms never[2] state a production function in these terms. A firm with twenty products and hundreds of inputs will not, and probably cannot, state a single equation production function. In such firms, the production function is a useful conceptual construct, but is not operational. A more operational form of the production function is the input-output matrix, which then is incorporated into a linear program. There are numerous operating examples, but such models are usually short run operating models, not part of longer run corporate planning models. One exception is the CIBA-GEIGY model reported in Rosenkranz (1979).

The economic theory of the firm considers only a narrow set of real world problems. But the following issues are fundamental and remain. Corporate planning models must deal with search for new opportunities, and an operational statement of production possibilities. The fundamental notions in economics are relevant, but they are not evident in the first level analysis in economics. We will make this bridge later in the paper, but would like to consider some other criticisms of the economic theory of the firm first.

CRITIQUE

Ansoff (1965, Chapter 2) states that any theory of corporate planning must include: a theory of search, and a theory of choice. The economic theory of the firm offers a theory of choice, but not a theory of search. There is no mechanism in the theory to guide one to search for products and inputs beyond the current opportunity set. Ansoff considered this result to be a most damaging criticism of economic theory for corporate planning. However, as we shall demonstrate later, a theory of search may include the use and application of economics, and further, that efficient search will rely heavily upon economic reasoning. That is, the received theory does not yield a theory of search, but an efficient search procedure includes economic reasoning. In this context, economic theory supplies appropriate questions more than it supplies answers.

A more general critique of the economic theory of the firm is the behavior theory by Cyert and March (1963). They also note that the economic theory of the firm does not supply a theory of search. Using data from observed firms, they supply a theory of decision making which suggests:

(1) Search is biased, myopic, and simple-minded, i.e. find a workable solution near to a present solution.

(2) Choice is not profit maximizing, but involves resolution of conflicting goals among sub-units on a continuing basis. That is, goals are not given, but are discovered through analysis and search.

(3) Uncertainty is avoided through continuing feedback.

(4) Learning is evident through adaptation of goals, attention rules, and search rules.

The implicit assumptions of free and perfect information, and free and optimal decision making are not present in real firms. There is considerable uncertainty, information is costly and decision-makers must be paid.

Leibenstein (1966) offers another critique of the economic theory of the firm. He argues that economics concentrates on the wrong problem. Namely, economics solves for allocative efficiency and the real issue is to achieve productive efficiency. To illustrate, consider the production possibilities for a firm, shown in Figure 1. Here, X_1, X_2 are two outputs. The production possibilities

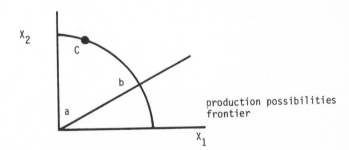

Figure 1. Typical production possibilities function for the firm

frontier represents the set of (X_1, X_2) products which can be made efficiently. Let us assume that the market prices, and resulting marginality conditions dictate the point C is optimal. Now, if the firm produces at point b, it suffers an opportunity loss by making a non-optimal combination of X_1, X_2. Point b represents an allocative inefficiency. However, point b is productive efficient, as it is not possible to obtain a greater quantity of X_1 without decreasing X_2, or vice versa. Now consider point a. It is not only allocative inefficient, but also productive inefficient, as it is possible to increase the quantity of X_1 and/or X_2 with existing inputs.

Leibenstein (1966) in his study of monopoly argues that productive inefficiency is far more serious than allocative inefficiency. Firms make both errors, but productive inefficiency results in the greater opportunity cost as lost profits. For corporate planning, the search for productive efficiency must be explicit. We cannot assume this issue away. In an empirical study, Schiff and Lewin (1970) found that firms choose to operate at less than efficient levels in order to minimize managerial effort and hedge against contingencies.

Shubik (1970) critiques the individual owner who is a profit maximizer assumption, no evident relation between economics and accounting, ignorances of internal organization, and lack of differentiation between GM and a local candy store as some issues which economists might begin to consider if they want to be more relevant.

THE NATURE OF CORPORATE MODELING

Corporate modeling is a process which can yield different models depending upon the firm, the intended use, and the modeling language. Quite simply the form of most corporate models is different than the form of the simple economic model of the firm. This difference follows for a variety of reasons.

Accounting provides the language and framework for most corporate planning. The budget is the primary resource allocation mechanism used in most firms. Consequently, corporate planning models are written in accounting terminology, and the focus is on the budget. The language of economics as marginal revenue, marginal costs, and marginal productivity is largely missing from these models. Further, the extreme emphasis on optimality and marginality conditions is also missing. The economic models have as their decision variables the levels of production and inputs. But firms operate with budgets as fundamental allocation devices rather than stating decisions in quantity terms, e.g. a firm which makes a wide variety of similar products may not plan for precise output quantities but a general level of effort which is stated in monetary terms, such as sales of $10,000,000. The result is that the language and form of corporate models create a facade of dissimilarity which clouds an underlying homology.

The organization of the firm is an important element in corporate modeling. Practical corporate models are usually modular with production, marketing, and finance modules. These are integrated to obtain the corporate model. Further, multi-business firms require separate modules for each business. The economic theory of the firm assumes an integrated model which does not capture the reality of the firm's structure and internal information network which support the actual decision making process. Exceptions include the work by Baligh and Burton (1976, 1979), Burton and Damon (1979), and Burton and Damon, and Obel (1979) where the organizational decision process is explicitly considered in the economic model. The unimodular economic model of the firm must be expanded for the corporate model.

MODEL SPECIFICATION

Corporate models are written as a large number of logical or mathematical relations which may be recursive or simultaneous in nature. Naylor (1979b) has developed a taxonomy of optimization, systems analysis and corporate simulation. As the simulation approach may appear most foreign to economic theory, we shall concentrate on that form of the corporate model. Economics helps specify the basic form for many of these equations.

The firm's demand equation is one example. Economic theory suggests the well-known downward sloping demand. Take the demand function:

$$Q_1 = a + bP_1 + cA_1$$

where: Q_1 is quantity demanded, P_1 is the price, and A_1 is advertising, a, b, c are parameters.

What does economic theory imply? A downward-sloping demand suggests that b is negative. Advertising which has any reason to it yields c positive. Economic theory gives qualitative results, and points up obvious errors in data and structure. But for corporate models, we want more precise quantitative relations than economic theory supplies. In this context, the corporate model can be viewed as the quantitative operationalization of qualitative results of economic theory. Further examples of corporate models reveal a strong guiding influence of economics on corporate models. The production function may be stated in accounting terms as:

$$COG(t) = 1.8 \ DirLAB(t)$$

where: COG is the cost of goods sold, and Dir LAB is direct labour.

First, it is a financial statement--not the usual physical quantity statement [Ijiri, et.al. (1963) developed a complete prototype in accounting terms using linear programming]. Second, it is incomplete as it only gives labour, product relationships. Yet it is a production function as it states the relation between inputs and outputs. But, it is a partial statement of a linear production function. The rest of the function will be contained in another accounting statement. Taken together, they could be reduced into a more familiar input-output vector.

The corporate model must contain a production function, and output demand and input supply functions. These relations are qualitatively determined by economic theory. Their (accounting) form may be foreign to the economists. But their content is not.

With corporate simulation models, for any given value of the managerial decision variables, we can generate the time paths of the endogenous variables. In other words, when we approach the corporate planner or manager, we ask him or her only two questions. First, 'What output variables are of particular interest to you?' Second, 'What sets of decision variables appear to be relevant and feasible?' With simulation we can then show the corporate decision maker the consequences of the proposed managerial strategy. In addition, the analyst or operations research specialist may also propose a few policies or decision rules for consideration by top management. These policies may be put to a similar test. The decision maker then selects the strategies or decision rules which are most compatible with his or her own preference function (which is unknown to the analyst). The results of initial simulation runs may suggest other decision variable configurations to try.

There are a number of advantages to the corporate simulation approach relative to the optimization approach and the target approach. First, with corporate simulation, it is not necessary to assume the availability of information about management's preferences. Second, corporate simulation models provide the decision maker with the type of information which he or she is most likely to require in order to make decisions. Third, with the corporate simulation approach, we are not restricted to any particular type of mathematical model or logical structure. With computer simulation, there are virtually no limitations placed on the type of model structure which may be utilized. The only limitations are those imposed by the size and speed of the computer available to the analyst and the imagination of the analyst. That is, we do not have to assume linearity, concavity, non-negativity or any of the other highly restrictive assumptions which are inherent in optimization approaches.

In order to be useful, any theory of corporate models proposed must be both dynamic and stochastic, and possess feedback characteristics. With such a model, it should be possible for events to occur both sequentially and simultaneously.

Time should be measured in discrete units, since corporate data typically is only available in discrete units. (This rules out the use of differential equations.) Simultaneous, stochastic difference equations possess a number of the desirable properties of a theory of corporate simulation and will be used as a conceptual framework for our theory. For expository purposes, we shall employ linear difference equations, although the approach can easily be generalized to non-linear systems.

It is convenient to think of a corporation in terms of three mutually interdependent sub-systems--production, marketing and finance with outputs given by Y_1, Y_2, and Y_3, respectively. The outputs of each of these subsystems depend on (1) managerial decisions, (2) exogenous inputs, (3) random error, and (4) outputs from other subsystems.

The variables and equations for the system are specified below:

Output variables

Y_1 = a vector of production output variables, e.g. inventory levels.

Y_2 = a vector of marketing output variables, e.g. sales.

Y_3 = a vector of financial output variables, e.g. profit, cash flow, ROI.

Decision variables

Z_1 = a vector of production decision variables, e.g. input quantities.

Z_2 = a vector of marketing decision variables, e.g. price and advertising.

Z_3 = a vector of financial decision variables, e.g. debt level and structure, etc.

Exogenous variables

X_1 = a vector of exogenous production variables, e.g. new technology, productivity, capacity.

X_2 = a vector of exogenous marketing variables, e.g. competitors' prices and price changes.

X_3 = a vector of exogenous financial variables, e.g. prime interest rate, long term economic forecast, inflation, price of oil, etc.

Production Equations

$$A_1 X_{1t} + B_1 Y_{1t} + \sum_{j=1}^{p} B_{1j}^1 Y_{1,t-j} + \sum_{j=0}^{p} B_{2j}^1 Y_{2,t-j} + \sum_{j=0}^{p} B_{3j}^1 Y_{3,t-j} \qquad (11)$$

$$+ C_1 Z_{1t} + D_1 = U_{1t}$$

Marketing Equations

$$A_2 X_{2t} + B_2 Y_{2t} + \sum_{j=0}^{p} B_{1j}^2 Y_{1,t-j} + \sum_{j=1}^{p} B_{2j}^2 Y_{2,t-j} + \sum_{j=0}^{p} B_{3j}^2 Y_{3,t-j} \qquad (12)$$

$$+ C_3 Z_{3t} + D_3 = U_{3t}$$

Finance Equations

$$A_3 X_{3t} + B_3 Y_{3t} + \sum_{j=0}^{p} B_{3j}^{1} Y_{1,t-j} + \sum_{j=0}^{p} B_{2j}^{3} Y_{2,t-j} + \sum_{j=1}^{p} B_{3j}^{3} Y_{3,t-j} \tag{13}$$

$$+ C_3 Z_{3t} + D_3 = U_{3t}$$

We contend that most of the corporate simulation models developed thus far can be cast in the mould of the analytical framework outlined above. Although some of the existing models do include non-linear equations, inequalities, and logical switches, none of these concepts represent serious departures from the structure which we have proposed. Non-linearities simply mean we use the Gauss-Seidel method to solve the system of equations rather than matrix inversion.

Inequalities can be transformed into equations through the use of slack variables. Logical switches can be used to correct different blocks of simultaneous and re-cursive difference equations.

Examples of financial planning models include American Telephone & Telegraph, Ross Labs, Xerox, and Santa Fe. Marketing models are an integral part of the models of Northwest Industries, the North Carolina National Bank, and the Canadian National Railways. Production models are included in the corporate planning models Labs, Xerox, and Santa Fe. Marketing models are an integral part of the models of Northwest Industries, the North Carolina National Bank, and the Canadian National Railways. Production models are included in the corporate planning models of The New York Times, Dresser Industries, and CIBA-GEIGY.

TOWARDS AN ECONOMIC THEORY OF CORPORATE PLANNING

An economic theory of corporate planning must go beyond the economic theory of the firm in many ways:

(1) The language is that of corporate planning models.

(2) Alternatives are stated in budgeting terms as well as production quantity terms.

(3) A theory of search as well as a theory of choice is important.

(4) Productive efficiency is to be obtained, not assumed.

(5) Multiple goals are to be generated, not a single goal assumed.

In this context, an economic theory of corporate planning incorporates economic reasoning as a guide in searching for answers.

Porter (1980) uses economics as a basis for division corporate strategy and his approach clearly moves in the direction proposed as it presents both a theory of choice and search in operational terms. Schenedel & Patton (1978) present a simultaneous equation econometric model which is applied to develop a corporate strategy. Economics as a basis for corporate planning is in the making. "What if" is one corporate planning tool which attempts to ferret out the trade-offs available to the corporation and highlight relevant contingencies.

ECONOMICS AND 'WHAT IF?'

'What if?'--the ubiquitous question of corporate planning.* The neophyte cannot

---

* See Business Week, January 2, 1980.

generate one 'What if?' question. The cynic can generate a million. Neither is very helpful. The idea is to generate a reasonable list of 'What if?' questions for which the answer and its implied change will make a difference. This is neither easy nor obvious. We need a theory of 'What if?' questioning--a theory of questioning and search. It is here that economic theory offers a guide.

The goal in 'What if?' questioning is to find a better solution than the current solution. Except by accident, any currently proposed solution can be improved upon, and is consequently non-optimal. 'What if?' is an attempt to search in the region of the current solution to find a better solution.[3]

Consider a company with an operating corporate model. The 'What if?' question is 'What if we increase production quantity by 10 percent?' Is this a better solution? It is a better solution if it adds to a goal of interest, say profit. So, the calculation for comparison is then:

profit (+ 10 per cent production) - profit (base production)

This is a familiar marginal profit calculation, and economic theory suggests that production should be increased until marginal profit becomes zero. We can also put this result in ratio form:

$$\frac{\text{profit (+ 10 per cent production) - profit (base production)}}{\text{1.1 production quantity - base production quantity}}$$

$$\frac{\text{change in profit}}{\text{change in production quantity}} = \frac{\Delta Y_3}{\Delta Z_1} \frac{\text{(profit)}}{\text{(output)}}$$

This resulting ratio is the usual marginal measure in the economic theory of the firm where the latter notion follows the earlier model specification. Economic theory suggests we would increase production by 10 per cent if the marginal profit were positive, i.e.

$$\frac{\Delta Y_3}{\Delta Z_1} > 0$$

This proposed solution would be better.[4] This result and others are summarized in Table 1, the 'What if?' response matrix. The important 'What if?' issues are listed down the left side. Important responses are suggested across the top.

This analysis illustrates the equivalent of a marginal revenue, marginal cost calculation for the firm. That is, we would increase production (output) quantity until marginal revenue equals marginal costs. This is the first production level decision given in an earlier section.

The two other standard economic questions concern technological and input balance. Again, 'What if?' search can be used:

(1) What if the firm increases its production capacity by one machine? Using the corporate model, the equivalent marginal product can be calculated,

$$\frac{\Delta Y_3}{\Delta X_1}$$

Table 1. The Substantive 'What if?' response matrix

'What if?' Questions	Output responses			
	ΔY_1 inventory levels	ΔY_2 sales profit	ΔY_3 cash flow	ROI
ΔZ_1 input quantities, production quantities			$\dfrac{\Delta Y_3(\text{profit})}{\Delta Z_1(\text{output})}$	
ΔZ_2 price advertising				
ΔZ_3 short term debt				
ΔX_1 productivity technology capacity			$\dfrac{\Delta Y_3}{\Delta X_1}$	
ΔX_2 competitors' price		$\dfrac{\Delta Y_2}{\Delta X_2}$		
ΔX_3 prime interest rate, inflation, price of oil			$\dfrac{\Delta Y_3}{\Delta X_3}$	

(2)   What if the rate of inflation is 20 per cent, what is the impact on cash flow and sales,

$$\frac{\Delta Y_3}{\Delta X_3} \quad , \quad \frac{\Delta Y_2}{\Delta X_2}$$

The result is quite simple. Efficient 'What if?' search follows the economic theory of the firm--both by supplying the questions to ask on prices, costs, and technology, and supplying the criterion for a better solution, namely is the marginal profit positive?

This oversimplifies the search and the analysis. It supplies the dimension of the questions, and the form of the answers. In more complex real situations the questions must be operational and the answers multidimensional.

The 'What if?' response matrix in Table 1 suggests any questions will have a multidimensional response impact. Usually, the impact will be mixed--a good impact on some variables, and bad for others, e.g. a 10 per cent price increase will usually decrease sales volume, force layoffs, but may increase profits. The appropriate action is unclear. How does one weigh the relative impact, and make the appropriate trade-offs? The economic theory of the firm is of little help. In that theory, the goal is to maximize profits; and it helps in selecting the best mix of products and inputs to meet that one goal, but it assumes away the problem of multiple goals.

The 'What if?' approach applied to the corporate model meets the requirements for an economic theory of corporate planning:

(1) The language of the corporate model is that of the manager and has a strong accounting orientation.

(2) The alternatives can be stated in operational budgeting terms.

(3) The 'What if?' approach is an implicit search theory which attempts to find marginal gains. The search is guided by economic questions concerning internal issues of technology, productivity, and capacity. External issues as competitor's prices, inflation, new opportunities, etc. are examined.

(4) 'What if?' questioning does not assume efficient productivity.

(5) The output responses on profit, sales, etc. do not assume a known unique objective, but assume there is a vector of important issues involving trade offs and choice. The operating utility function need not be known a priori, but is discovered in the search process.

Briefly, the economic theory of the firm provides a basic but incomplete framework for a theory of corporate planning. The essential emphasis in both is efficient resource allocation. Economic theory supplies the basic ingredients of the model and the important questions. But the operationalization for corporate planning must be embellished.

TOWARDS A PROCEDURAL RATIONALITY IN CORPORATE PLANNING

The development of rational procedures is a difficult undertaking. There is no highly developed framework as microeconomic theory is for substantive issues.

There are two levels of consideration:

- the rational procedures themselves for corporate planning, and,

- the meta procedures, or rational procedures to develop the organization's rational procedures. Both are formidable. Each requires creation as well as analysis. Unlike many substantive problems solving and decision making situations, the criteria for good procedures are wanting in operational terms. Elementary notions of effectiveness and efficiency are not operationally defined and measured. Nonetheless, the challenge is clear. If economics and other social sciences are to maintain their relevancy, we must take up the tough issues of creating a procedural rationality in this very important area of corporate planning.

There are procedures or rational steps in decision making. A first level text will list the steps of the scientific method:

- define the problem
- gather relevant data
- state the alternatives
- choose the best alternative.

It sounds simple. But that is not the way it happens. Cohen, March, and Olsen (1972) suggest the garbage can model is a better description: alternatives without problems, choices without data, data without relevancy, problems without alternatives, etc. Of course, the scientific method is a possible procedure, but only one of many, and in fact the rare one. Nonetheless, elaboration and modification of the scientific method has been proposed for corporate planning. These procedures are prescriptions of what an organization should do to develop a good corporate plan.

Naylor (1979) has suggested one such rational operationalization process for the development of a corporate planning model. That procedure includes the eight steps listed below.

1. Identification of stakeholders.
2. Review of goals and objectives.
3. Specification of corporate constraints.
4. Review of existing strategic options.
5. Search for additional strategic options.
6. Sort out those strategic options worthy of serious consideration.
7. Evaluate strategic options.
8. Selection of a set of strategic options.

1. Identification of stakeholders

Strategic decisions whether at the corporate, division, or department level are not made in a vacuum. Managers of corporations exist in an environment which is characterized by multiple constituencies--investors, other managers, employees, consumers, government, and the general public. More often than not, these different stakeholders have conflicting objectives with regard to how the corporation should be managed.

Investors want high earnings per share and a satisfactory dividend payout rate. Other managers are concerned with their own salaries, the size of their staff, and territorial rights within the company. Employees will press for high salaries and wages, liberal fringe benefits, and stable employment. Consumers want high quality, excellent service and support, and low prices. Finally, to the extent that the government represents the general public then the government is interested in the overall social welfare implications of strategic decisions.

The problem is a practical difficulty in assigning weights or priorities to these conflicting goals and objectives. To be sure there is no shortage of totally theoretical approaches such as utility theory, social welfare theory, and goal programming which have been proposed by academic economists and management scientists. But these techniques are either based on assumptions which are unrealistic or data requirements which are not readily available.

The upshot of all of this is merely to say that one of the principal roles of corporate managers is to be able to somehow balance these conflicting objectives in such a way that the company not only survives but actually grows and provides a useful service to various constituencies.

2. Review of goals and objectives

Obviously, the selection of corporate strategies is void of meaning if it is not preceded by the definition of well defined goals and objectives for each level of the company. Naylor (1980, Chapter 6) describes in detail a process for formulating corporate, division, and department goals and objectives.

3. Specification of corporate constraints

Corporate growth and development is often impeded by a variety of constraints which may be imposed on the company by government, outside financiers, technology, availability of inputs into the production process, and the personal goals of either managers or owners of the corporation. These constraints must be understood and dealt with by management as they go through the strategic decision process.

For example, banks, other financial institutions and public utilities are restricted by law as to the types of businesses which they may engage. A bank cannot open a department store or even a management consulting firm. Expansion in certain foreign countries may be risky or impossible as a result of a broad spectrum of political constraints ranging from the threat of nationalization or the possibility of a military takeover of the government. Outside financiers may impose limitations on debt, dividend payout, executive salaries, and capital expenditures.

Strategic planning may prove to be a useful vehicle for ascertaining the costs associated with some of these constraints so as to determine whether it might prove worthwhile for management to invest the time and money required to either eliminate a particular constraint or alleviate the negative impact of the constraint. Information of this type can prove to be extremely valuable to management in attempting to make strategic decisions.

4. Review of the existing strategic options

The next step in the strategic decision making process is to review those strategic options which are already being exercised or are known to be available. This is usually done annually as part of the strategic planning process, but many companies find it useful to repeat this process on a quarterly or semi-annual basis.

The purpose of this review is to at least make a preliminary judgment on the adequacy of the existing set of strategic options. Among the questions to be answered at this stage are the following. Will the strategic options available to us provide for an adequate return on investment? Are we protected from currency devaluations? Can we survive another major recession with our present mix of businesses? Can we improve our market share sufficiently to produce enough cash to finance the construction of a more efficient plant?

The results of this review of the current inventory of strategic options will play a major role in determining whether or not the company should consider a corporate development strategy to acquire new businesses or whether the company should pursue international markets and businesses.

Some companies have used the PIMS methodology to evaluate the effects of alternative strategies based on a cross-section of companies. That is, with the PIMS database one can ascertain how an average company in the PIMS sample might have fared if it followed a particular strategy or set of strategies. Subject to some well known limitations of the PIMS approach, this may be a viable way to screen existing strategy options. General Electric was one of the earlier companies to use this approach for screening strategic options.

5. Search for additional strategic options

The successful search for new business strategies can certainly be enhanced by modern scientific analysis, data retrieval, and search procedure. We have outlined one substantively rational approach. But this is one aspect of management where the executive must be free to consider the impossible and to respond to his or her entrepreneurial instincts which say that a particular deal has a chance of success or not. An attempt to overformalize the search for new strategic options can easily stifle creativity and not produce the types of strategies which are really needed to run the company. The goal in devising a search strategy is to guide costly search, not to stifle it and eliminate investigation of the seemingly unreasonable alternative a priori.

An integral part of corporate development planning and multi-national planning is the search for additional strategic options.

6. Sort out those strategic options worthy of serious consideration

The next step in the strategic decision process involves reducing the number of strategic options under consideration down to relatively small number of options which merit more rigorous evaluation and consideration. Not unlike several other steps in our decision process, step 6 is an intuitive step.

Basically this is an analytical and <u>subjective</u> evaluation of the strategic options which have been defined in light of given goals and objectives and given corporate constraints and policies. Strategies which clearly violate corporate policies and constraints can be eliminated at this stage or they may call for policy changes. Strategies which contribute only marginally to major goals and objectives should be dropped from further consideration. Only those strategies which survive this critical stage should be subjected to the rigorous analysis provided by the portfolio models of the Boston Consulting Group (Henderson, 1979) and the type of corporate planning models described in Naylor (1979a).

7. Evaluate strategic options

This step in the decision making process involves the <u>objective</u> evaluation of alternative strategies using portfolio models and 'What if?' computer simulation models. Those strategies which were not rejected in step 6 must now be subjected to serious analysis and evaluation.

Specifically, computer based planning models can be used to simulate the effects of alternative financial, marketing, and production strategies on the behavior of the company, division, or department. Frequently, quite simple financial planning models can prove to be extremely powerful analytical tools for strategic planning.

This step in the decision process represents an important interface between modern scientific management tools and the intuition and good judgment of an experienced manager.

The information which is generated by the analysis produced in this step will provide the basis for strategic decisions in step 8.

8. Selection of a set of strategic options

The eighth and final step of the decision process represents the moment of truth on the part of the manager. A decision must be made on the set of business strategies which will actually be implemented.

The toughest part of the strategic decision problem is that the evaluations produced in step 7 generate a multiplicity of output measures. In other words, we are once again confronted with multiple stakeholders who have conflicting objectives, but now we have multiple measures of performance on which to base a decision.

The analytical planning tools available to managers permit them to evaluate the effects of alternative strategies either on a single output measure or a host of output variables.

In terms of our earlier criteria: search is an integral part of the procedures, and goals are to be discovered - not given <u>a priori</u>. Of course, analysis of the generated alternatives is part of the procedures.

Cohen and Cyert (1973, p. 349) offer a different nine step procedure in strategy formulation, implementation, and monitoring:

1. formulation of goals;
2. analysis of the environment;
3. assigning quantitative values to the goals;
4. the microprocess of strategy formulation;
5. the gap analysis;
6. strategic search;
7. selecting the portfolio of strategic alternatives;

8. implementation of the strategic program;
9. measurement, feedback, and control.

If one were to juxtapose two sets of procedures, they are quite similar in detail, and certainly akin in spirit. The one important distinction is the explicit attention to implementation and control in Cohen and Cyert's steps 8 and 9. These steps include consideration of the budgeting process, the "rules of the game", the rewards for individuals, etc. "It is critical as part of the implementation process to examine the formal organization structure" (p. 363). This notion of procedure goes beyond mere decision making to a concern for how the organization will implement the decisions.

An alternative approach is to start with a description of the organization and then to indicate how the organization will behave - will it search for strategic alternatives, will it consider all the stakeholders, will the decisions be made on appropriate information or not? This view suggests the procedures are embedded to a large extent in the organization itself, and thus, the tools of the corporate planner include the organization and its procedure; i.e., does the organization proceed rationality concerning corporate strategy. Given this view, what are the organizational elements of procedural rationality for corporate planning.

ORGANIZATIONAL ELEMENTS OF PROCEDURAL RATIONALITY FOR CORPORATE PLANNING

Baligh and Damon (1980) propose one scheme for describing an organization. This description is in managerially operational terms as the elements are the "Knobs" which a manager can change. Further, this description provides a framework for predicting the outcomes for the organization. That is, one can relate the description to the performance of the organization. Given these two properties of the description, it serves as an intermediary between those controllable managerial elements and the organization's performance. Baligh and Damon's (1980, p. 136-7) description includes:

- relevant decision variables,
- relevant parameters,
- relevant decisionmakers,
- assignment of decision variables to decisionmakers,
- assignment of parameters to decisionmakers,
- messages among decisionmakers concerning decision variable values,
- messages among decisionmakers concerning parameter values,
- questions among decisionmakers concerning decision variables,
- questions among decisionmakers concerning parameters decision rules among decisionmakers, and
- incentives and rewards for decisionmakers.

This organizational description can be viewed as a formalization of Jacob Marschak's (1959) description: "Who decides what based upon what information?"

Given the description of an organization in these terms, then the test of procedural rationality - will it do corporate planning? It is not an easy question.

This framework incorporates the issues of choice and search; but more importantly, what are procedures to search and choose. Within planning, and corporate planning, these issues have been the concern of Keen and Morton (1978), and Galbraith and Nathanson (1978). They bring these issues out of the domain of mere implementation; i.e. after we know what we want to do, we will find a way to do it.

Keen and Morton (1978, p. 187) state that for Decision Support systems design and implementation are inseparable. Later (p. 211), they write: "implementation requires a strategy". Here, we are arguing that the organization for procedural rationality is the strategy of implementation. No corporate strategy, regardless of its substantive rationality, is going to be implemented without a consideration of the organization and how it works. Clearly, Keen and Morton concentrate on the information system, but inseparability requires the consideration of the entirety of the organization.

Galbraith and Nathanson (1978) build upon Chandler's (1962) pioneering work, and later research. They propose a continuing sequence of strategies and structures where the two should "fit" in order to obtain acceptable performance (pp. 282-3). Here we cannot replicate the argument, but the point is that the organizational structure must be part of the corporate planning problem.

To elaborate, consider in more detail the question of incentives and rewards. It is well known that many managers do not engage in long range corporate planning. Why not? Rhetorically, it is not in their best interest to do so. So, the issue is how to make it in their best interests. Cohen and Cyert (1973, p. 365) point out that the profit center orientation with its short run concern may jeopardize long run corporate health. The problem is well known. Can we do anything about it? Behavioral scientists tell us that "rewarding A while hoping for B" is folly. You won't get "B". So, the rewards are part of the corporate planner's tools. Professor Shubik states it succinctly, "Don't forget to tip Murphy, the bartender". Or, stated differently, "Don't be surprised that the drinks are watered, if the bartender knows you can't tip".

Clearly, the issues of procedural rationality in corporate planning has not escaped the corporate planners in general and economists in particular. Naylor (1978, 1979) discusses organizational prerequisites for corporate planning. Many books, such as Hofer and Schendel (1978), King and Cleland (1978), explicitly treat the procedure of implementation. The question remains whether we can devise an approach which augments these ad hoc considerations of a rational procedure.

TOWARDS A SUBSTANTIVE RATIONALITY TO DEVISE PROCEDURAL RATIONALITIES

A colleague, whose forte is the management of interdisciplinary research efforts, quips, "I always like to have economists around, 'cause they think good." Economists bring a powerful logical analysis to bear on substantive issues--they understand clear thought, hard analysis, and the fundamental notion of a trade-off. Clearly, this is where the economist is at his best. In more general terms, economists have been reluctant to take up those more demanding issues of organizational process rationality. My friend says, "You sometimes have to help economists in choosing interesting issues." As a sociologist, he is intimately concerned with organizational process and procedure.

But economists are not without their exceptions. Herbert Simon's work by itself fills the void. His concept of bounded rationality (1959) introduces the rationality of satisfying in lieu of optimization. For the organization, this one concept has important implications about the way an individual and a large group can proceed, and do proceed. Williamson (1975) uses Simon's concept of bounded rationality together with the notions information impactedness (everyone has different pieces of information), and opportunism (everyone will use his own information for his own benefit at potential loss for the corporation) to devise a theory of procedural rationality, or internal organization applying the economic reasoning common to substantive issues. Galbraith and Nathanson (1978, p. 251) write "Williamson makes an argument that is obvious to business policy and organization theorists but not necessarily to economists: internal organization makes an economic difference". Deja vu, perhaps? But this would miss the point. Economic reasoning is relevant to organizational issues, and the challenge is to use the substantive rationality for procedurally rational questions.

Can we state procedural issues in substantive terms. Can we apply the economists'

TABLE 2

The Procedural "What If" Matrix

Potential changes in **Organizational Elements** lead to likely changes in **Performance**

Organizational Elements	The kinds of alternatives generated	The character of investments undertaken	Efficiency in reaching a decision	Risk taking behavior of decision makers	Impact on short run cash flow	Profits
relevant decisions to set						
relevant parameters to read						
assignment of decisions to decision-makers						
messages concerning decisions						
messages concerning parameters						
incentives and rewards						

reasoning to those difficult procedural questions? Consider a modified "What if" matrix for procedural issues in Table 2. The left hand side lists the organizational variables given previously and the column headings are some organizational performance outcomes which are of interest and relevance. As the "what if" matrix column and headings for substantive analysis in Table 1 must be modified for the particular corporation, their entries are illustrative. An example question would be "What if" we changed the incentive and reward system for decision managers, how would that impact upon the likely opportunities for investment for the corporation? We may not be able to say definitely - but it is important to state the direction of the change (+ or -). The entries in matrix are not easy to obtain. But evidence exists for some alternatives.

Consider the composite of two sets of organizational elements: the U-(unitary) and M-(multidivisional) forms of corporate organization. (The U-form yields a set of values for the organizational elements; the M-form another.) Which one is likely to perform better? Williamson (1975, p. 150) proposes the M-form hypothesis:

> The organization and operation of the large enterprise along the lines of the M-form favors goal pursuit and least-cost behavior more nearly associated with the neoclassical profit maximization hypothesis than does the U-form organizational alternative.

Assuming the hypothesis is substantiated, as it is, then the large enterprise will do better on goal pursuit, costs, and profits organized in the M-form. Williamson's argument rests upon bounded rationality, information impactedness, and opportunism. Ouchi (1977) summarizes Williamson's argument as the "informational imperative" of organization. Burton and Obel (1980) use a computer simulation to test the informational imperative. They found that the M-form of organization reaches better planning decisions with the same planning effort in the U-form, i.e. the M-form is more efficient. In terms of a modified Table 2, a change from U-form to M-form increases the efficiency in obtaining good decisions.

In terms of Table 2, Burton and Obel (1980) investigate the impact of varying the "relevant parameters to read" for initiating the planning process using a computer simulation. They found that crude environmental information yielded better points of departure for setting plans than internal historical information. In an earlier study, Burton, Damon, and Obel (1979) found a decomposition by short run-long run yielded better solutions than an "existing business-new ventures" decomposition. Tuggle and Gerwin (1980) use a computer simulation to investigate the impact of firm's sensitivity to its environment on strategy and choice.

An important problem is devising appropriate incentives and rewards for decision makers to do corporate planning i.e. search, choice, and implement. A great deal of our knowledge is intuitive, anecdotal, and ad hoc. Agency theory, where the issue is to devise a contract and reward for an agent such that he will act in the best interests of the principal when the agent has different and better information and acts in his own best interest, i.e. information impactedness and opportunism, is a promising approach. To date, the applications have been in finance and accounting (e.g. Baiman and Demski, 1980). Laughhunn, Payne and Crum (1980) have found managers are not risk averse in some situations contrary to normal assumptions. Incentives and rewards greatly impact performance but not as simply as often assumed.

In terms of the procedural "What if" Matrix, these studies yield tentative qualitative answers. With the exception of Williamson's global performance measure of "goal pursuit... least-cost behavior...neoclassical profit maximization" the results are limited to a single performance outcome, e.g. efficiency in obtaining a good solution. For the organizational elements, the comparison is frequently a small set of alternatives, e.g. crude environmental information vs. historical information. The majority of the cells in the procedure "What if" matrix are "question marks," which only points up the opportunity for the economists to apply the rigor of economic reasoning to these important procedural and organization issues.   See Burton and Kuhn (1981) and Hall and Saias (1980) for discussions which begin to fill in the cells.

One point remains.   The particular organizational elements and performance outcomes in Table 2 are illustrative.   There are others.   E.g. a taxonomy of authority and responsibility is possible.   The organizational elements shown in Table 2 (Baligh and Damon, 1980) describe the corporation in a procedural fashion which reflects an "information processing and decisionmaking" model of the firm.   The performance outcomes relating to the nature of the search, the efficiency in decisionmaking, etc. reflect traditional concerns of the economists.   These organizational elements and performance measures are illustrative, but also generic. They are likely to be modified in detail rather than fundamental concern.

IMPLICATIONS FOR THE CORPORATE PLANNER AND ECONOMIST

The challenge is worthy of our best efforts - bringing the economist's traditional rigor and logic to the procedural issues for corporate planning.   The form of both the questions and answers will be different, but the analysis is still applicable. Answers will not be optimal conditions; the best we can do is to divide procedural alternatives in those which are reasonable, and those which are dumb.   This lacks the elegance of microeconomics, but it gains relevancy.   This is the trade off and one which is reasonable for some to accept.

FOOTNOTES

[1] The logic of the differential calculus requires a continuous production function with non-vanishing first and second order partial derivatives with perfectly divisible inputs and outputs. In order to obtain a finite solution for perfectly competitive markets, the production function must be concave.

[2] 'well, hardly ever' _a la_ Gilbert and Sullivan.

[3] In a formal sense, the current solution yields a point value on a multi-dimensional response function and the approach is to explore the nature of the function in the neighborhood of the point by generating the gradient. In the elementary economic theory of the firm, the response function is given.

[4] The profit and output subscripts are suppressed.

REFERENCES

[1] Ackoff, Russell L. A Concept of Corporate Planning, Wiley-Interscience, New York, 1970.

[2] Ansoff, H. Igor. Corporate Strategy, McGraw-Hill, New York, 1965.

[3] Baiman, Stanley and Joel S. Demski. 'Variance Analysis Procedures as Motivational Services', Management Science, Vol. 26, No. 6, August 1980, pp. 840-848.

[4] Baligh, Helmy H., and Richard M. Burton. 'Organization structure and cooperative market relations', Omega-The International Journal of Management Science, 4, 1976, pp. 583-593.

[5] Baligh, Helmy H., and Richard M. Burton. 'The marketing concept and the organization's structure', Long Range Planning, 12, April 1979, pp. 92-96.

[6] Baligh, Helmy H., and William W. Damon, 'Foundations for a Systematic Process of Organization Structure Design', Journal of Information and Optimization Sciences, Vol. 1, No. 2, 1980, pp. 133-165.

[7] Baumol, William J., 'Entrepreneurship in economic theory', American Economic Review, LVIII, May 1968, pp. 64-71.

[8] Bonini, Charles P. Simulation of Information and Decision Systems in the Firm, Prentice-Hall, Englewood Cliffs, NJ, 1963.

[9] Boulding, Kenneth E. 'The present position of the theory of the firm', in Linear Programming and Theory of the Firm, edited by Kenneth E. Boulding and W. Allen Spivey, Macmillan, New York, 1960.

[10] Burton, Richard M., and William Damon. 'Budgets for integrating decentralized investment and production planning', Omega-The International Journal of Management Science, 7, 1979, pp. 113-117.

[11] Burton, Richard M., William Damon, and Brge Obel. 'An organizational model of integrated budgeting for short run operations and long run investments', Journal of Operational Research Society, 30, 1979, pp. 575-585.

[12] Burton, Richard M. and Arthur J. Kuhn, "Structure follows Strategy--the Counter Hypothesis", 1980, Duke University Working Paper.

[13] Burton, Richard M. and Thomas H. Naylor, 'Economic Theory in Corporate Planning' Strategic Management Journal, Vol. 1, No. 3, July-September 1980, pp. 249-263.

[14] Burton, Richard M., and Brge Obel, 'The Efficiency of the Price, Budget and Mixed Approaches Under Varying A Priori Information Levels for Decentralized Planning', Management Science, Vol. 26, No. 4, April 1980 a, pp. 401-417.

[15] Burton, Richard M. and Brge Obel, 'A Computer Simulation Test of the M-Form Hypothesis', Administrative Science Quarterly, Vol. 25, No. 3, September 1980 b, pp. 457-466.

[16] Caveg, Richard E. 'Industrial Organization, Corporate Strategy and Structure', Journal of Economic Literature, Vol. XVIII, March 1980, pp. 64-91.

[17] Cleland, Sherrill. 'A short essay on a managerial theory of the firm', in Linear Programming and Theory of the Firm, edited by Kenneth E. Boulding and W. A. Spivey, Macmillan, New York, 1960.

[18] Cohen, Kalman J., and Richard M. Cyert. Theory of the Firm: Resource allocation in a Market Economy, Prentice-Hall, Englewood Cliffs, NJ, 1965.

[19] Cohen, Kalman J. and Richard M. Cyert, 'Strategy: Formulation, Implementation, and Monitoring', The Journal of Business, Vol. 36, No. 3, July 1973. pp. 349-367.

[20] Cohen, Michael D., James G. March and John P. Olsen, 'A Garbage Can Model of Organizational Choice', Administrative Science Quarterly, Vol. 17, 1972, pp. 11-25.

[21] Cyert, Richard M., and James G. March. A Behavioral Theory of the Firm. Prentice-Hall, Englewood Cliffs, NJ, 1963.

[22] Dorfman, R. Application of Linear Programming to the Theory of the Firm. University of California Press, Berkeley, 1951.

[23] Galbraith, Jay R. and Daniel A. Nathanson, Strategy Implementation: The Role of Structure and Process, 1978, West Publishing Co., St. Paul, MN, 1978, abridged in Schendel & Hofer (eds.)

[24] Grinyer, Peter H., and Jeff Wooller. Corporate Models Today, The Institute of Chartered Accountants, London, 1975.

[25] Hall, D. J. and M. A. Saias, 'Strategy Follows Structure', Strategic Management Journal, Vol. 2, No. 2, April-June 1980, pp. 149-163.

[26] Henderson, Bruce D. Henderson on Corporate Strategy, Abt Books, Cambridge, MA, 1979.

[27] Iriri, Y., F. K. Levy, and R. C. Lyon. 'A Linear programming model for budgeting and financial planning', Journal of Accounting Research, 1, Autumn 1963, pp. 198-212.

[28] Keen, Peter W. and Michael S. Scott Morton, Decision Support Systems: An organizational Perspective, Addison Wesley Publishing Co. Inc., Reading, MA, 1978.

[29] King, William R., and David, I. Cleland. Strategic Planning and Policy, Van Nostrand Reinhold, New York, 1978.

[30] Lanstein, Ronald J. and William W. Jahuke, 'Applying Capital market theory to investing', Interfaces, Vol. 9, No. 2, Part 2, February 1979, pp. 23-38.

[31] Laughhunn, Dan J., John W. Payne, and Roy Crum, 'Managerial Risk Preferences for Below Target Returns', Management Science, Vol. 25, December 1980.

[32] Leibenstein, Harvey. 'Allocative efficiency vs. "X-efficiency"', The American Economic Review, LVI, June 1966, pp. 394-415.

[33] Lorange, Peter, and Richard F. Vancil. Strategic Planning Systems, Prentice-Hall, Englewood Cliffs, NJ, 1977.

[34] Lorange, Peter. Corporate Planning: An Executive Viewpoint, Prentice-Hall, Inc.,Englewood Cliffs, NJ, Prentice-Hall, Inc., 1980.

[35] Marglois, Julius. 'The analysis of the firm: rationalism, conventionalism and behaviorism', Journal of Business, XXXI, July 1958.

[36] Marschak, Jacob. 'Efficient and Viable organizational Forms', Mason Haire, (ed.). Modern Organization Theory, New York, John Wiley and Sons, 1959.

[37] Mattessich, Richard. Simulation of the Firm Through a Budget Computer Program, Richard D. Irwin, Homewood, IL, 1964.

[38] Naylor, Thomas H., Joseph L. Balintfy, Donald S. Burdick, and Kong Chu, Computer Simulation Techniques, Wiley, New York, 1966.

[39] Naylor, Thomas H. The Design of Computer Simulation Experiments, Duke University Press, Durham, NC, 1969.

[40] Naylor, Thomas H., and John M. Vernon. Microeconomics and Decision Models of the Firm, Harcourt, Brace & World, New York, 1969.

[41] Naylor, Thomas H. Computer Simulation Experiments with Models of Economic Systems, John Wiley, New York, 1970.

[42] Naylor, Thomas H. The Politics of Corporate Planning and Modeling, Planning Executives Institute, Oxford, Ohio, 1978.

[43] Naylor, Thomas H. Corporate Planning Models, Addison-Wesley, Reading, MA, 1979 a.

[44] Naylor, Thomas H. 'Organizing for Strategic Planning', Managerial Planning, July/August 1979 b.

[45] Naylor, Thomas H. Strategic Planning Management, Planning Executives Institute, Oxford, Ohio, 1980.

[46] Ouchi, William G. 'Review of Markets and Hierarchies: Analysis and Antitrust', Administrative Science Quarterly, Vol. 22, pp. 540-54.

[47] Porter, Michael C. Competitive Strategy Techniques for Analyzing Industries and Competitors, The Free Press, New York, 1980.

[48] Robinson, Joan. Economic Philosophy, Aldine Publishing Company, Chicago, 1963.

[49] Rosenkranz, Friedrich. An Introduction to Corporate Modeling, Duke University Press, Durham, NC, 1979.

[50] Schendel, Dan and G. Richard Patton. 'A simultaneous equation model of corporate strategy', Management Science, Vol 24, No. 14, Nov. 1978, pp. 1611-1621.

[51] Schendel, Dan E., and Charles W. Hofer, (editors). Strategic Management: A New View of Business Policy and Planning, Little, Brown and Co., Boston, (Inc.), 1979.

[52] Schiff, M., and A. Y. Lewin. 'The impact of people on budgets', The Accounting Review, XLV, 1970, pp. 259-268.

[53] Schrieber, Albert N. (Editor). Corporate Simulation Models, Seattle: School of Business, University of Washington, 1970.

[54] Shubik, Martin. 'Simulation of the firm and industry', American Economic Review, L, December 1960.

[55] Shubik, Martin. 'A curmudgeon's guide to microeconomics', Journal of Economic Literature, 8, June 1970, pp. 405-434.

[56] Simon, Herbert A. 'Theories of decision-making in economics and behavioral science', American Economic Review, ILIX, June 1959.

[57] Simon, Herbert A. 'Rationality as process and as product of thought', The American Economic Review, 68, May 1978, pp. 1-16.

[58] Taylor, Bernard, and John R. Sparks. Corporate Strategy and Planning, A Halsted Press Book, Wiley, New York, 1977.

[59] Thorelli, Hans B., Strategy + Structure = Performance, Indiana University Press, Bloomington, 1978.

[60] Tinbergen, J. On the Theory of Economic Policy, North-Holland Publishing Company, Amsterdam, 1955.

[61] Tuggle, Francis D. and Donald Gerwin. 'An Information processing model of organizational perception, strategy and choice', Management Science, Vol. 26, No. 6, June 1980, pp. 575-592.

[62] Williamson, Oliver E. The Economics of Discretionary Behavior: Managerial Objectives in a Theory of the Firm, Prentice-Hall, Englewood Cliffs, NJ, 1964.

[63] Williamson, Oliver E. Markets and Hierarchies: Analysis and Antitrust Implications: A Study in the Economics of Internal Organization, The Free Press, New York, 1975.

ECONOMICS AS A CONCEPTUAL FRAMEWORK
FOR STRATEGIC PLANNING AND MODELING

Martin Shubik

Yale University
New Haven, Connecticut
U.S.A.

WHO PLANS AND WHO DECIDES

Possibly one of the most overworked words in the writings on corporate decision-making is the word "decisionmaker." The process of the direction of a major corporate enterprise is a complex of the interplay of many individuals constrained by the structure and history of the organization.

Those individuals who are frequently called top decisionmakers may better be described as "responsibility-takers" and "environment-setters". When we view the ongoing processes of the corporation, no individual is going to instantly reverse or quickly change the inertial forces that are present. The wise and powerful manager or entrepreneur will redirect them in the ways he sees fit. But the redirection is a process much like improving the performance of simulation. Parameters are reset and routines are changed. The environment is modified in a manner consistent with the optimal redirection of the organization. The top decisionmaker is the responsibility taker for the resetting of the environment.

The optimal birth, growth, maturity, and eventual death or transmutation of a corporation calls for many different types of individuals and the economist is only one among these. A crude categorization of the different types involved includes:

> the explorer and entrepreneur,
> the hero or warrior,
> the poet, inventor and scientist,
> the administrator and manager,
> the economist and planner,
> and the lawyers, accountants, and other advisors and consultants.

An organization run by heroes, entrepreneurs and poets may be a spectacular and exciting place to be. But the long term prognosis for it in general will not be good. An organization run only by managers, economists, lawyers, and accountants may function smoothly, but it runs the danger of being without the soul and spark that enabled the growth of organizations which brought into reality the major innovations from the cotton gin to the telephone, automobile, and high speed digital computer. Vision and good ideas without the delivery system to convert them into actualities may easily die. Institutions with great economic sense and good management must have the vision and imagination needed to keep them vital.

In the earlier stages of an economic organization, vision, heroism, will power, and entrepreneurship alone may be enough to carry the day. The accountants, planners, economists, and managers may hardly play a role. Success, however, will, in general, bring both growth and change. The entrepreneurial and visionary roles must be tempered by management and control. Size requires organization and routine. Control requires not only the taking of responsibility, but the organization of an information system that enables this responsibility to be discharged wisely. Information by itself is necessary, but not enough. It must be organized and interpreted purposefully. This activity calls for a planning process.

It has been said of the Holy Grail that "The Grail is in the seeking not the cup." So it is with corporate planning. The product is the process and not a particular plan. This fact has been recognized not only by the words of the managements of the major economic enterprises, but by their deeds. Thirty years ago a corporate planning group was the exception; twenty years ago the idea of a corporate model or simulator was something that only the most venturesome considered; ten years ago a survey by Gershefski (1970) indicated of the order of a hundred models built or in the building. Today the models are in the hundreds and corporate planning is a fact of life in any large and most middle-sized corporations. The size and complexity of modern enterprise makes this a virtual necessity.

CORPORATE ECONOMICS AND THE PLANNING SUPPORT FUNCTION

The economy is not the world. Economic activity and so-called economic motivation and even profit maximization are by no means the only drives which characterize desirable behavior in all organizations. But in both governmental bureaucracy and in the business sector even the wildest of visionaries needs his vision tempered by economic sense.

The simple concept of <u>opportunity cost</u> central to economic thinking contains many lessons for both bureaucratic behavior and even personal behavior. It implies one of the key concepts of planning, which is that you must always evaluate and compare alternatives. The famous slogan attributed to Milton Friedman stresses this in a different way. "There is no such thing as a free lunch" translates into asking the question what are my costs in attending this lunch and my alternative opportunities at this time. Nothing is costless if the resources, be they only time, can be invested in doing something else. At the level of personal relations the statement "I am sorry I did not have time to see you this afternoon" can be fruitfully reinterpreted as "I had a higher valued alternative to which I allocated the time I could have spent seeing you." At the corporate level, the choice is never do X but at least "do X or Y."

The key words choice or decision imply the presence of alternatives. The concept of opportunity cost stresses not only alternatives, but that there are different opportunities and costs attached to each of the alternatives.

The word opportunity calls attention to the other key factor in the economic problem: one which is not strictly economic, but which is critical to all planning. What are the goals of the firm, organization or individual? You cannot tell an opportunity from an invitation to disaster unless you know what you want, or at least what you do not want.

In short, the economic problem calls for the perception and understanding of:

>   alternatives,
>   goals,
>   and costs.

As we, in general, do not exist in isolation we must take into account the competitive element beyond the firm. This calls for an understanding of two further key elements:

>   the rules of competition
>   and the nature and abilities of competitors.

These five features, which on the surface are simple and to many of us almost obvious, lead to enormous ramifications. The central importance of understanding one's goals cannot be overstressed. The economic analyst cannot define the goals for the corporation but he can provide the objective mirror to help corporate managers, directors, and entrepreneurs look into their own minds to form a better understanding of their goals. Or to at least provide them with a self-awareness that although they do not know precisely what they want, at least they feel that they have a direction which is broadly consistent with their perceptions and self-image.

In the probing to understand goals and alternatives, the skilled corporate economist is best compared with the skilled psychoanalyst. He is the psychoanalyst for a complex socio-biological institution known as the corporation or firm. He is not the management. He should not even attempt to play the role of conscience of management. He is the physician with imperfect, but highly relevant, means to promote better self-understanding and consistency of behavior for corporate direction.

The hardest and most critical task for the economist is to help in the understanding of the goals and motivating forces of the organization. This task is probably harder for not-for-profit organizations such as government bureaucracies than it is for business firms. Making a profit is by no means everything, but it serves as an important component of the goals of a healthy business enterprise. Goal formation for the Department of Health, Education and Welfare contrasts with goal formation for a small insurance company.

The study and the selection of alternatives cannot be separated from the perception of goals. It is considerably easier to find something if you know what you are looking for than if you do not.

The perception of goals by a good management provides the screening device in the selection of alternatives to study in depth and to eventually pursue. The selection of alternatives requires not only the guidance of volition, it requires a great amount of knowledge about technological and economic fact in particular, and the environment in general.

It is a central part of the job of the corporate planner to know "the rules of the game" and who the players are. Knowledge of the general external and internal environment is a basic prerequisite to planning. A good planning group in a large corporation may need to include political scientists and others who understand bureaucratic structure. But the information and understanding of the political bureaucratic and technological environment are basic inputs needed in the formulation of the economic problems of planning and not a substitute for them.

In this section it has been suggested that the central concerns of the economist give rise to a way of thought and a language which has a natural use in the development of an understanding of corporate goals, environment, costs, and alternatives.

It has already been stressed, and is stressed again, that the language and talents of the economist are particularly attuned to providing the conceptual basis for corporate planning. Furthermore, good corporate planning is a vital, but not sufficient, factor in the direction of the firm. It organizes and presents much of the information that reaches the corporate brain. It is not the brain itself. The planning group constitutes a key set of advisors and professional consultants to management--they are not management. They have neither environment-setting nor a general responsibility-taking role. They service those whose main concern is with these roles.

Good planners and economists may eventually become chief executive officers, but not merely because they are competent in providing the planning support needed for the direction of an ongoing enterprise. Being a first class economist or planner does not preclude an individual from having executive talents, but it is no substitute for other talents needed for direction.

PLANNING, ANTICIPATING AND FORECASTING

Corporate planning is a vital high level feedback process of the firm. Forecasting is a far more product oriented than process oriented occupation. Forecasting has been a time honored profession since long before the existence of the oracle of Delphi.

Corporate planners are natural consumers of forecasting but their responsibility goes far beyond that of producing forecasts. The planners need to know why forecasts are needed and how sensitive their plans will be to error in the forecasts. They relate the forecasts to the decision system. They integrate them by placing them in a basic economic context.

The forecasters alone offer little to the firm without the planners or anticipators. A management which uses forecasting directly is implicitly assuming the burden of its own planning staff support. And this is a burden which can now be efficiently delegated.

Pro forma financial statements based upon a set of "what if" assumptions concerning the degree of error in a forecast are frequently not exciting, but they are highly useful. If they are produced by a responsible planner, they provide the needed insights concerning the accuracy of the forecasting activity and its relevance to the decisionmaking process.

Forecasting is not necessarily the main province of the economist. Technological forecasts are vital for many corporations. Political forecasts may be critical. Social forecasts concerning changes in habits and modes of existence or changes in family size are undoubtedly of great importance to the perception of markets.

The state of forecasting depends upon the development of scientific enquiring in many different disciplines. Forecasts of the weather, population growth, the rate of innovation, or success in oil exploration each call for special bodies of knowledge. But even when one is merely forecasting, the more closely related the forecast is to human activity, the more dependent it is upon correct assessments of many of the intangibles of the environment.

A sensitive study by Ascher (1978) on forecasting stresses that the critical feature in forecasts on items such as energy consumption or population is the picking of a good underlying model and relevant variables and not the degree of statistical sophistication of the data processing.

This observation is consistent with the basic theme being developed here. The central job of a corporate planning group is not number crunching but the organization of information and the interpretation of what the information means in terms of the decision process. If the planning group is doing its job, it will challenge the concepts of those providing it with forecasts and it will motivate those using its services to improve their concepts of goals and purpose.

Forecasting is important. It requires many different skills. It is not an economic activity in and of itself. Forecasts are a natural input to the planning process and as such they must be processed for conceptual validation and economic relevance in terms of their influence in the weighing of alternatives.

PLANNING AND ECONOMICS

Two important and intertwined activities in economics are theory development and measurement. There is a growing body of work devoted to the methodology and the theory of measurement; there are activities devoted to data gathering and the organization of data bases. Econometrics and data base construction, along with modern accounting, are all valuable tools used in planning. They interface with economic theory and planning at the point of model construction and conceptualization.

The central job of the planners is to help to identify for managers the key relevant concepts, models and variables for the perceived goals or direction of the firm. In attempting to do this the central tool is provided by the teachings and language of economic theory.

The imaginative use of economic theory in planning will appear to be ad hoc in the pejorative sense of this phrase. The opposite is true. Good economic analysis provides a means to identify the best model for the purposes at hand. This does not mean that it lacks abstraction. On the contrary, it means that the abstractions are at a higher level than those usually thought to be the key economic entities such as price, production and profit. These items are particular manifestations of the process of strategic choice governed by economic sense. Depending upon the organization and the time in its life, the key economic factors may be diversification, innovation, divestment, survival liquidation or many others. One cannot specify these a priori, nor is it fruitful to list all of them in every instance and to develop large taxonomies. A feature of good planning is to have the techniques and ability to select the relevant factors and to construct the appropriate verbal, numerical diagrammatic analytic models or simulators with speed and parsimony.

The metalanguage of economic choice introduces the overall concepts of goals, alternatives, costs, strategic environment, competition, efficiency and optimality. The more specialized languages of economics provide the refinements needed to operationalize these relatively broad concepts in terms of specific institutions. In the comments that follow, no attempt is made to be exhaustive. A few instances of special bodies of knowledge are presented.

A major division in economic theorizing is into macro and microeconomic theorizing. The work on macroeconomics is a critical conceptual input into the overall national economic models which frequently serve to provide much of the context of the overall economic environment. The economics of corporate planning is such that it will rarely be reasonable to build one's own national economic model. What is needed is the capacity to judge the quality of available macromodels and their importance to the planning process.

The remarks made here are restricted to microeconomic theorizing, because for the corporation (but not necessarily for a government agency) they are more relevant than macroeconomic theory.

Among the specialized disciplines of microeconomics relevant to planning there are:

> The theory of the firm;
> oligopoly theory;
> industrial organization;
> production
> labor
> finance

and

> marketing.

At a greater level abstraction there is:

> game theory
> utility theory

and

> information economics.

The theory of the firm is central to the contribution of economics to planning.

It has undergone at least three major transformations in the last fifty years.
The old theory stressed price and quantity, and in essence simplistically aggregrated most of its models into a single product, single and simple profit view of
the world. Its main attraction was simplicity and understandability. In particular, it is worth noting that in the development of neo-classical economics in
England, it had a direct operational use in eighteenth and nineteenth century
policymaking. Brevity and simplicity in presentation is still, today, an important factor in presenting results to high level personnel. Simplicity in presentation does not necessarily imply simplicity in concept or in thougth. Unfortunately, this connection is often true.

The growth of mathematical methods and computation caused a revolution in microeconomic analysis. It was not merely that more could be calculated. The difference was qualitative as well as quantitative. Prior to the advent of programming and computation, simple smooth one dimensional production and demand curves
were used because they could be drawn with ease and they were made differentiable
because the differential calculus could be used to solve optimization problems.
The approximations to reality had to be kept in line with the ability to analyze.
As the ability to analyze increased, it was possible to improve the approximations
to reality and have the models of the firm used by the economist come closer to
the models of the firm perceived by the manager.

The growth of behavioral understanding, computer technology and mathematical
methods, produced yet another revolution in microeconomic analysis which still
goes under the name of the behavioral theory of the firm. In the earlier theory,
in essence, the firm was the atom. There was no curiosity concerning its subatomic structure. The original trend in mathematical microeconomic theory was
towards a noninstitutional bloodless simple maximizing view of the firm. This has
been drastically revised by subsequent developments. The firm as an institutionally oriented complex goal defining, problem solving and adapting entity has
become the object of serious research.

These two new developments have their direct counterparts in the growth of corporate planning. The analytical computational optimizing models and the simulations are bridging the gap between theory and practice.

Industrial organization and marketing were for many years regarded as the stepchildren of economic theory. Those professionals who earned their living teaching
or consulting on these topics were rated for their ability to tell "war stories,"
to recount facts about everything and to be able to abstract and generalize very
little. The development of economic theory until as late as the 1950s was such
that institutional richness was regarded as an indicator of analytical weakness.
This has changed overwhelmingly in the last ten to twenty years. Along with the
simulations of specific firms has come a new industrial organization. It can
best be described by the somewhat forbidding but accurate title of "mathematical
institutional economics." The recognition of the need for detailed institutional
understanding and the behavioral structure of the firm has been reconciled with
the recognition of the need for abstraction, calculation and the use of mathematical methods.

The change in the study of industrial organization is being paralleled by the
changes in marketing. To some, because it clearly deals with competitive interaction, the new marketing has been regarded as equivalent to strategic planning in
general. This may be true for distribution and retailing firms. It is not so for
firms in which production or finance plays an important role. As in industrial
organization, so in marketing both the behavioral and the analytical approaches
are growing individually together. The availability of data processing and
handling technology has made the growth and use of detailed data bases an economic
reality. But along with the profusion of our ability to produce and to "crunch"
numbers, the need to control these activities by having better concepts and
theories has also grown.

It has undergone at least three major transformations in the last fifty years. The old theory stressed price and quantity, and in essence simplistically aggregrated most of its models into a single product, single and simple profit view of the world. Its main attraction was simplicity and understandability. In particular, it is worth noting that in the development of neo-classical economics in England, it had a direct operational use in eighteenth and nineteenth century policymaking. Brevity and simplicity in presentation is still, today, an important factor in presenting results to high level personnel. Simplicity in presentation does not necessarily imply simplicity in concept or in thought. Unfortunately, this connection is often true.

The growth of mathematical methods and computation caused a revolution in microeconomic analysis. It was not merely that more could be calculated. The difference was qualitative as well as quantitative. Prior to the advent of programming and computation, simple smooth one dimensional production and demand curves were used because they could be drawn with ease and they were made differentiable because the differential calculus could be used to solve optimization problems. The approximations to reality had to be kept in line with the ability to analyze. As the ability to analyze increased, it was possible to improve the approximations to reality and have the models of the firm used by the economist come closer to the models of the firm perceived by the manager.

The growth of behavioral understanding, computer technology and mathematical methods, produced yet another revolution in microeconomic analysis which still goes under the name of the behavioral theory of the firm. In the earlier theory, in essence, the firm was the atom. There was no curiosity concerning its subatomic structure. The original trend in mathematical microeconomic theory was towards a noninstitutional bloodless simple maximizing view of the firm. This has been drastically revised by subsequent developments. The firm as an institutionally oriented complex goal defining, problem solving and adapting entity has become the object of serious research.

These two new developments have their direct counterparts in the growth of corporate planning. The analytical computational optimizing models and the simulations are bridging the gap between theory and practice.

Industrial organization and marketing were for many years regarded as the stepchildren of economic theory. Those professionals who earned their living teaching or consulting on these topics were rated for their ability to tell "war stories," to recount facts about everything and to be able to abstract and generalize very little. The development of economic theory until as late as the 1950s was such that institutional richness was regarded as an indicator of analytical weakness. This has changed overwhelmingly in the last ten to twenty years. Along with the simulations of specific firms has come a new industrial organization. It can best be described by the somewhat forbidding but accurate title of "mathematical institutional economics." The recognition of the need for detailed institutional understanding and the behavioral structure of the firm has been reconciled with the recognition of the need for abstraction, calculation and the use of mathematical methods.

The change in the study of industrial organization is being paralleled by the changes in marketing. To some, because it clearly deals with competitive interaction, the new marketing has been regarded as equivalent to strategic planning in general. This may be true for distribution and retailing firms. It is not so for firms in which production or finance plays an important role. As in industrial organization, so in marketing both the behavioral and the analytical approaches are growing individually together. The availability of data processing and handling technology has made the growth and use of detailed data bases an economic reality. But along with the profusion of our ability to produce and to "crunch" numbers, the need to control these activities by having better concepts and theories has also grown.

It has undergone at least three major transformations in the last fifty years. The old theory stressed price and quantity, and in essence simplistically aggregated most of its models into a single product, single and simple profit view of the world. Its main attraction was simplicity and understandability. In particular, it is worth noting that in the development of neo-classical economics in England, it had a direct operational use in eighteenth and nineteenth century policymaking. Brevity and simplicity in presentation is still, today, an important factor in presenting results to high level personnel. Simplicity in presentation does not necessarily imply simplicity in concept or in thought. Unfortunately, this connection is often true.

The growth of mathematical methods and computation caused a revolution in microeconomic analysis. It was not merely that more could be calculated. The difference was qualitative as well as quantitative. Prior to the advent of programming and computation, simple smooth one dimensional production and demand curves were used because they could be drawn with ease and they were made differentiable because the differential calculus could be used to solve optimization problems. The approximations to reality had to be kept in line with the ability to analyze. As the ability to analyze increased, it was possible to improve the approximations to reality and have the models of the firm used by the economist come closer to the models of the firm perceived by the manager.

The growth of behavioral understanding, computer technology and mathematical methods, produced yet another revolution in microeconomic analysis which still goes under the name of the behavioral theory of the firm. In the earlier theory, in essence, the firm was the atom. There was no curiosity concerning its subatomic structure. The original trend in mathematical microeconomic theory was towards a noninstitutional bloodless simple maximizing view of the firm. This has been drastically revised by subsequent developments. The firm as an institutionally oriented complex goal defining, problem solving and adapting entity has become the object of serious research.

These two new developments have their direct counterparts in the growth of corporate planning. The analytical computational optimizing models and the simulations are bridging the gap between theory and practice.

Industrial organization and marketing were for many years regarded as the stepchildren of economic theory. Those professionals who earned their living teaching or consulting on these topics were rated for their ability to tell "war stories," to recount facts about everything and to be able to abstract and generalize very little. The development of economic theory until as late as the 1950s was such that institutional richness was regarded as an indicator of analytical weakness. This has changed overwhelmingly in the last ten to twenty years. Along with the simulations of specific firms has come a new industrial organization. It can best be described by the somewhat forbidding but accurate title of "mathematical institutional economics." The recognition of the need for detailed institutional understanding and the behavioral structure of the firm has been reconciled with the recognition of the need for abstraction, calculation and the use of mathematical methods.

The change in the study of industrial organization is being paralleled by the changes in marketing. To some, because it clearly deals with competitive interaction, the new marketing has been regarded as equivalent to strategic planning in general. This may be true for distribution and retailing firms. It is not so for firms in which production or finance plays an important role. As in industrial organization, so in marketing both the behavioral and the analytical approaches are growing individually together. The availability of data processing and handling technology has made the growth and use of detailed data bases an economic reality. But along with the profusion of our ability to produce and to "crunch" numbers, the need to control these activities by having better concepts and theories has also grown.

Along with a more complex society has come the increasing need for some industries to cope with development and production processes which may last over ten to twenty years. The building of a nuclear reactor or a major ship may take ten years or more even without major development or innovation. The uncertainties which must be absorbed over periods of high investment involving exposure for over a decade make long range planning a necessity. The specifics of both the production process and of the problems pertaining to the development, maintenance, morale and efficiency of the labor force are recognized as important subfields of the discipline of economics.

In most corporations neither production and engineering nor personnel and labor policy are the proper domain of corporate planning. Yet the inputs from both of these activities must be obtained and interpreted in terms of the economics of strategic coordination.

Finance and accounting were until the last ten to twenty years both regarded as useful, but not quite academically first rank subjects. Also like marketing, they were stepchildren of economics. The corporations needed them and the business schools taught them. But except for the stories of the occasional wicked wolf of Wall Street whose financial coups in the foreign world of paper were reported in the press, the concept of linking finance accounting and corporate strategy was a new concept to virtually all but the most sophisticated of industries. This began to change in the last thirty years. And possibly certain aspects of finance, having caught up with economic theory and practice, have overshot the market. An example will make this clear. The emphasis on portfolio theory out of institutional context has been overdone. Even the largest of the industrial conglomerates must face up to the institutional facts that a portfolio of paper is different from the ownership and operation of a hundred divisions. The simplistic, although appealing classifications of the Boston Consulting Group may, from one point of view, be regarded as a watered down version of the language of a merger-and-acquisition oriented banker who need not pay too much attention to the organizational stress caused in a conglomerate by milking department A to nurture department B while terminating C.

Birth, growth, and death are natural human and organizational processes and they require the full sweep of time if they are to avoid pathologies. The severing of a department from the General Electric Corporation is not the same as the selling of a block of share of G.E. to the same value. The human equation is different. Th strategic importance of finance has finally been recognized by virtually all industries. Perhaps it has been over-recognized. Corporations may hold portfolios of stocks and bonds. When they start to think that they also hold portfolios of firms and people, they have lost touch with institutional reality.

Last in our listing of substantive areas of microeconomic theory is the theory of oligopoly which is developing into an exotic blend of industrial organizations, mathematical economics, behavioral study, marketing, and the theory of games. Possibly one of the most difficult of all of the planning tasks is to take into realistic account the competitive interaction among firms. The competition must be appropriately accounted for, but in the immortal words of a great American philosopher Pogo, frequently the case is "we have met the enemy and he is us!"

The last three topics noted in the list of economic enquiry are game theory, utility theory, and information economics. They are simultaneously more arcane and exotic than the other topics already described, yet they are also directly related to the current and future developments in the theory and practice of planning. If economics is the language of much of corporate strategic planning, game theory is the language of strategic planning in general.

The basic concepts underlying the theory of games are: the rules of the game (the environment); the players (the competition); the payoffs, moves, choices, alternatives, information conditions and strategies.

These elements lead naturally to the operational definitions of concepts such as viability and maneuverability. The concepts at this level are equally well applicable to military, diplomatic, governmental and economic strategic planning. John McDonald's informal, but stimulating book on "The Game of Business," provides light but suggestive reading on strategic analysis.

Utility theory in spite of its forbidding title (it could be called preference theory--but that is scarcely better) helps to raise basic questions concerning the feasibility of constructing logically consistent goals for the firm when there are multiple objectives to be pursued or when there are group preferences or fiduciary roles to be taken into account.

Last in the list is the growing work on information economics based upon the somewhat pessimistic but frequently realistic assumptions that information is imperfect and expensive to obtain and that frequently it pays one individual in an organization to conceal knowledge from the other.

The amount of directly applied utility theory and information economics is low if measured purely in terms of pointing to specific problems and direct calculations associated with them. But this is not the only way that theory impinges upon practice. The change in the way of thinking about a problem; the way in which questions are asked and the manner in which answers are structured can all be manifestations of application at a level other than computational. And frequently it is the higher level of application that has the major impact. New ways of thinking about problems may precede new calculations.

ECONOMICS, PLANNING, MODELS AND SIMULATIONS

There are financial models, investment studies, merger and acquisition calculations, market simulations, product development studies, personnel turnover simulations, production-inventory scheduling systems, market games and many other direct planning applications of analytical models and simulations in business; weapons evaluation models, nuclear exchange simulations, war games and a host of other special applications exist in military planning.

Underlying all of these approaches is the basic unifying theme of purposeful resource allocation in a competitive environment. The purposes of the planning may differ considerably but the underlying theme binding all together is the same. It is a theme of economic analysis.

Those engaged in corporate planning vary their methods and utilize techniques appropriate to the problem at hand. For some the elaborate computation offers the best opportunity; for others a simulation is called for. For still others the judicious use of a special planning computer language to produce pro forma financial statements is all that is needed. In other instances a verbal report or a diagram tells the story.

There are many techniques and the development of the computer has enlarged the scope of the techniques. But planning is not achieved by technique alone. The fundamental ingredient is insight and the basic insight is economic. The world of the corporation stretches far beyond the economic but the unifying theme and sense of proportion is provided from this source.

REFERENCES

[1] Ascher, William. Forecasting an Appraisal for Policy-Makers and Planners. Baltimore, MD: The Johns Hopkins University Press, 1978.

[2] Gershefski, George W. "Corporate Models - The State of the Art." In Albert N. Schrieber (ed.), Corporate Simulation Models, Seattle, WA: University of Washington Press, 1970.

[3] McDonald, John. The Game of Business. New York: Doubleday & Company, Inc., 1975.

INDUSTRIAL ORGANIZATION AND THE EVOLUTION OF
CONCEPTS FOR STRATEGIC PLANNING

Michael E. Porter

Graduate School of Business Administration
Harvard University
Boston, Massachusetts
U.S.A.

INTRODUCTION

From its birth in the 1950s, the strategic planning field has grown into a major and accepted part of the territory of management. Along the way, a wide variety of analytical techniques have been introduced to aid managers in formulating business strategy, many of which have grown out of the practice of strategic consulting firms. Yet as provocative and widely used as some of these planning concepts have been, it is becoming increasingly recognized that they leave many questions unanswered that are at the heart of business strategy formulation.

This paper will trace the historical development of concepts for business strategy formulation through what I will argue have been two major phases. The aim of this will be to make some of the unanswered questions raised by contemporary strategic planning techniques explicit. Having done so, I will argue that research growing out of the field of industry organization economics promises to trigger a new, third phase in the development of the strategy field and provide the beginnings of answers to these questions. Some of the essential concepts from this recent literature on competitive strategy will be briefly reviewed and the frontiers that research is taking identified.

THE EVOLUTION OF CONCEPTS FOR BUSINESS STRATEGY

The first phase of the modern strategic planning field had its beginnings in the work of Andrews, Christensen, Learned and others at the Harvard Business School that culminated in the development of the concept of corporate strategy in the early 1960s. Prior to the formal articulation of the concept of strategy and the intellectual apparatus it provided, discussions of policy cases at Harvard were exercises in searching for the core issue facing a company. The core issue was one that, if identified, would tie the other symptoms and problems in a company's situation together and provide the insight to needed solutions.

The concept of strategy was an analytical construct that allowed this core issue to be articulated as the so-called "purpose" of the firm. According to the classic treatment appearing first in 1965 in the policy textbook by Learned, Christensen, Andrews and Guth (LCAG), strategy was defined as the essential concept of how a firm was attempting to compete in its environment, encompassing a choice of goals as well as operating policies in each functional area of the business such as product line, served markets, marketing, manufacturing and so on. The goals of the firm were broadly conceived to encompass both economic and noneconomic considerations such as social obligations, treatment of employees, organizational climate and others. Effective strategy formulation from a normative standpoint was the relating of four key elements shown in Figure 1.

Broadly speaking, the aim of business strategy was to match the internal competences and values of the firm to its external environment, and LCAG offered a series of very general but logically compelling consistency tests which helped the firm probe its strategy to see if it truly related these elements. These consis-

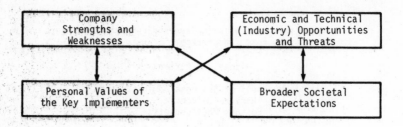

Figure 1. The Components of Business Strategy

tency tests stressed the need for a firm's operating policies in each functional area to be interrelated as well as the need for the entire group of functional policies to make sense given the environment. The high performing (high return on investment) firm in LCAG's framework was one that had found or created a position in its industry where such consistency was present.

The concept of strategy emerged out of the crying need to help the practitioner (particularly the general manager) translate the chaos of events and decisions he faced every day into an orderly way of sizing up the firm's position in its environment. As a result, the early policy literature on strategy formulation subsequent to LCAG was largely process oriented, translating the basic LCAG paradigm and extensions of it into a sequence of logical (and very general) analytical steps (cf., Ansoff, 1965). This work attempted to convert the elegant prose of LCAG into flowcharts composed of a concrete series of questions the firm had to answer in developing its strategy. Some of the early strategic planning methodologies developed at firms such as Stanford Research Institute and Arthur D. Little took this form, and this sort of literature has continued to appear.

The pioneering research on the concept of strategy had a powerful impact on business practice, and was responsible for stimulating the development of formal processes for strategic planning in many companies. The need to develop strategy was perceived by sophisticated managements as compelling. The powerful questions raised by the LCAG framework were obviously relevant: What are the opportunities and threats in my industry? What are my company's strengths and weaknesses? Is my strategy consistent internally and with the environment?

As relevant as the questions were, however, the LCAG framework and its followers provided few answers, or provided answers of only the most general sort. The firm was left to its own devices to develop answers suitable to its industry and competitive situation. Thus a vacuum was created, one that caused many managers to look for ways to fill it given the high stakes involved.

Strategic Planning Concepts

This vacuum was soon filled by a large body of analytical tools I will term "strategic planning concepts," which represented the second phase in the development of the strategy field. The grandfather of the new planning concepts was the experience curve, popularized by the Boston Consulting Group beginning in the late 1960s. Soon after and in the subsequent years came such concepts as the growth/share portfolio matrix, the McKinsey/General Electric/Shell attractiveness screen, the product life cycle-based framework identified with Arthur D. Little, Inc., the statistically derived findings and models of the PIMS Program,[1] and a plethora of planning and forecasting models.[2] Except for the planning and forecasting models, the initiative in developing and using these concepts lay with practicing consulting firms. Scholars in business schools largely took the role of bystanders, disseminators or critics of the new planning concepts with a few notable exceptions.

Any observer of the strategic planning field is well aware of the great impact that these concepts have had and continue to have on practice in the field, and the degree to which discussion of them occupies the pages of academic journals. We see explicit mention of the use of these concepts in the annual reports of major corporations such as Norton, Becton-Dickinson, Texas Instruments, and a thriving consulting industry providing services in their application.

Unanswered Questions

As companies experimented with using these strategic planning concepts in practice and scholars have examined them, it has become apparent that the new concepts left many questions unanswered just as the LCAG framework had. The LCAG was completely situational and offered no generalizations about strategy, but the new planning concepts went to the other extreme. By and large, the new planning concepts abstracted from competition to identify a small number of key strategic variables deemed to be important, and constructed entire theories of strategy around them. Yet the process of abstraction from the complexity of industry competition carries with it its own set of dangers, because implicit in all of the planning concepts are subtle questions that have to be answered before the prescriptions of the concepts can be confidently followed.

Just a few of the most essential unanswered questions raised by each of the strategic planning concepts are as follows, which provide the analytical agenda that any new conceptual framework for business strategy must address:[3]

Experience Curve

Experience curve theory contains many unanswered questions about the relationship of the experience curve to other competitive phenomena, and the particular shape, defensibility and properties of the experience curve itself:

1. How important is the experience curve compared to other entry barriers? Experience curve theory admits no other entry barriers or competitive advantages as significant. Yet we know that other barriers exist and must be considered in strategy development.

2. In what kinds of industries will the experience curve be steep and why? How long will the experience curve continue at a given slope? There is much evidence that the slope and duration of the experience curve vary greatly among industries, and that the particular value added elements driving the curve differ significantly from business to business. The operational significance of the experience curve for business strategy depends critically on understanding these differences among businesses, as well as the way in which the rate of cost decline may change with industry evolution.

3. What is the strategic significance of the mix between cost declines due to economies of scale and those due to learning effects? Economies of scale and learning have fundamentally different strategic implications, and their presence can yield contradictory prescriptions. Yet the experience curve formulation mixes the two.

4. Under what circumstances can experience be kept proprietary, and under what circumstances does imitation or copying provide advantages to followers over leaders? The crucial and usually unstated assumption in learning curve theory is that the learning can be kept proprietary. Yet no research has identified when or how this can be done, or the mechanism by which followers can imitate experience.

5. Under what circumstances can followers leapfrog the technology of leaders and jump onto a new experience curve? Technological change provides a discontinuity which can destroy the entry barrier due to the experience curve. No propositions for either exploiting or guarding against this eventuality are articulated in the theory.

6. Under what circumstances is experience transferable among related businesses? While it is widely recognized that experience can be transferable, the concept does not allow an identification of the boundaries of transferability or the strategic implications.

Growth/Share Matrix

The growth/share matrix contains many unanswered questions about the sufficiency of the axes to capture the strategic situation of business units, and the way in which businesses are plotted in practice:

1. How do we define market boundaries in order to meaningfully calculate relative market share? The strategic prescription of the growth/share matrix depends critically on how the market is defined and market share calculated. Yet the model provides no guidance for assessing market boundaries, or which competitors to exclude or include.

2. What other firm and industry characteristics can influence the competitive position of a business unit besides share? Few believe that share is the only determinant of competitive position. Yet nothing but share is included in the model.

3. How can we factor in the behavior of competitors? The model ignores competitors altogether, except in the most indirect way through relative share. Yet competitors can nullify the effectiveness of any of the alternative strategies the model suggests.

4. How can we assess the fundamental attractiveness of the industry, because market leaders in some industries have low levels of return on investment? The model implicitly assumes that all industries are equally attractive if the firm has a leading share. Empirical data raises serious questions about this view.

5. How can we deal with interrelationships among the business units, whose presence nullifies the logic of the model? The model assumes independence among business units, yet independence among units is pervasive and often a major source of strategic leverage.

6. How do we select among question marks to invest in? Since all but one competitor in each industry is not a question mark or a dog (depending on market growth), this will be a pervasive problem.

McKinsey/General Electric/Shell Screen

The McKinsey/GE/Shell Screen raises many unanswered questions about the analysis required to plot a business, the sufficiency of the axes to determine strategic choices, and the logical relationship between where the business is plotted and the indicated strategy:

1. <u>What determines industry attractiveness?</u>   Lists of factors are sometimes given, but they lack comprehensiveness and mix cause and effect.

2. <u>What determines the strength of a competitive position?</u>   Lists of factors are sometimes given, but they lack comprehensiveness and mix cause and effect.

3. <u>How can we forecast future industry attractiveness?</u>   Future attractiveness should be as or more important than current industry conditions, yet is outside the model.

4. <u>How can we factor in the behavior of competitors?</u> Competitor behavior, though essential to the success or failure of any of the strategies in the model, is ignored.

5. <u>How can we avoid the "marginal versus average" fallacy?</u>   Just because the position of a business unit is strong and it may be earning high average returns does not imply that a firm should make additional investments in the business. Average return on investment may be high, but return on marginal investment may be low or even negative!

Product Life Cycle

The product life cycle model raises serious unanswered questions about its generality and the specific strategic implications identified:

1. <u>When does the product cycle pattern of industry evolution occur, and what causes other patterns to occur?</u>   Extensive literature illustrates that the product life cycle pattern of industry evolution is not generalizable. Thus the model can trap a firm into taking the wrong action or making the life cycle occur as a self-fulfilling prophecy.

2. <u>How can the firm choose among strategic alternatives for competing in the various life cycle phases?</u>   The model posits alternatives for appropriate behavior during the various life cycle phases. Yet the choice among these alternatives defines the success or failure of the firm. Further, the alternatives presented presume the life cycle will occur, rather than help the company find creative ways to overcome it.

3. <u>How can we factor in the behavior of competitors?</u> As with the other planning concepts, no explicit framework for integrating competitors into the analysis is part of the model.

PIMS

PIMS raises many unanswered questions about the underlying model of competition, the generality of the findings and the appropriateness of the data and statistical procedures:

1. <u>What general theory of competition explains the large collection of findings proposed by PIMS?</u> The numerous PIMS findings are empirical regularities which are then rationalized with ad hoc, though often persuasive, explanations. Even discounting the methodological difficulties inherent in PIMS statistical procedures, there is no theory tying the findings together and forming an integrated whole. Without such a theory it is difficult to feel secure about

particular strategic implications asserted by PIMS.

2. <u>Does PIMS include the right measures of market attractiveness and a business unit's competitive position?</u> While the PIMS data includes many measures of strategic position, without an underlying theory there is little comfort that all the right variables are included or that they are interacted properly.

3. <u>Is the PIMS concept of served market meaningful for capturing the firm's competitive arena?</u> PIMS concept of served market implies very narrow market definitions. Such things as potential entrants, substitution, and competitor shared costs are left out of such a procedure, yet bode very large as strategic issues in practice.

4. <u>Do the findings of the PIMS analysis apply with equal force in every industry?</u> PIMS is built on the premise of general laws of the market place. Yet a cross sectional regression finding on advertising, for example, is unlikely to apply equally to a consumer and an industrial business.

Planning and Forecasting Models

The planning and forecasting models raise unanswered questions about their appropriateness as abstractions of reality, and their data inputs:

1. <u>Which of the models is a good abstraction of how competitive processes work?</u> All planning and forecasting models are abstractions of competitive processes, chosen to expose the phenomena under study. What evidence is there that the particular abstractions employed capture the essential features of competition in a particular setting?

2. <u>What determines the crucial inputs to the models such as future prices, market growth, competitor behavior, etc.?</u> Most planning and forecasting models require inputs such as future prices, capacities, shares, etc. Yet the determination of these inputs is usually ad hoc and not based on a broad theory of competition. Further, many of these inputs taken as exogenous are really endogenously determined.

The Need for a Competitive Analysis Framework

Viewing these unanswered questions as a group, some striking themes emerge. Running through these unanswered questions about the strategic planning concepts is the need for a framework to comprehensively understand industry structure and the behavior of competitors and to translate these into operational strategic recommendations. It is clear from the discussion above that the strategic planning concepts that have emerged have been built, by and large, on views of competition stressing one or a few aspects of industry structure. Nowhere is there a comprehensive approach to understanding industry attractiveness. In addition, the planning concepts as a group have been almost totally lacking in in-depth treatments of competitors, focusing rather on external environmental changes, or relative cost, or other variables. Relative competitive position, then, can only be partially assessed. In the case of PIMS, the number of aspects of the environment considered has been large but there has been no model of competition tying them together. Finally, the treatment of strategic alternatives in the strategic planning concepts has largely stopped with broad statements such as "hold," "build" and the like. These have lacked operational content and not always been linked explicitly with the source of sustainable competitive advantage the firm was to possess.

INDUSTRIAL ORGANIZATION AS A BUSINESS STRATEGY FRAMEWORK

While the strategic planning concepts have developed through these two phases, economists were workng in a field known as industrial organization that considered the problems of applied microeconomics. Long orphans in the economics profession because their research was not mathematical, scholars in industrial organization evolved a paradigm aimed at explaining a firm's economic performance in its industry. This research was almost solely directed towards the concerns of public policy towards business, and in fact it became a key underpinning of antitrust analysis.

The essence of the industrial organization paradigm developed by Edward Mason, Joe Bain, and their followers was that a firm's performance in the market place depended critically on the characteristics of the industry environment in which it competed. This was expressed in the now familiar structure-conduct-performance trilogy shown in Figure 2.

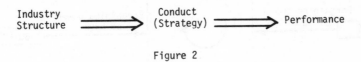

Figure 2

Industry structure determined the behavior or conduct of firms, whose joint conduct then determined the collective performance of the firms in the industry (Bain, 1958: Mason, 1953). Performance was defined broadly and in the economist's sense of social performance, encompassing dimensions such as allocative efficiency (profitability), technical efficiency (cost minimization), innovativeness and others. Firm conduct was the firm's choice of key decision variables such as price, advertising, capacity and quality. Thus in business administration terms, conduct could be viewed as the economic dimensions of firm strategy. Finally, industry structure was defined as the relatively stable economic and technical dimensions of an industry that provided the context in which competition occurred (Bain, 1972). The primary elements of structure identified as important to performance in IO research were barriers to entry (Bain, 1956), the number and size distribution of firms, product differentiation and the overall elasticity of demand (Bain, 1968). A final crucial aspect of the Bain/Mason paradigm was the view that since structure determined firms' conduct (strategy) which jointly determined performance, we could ignore conduct and look directly at industry structure in trying to explain performance. Conduct (or strategy) merely reflected the environment the firm operated in.

An important branch of industrial organization research was so-called oligopoly theory, or the study of competitive interactions in markets where one firm's actions affect its rivals (for a survey see Scherer, 1970). Oligopoly theory sought to flush out the link between industry structure and firm-to-firm rivalry, providing a rich set of determinants of the difficulty firms faced in coordinating their actions in the market place (for the classic analysis, see Fellner, 1949). It filled a gaping hole for the analysis of real life markets that had been left by economists' traditional exclusive focus on the polar cases of pure competition and pure monopoly. Game theory, born at nearly the same time as the Bain/Mason paradigm itself, introduced a potentially rich framework for examining competitive interaction, embodying concepts like commitment and deterrence which offered intriguing insights into making moves and countermoves (Van Neumann and Morganstern, 1953; Schelling, 1960). Game theory took its place in industrial organization as a part of the general topic of oligopoly theory.

The Bain/Mason paradigm was a promising beginning at what was missing in the strategic planning concepts of the 1970s -- a broad theory of competition.

M.E. Porter

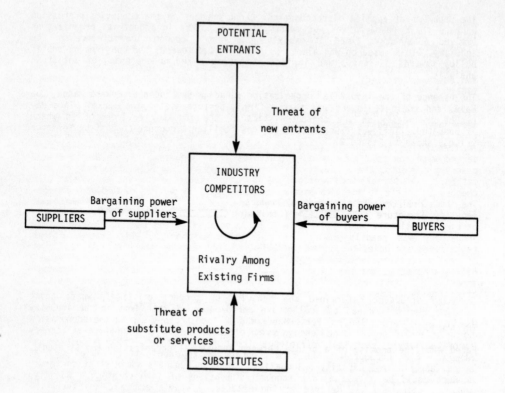

Figure 3

<u>Fundamental Determinants of Industry Competition</u>

Nevertheless, there was little integration of industrial organization concepts into the strategy field. No small barrier to this integration was the fact that researchers in the two areas were working in separate fields with very different traditions and different types of accepted training. Yet a variety of more substantive issues also stood in the way of integration of industrial organization and business strategy, which I have discussed in some detail elsewhere (Porter, 1981).

First, industrial organization research was framed in public policy terms and had never been plumbed to consider the implications for business strategy. In addition, industrial organization was concerned with industries and assumed the firms in them to be essentially identical, while strategic planning was vitally concerned with how to create unique strategies in an industry. As in the strategic planning concepts, the analysis of competitors was missing from industrial organization. Industrial organization was largely static while it was clear that changes in strategic position most often took place in periods of industry change. The industrial organization framework was stark and built on a few key elements of industry structure such as seller concentration and broad categories of entry barriers, while the manifold richness of factors affecting competition in actual industries was readily apparent to strategic planners. Game theory offered tantalizing analogies for competition, but did not address the practical realities of real markets including the feasibly available data about the payoffs of alternative strategies and the constraints of imperfectly known competitors. And most importantly industrial organization assumed away conduct (strategy) as relevant to affecting performance while great strategists had long found ways to change industry structure in their favor.

THE NEW BRIDGE

Faced with the promise of a bridge between industrial organization and strategic planning, but a substantial gap to overcome, research has been progressing in recent years to forge a framework for strategic planning growing out of the roots of industrial organization. The beginnings of such a framework, which I will term the competitive strategy framework, are beginning to emerge, the most comprehensive statement articulated in Porter (1980).

The core of the framework, drawing from the industrial organization tradition, is that in any competitive industry there are five basic competitive forces at work as shown in Figure 3. The collective strength of these five forces determines the fundamental potential for firms in the industry to earn returns on investment in excess of the opportunity cost of capital. Thus the collective strength of the five forces is the essential determinant of industry attractiveness, one of the important building blocks in strategic planning.

Underlying each of the five competitive forces is a number of economic and technical determinants of its strength in a particular industry. These economic and technical industry characteristics are the industry structure. The competitive strategy framework identifies the economic and technical determinants of each force in some detail. For example, the threat of entry is a function of 7 types of structural entry barriers and the expected retaliation of incumbents, itself a function of some predictable industry characteristics.[4] The underlying economic and technical determinants of the competitive forces define the "rules of competition" in the industry, with which the firm must cope strategically.

Business strategy, viewed in the context of the framework, is the creation of a defensible position vis-à-vis the competitive forces. The firm can find positions in its industry that are more defensible against the forces than others. Moreover, industry structure changes over time in industries and can provide the opportunity for strategic repositioning. Most importantly, though, the firm through strategy can influence every one of the five competitive forces in its favor. A central axiom of the competitive strategy framework is that although the industry structure is to some extent defined by exogenous economic and technical factors, strategy can unlock the constraints of industry structure. Hence the promise is present for the firm to change the rules of competition in its industry in its favor, and additional parts of the framework identify approaches to changing each competitive force in some detail. The competitive strategy framework thus provides meat to the previously empty phrase "rules of competition" by identifying the fundamental factors that determine the rules in a particular industry.

Starting from the core concept of industry structural analysis, the competitive strategy framework adds a number of additional analytical building blocks. Oligopoly and game theory provide the foundation for an approach to profiling competitors to predict their likely behavior. Forms of information flow in markets (or market signals) are identified, and the considerations in making offensive and defensive moves are developed. These parts of the framework thus draw in the analysis of competitors.

Industry structure and competitor analysis are integrated in the theory of strategic groups (Porter, 1980, Chapter 7; Caves and Porter, 1977). This theory addresses the underlying causes of differences in attractiveness among different strategic positions within an industry, bringing structural analysis down to the level of the individual firms. Part of the strategic group model is a generalization of entry barriers into what are termed "mobility barriers," or impediments to the shift of firms from one strategic configuration to another within an industry. The group model also facilitates the construction of strategic maps that chart the relative positions of competitors.

The strategic group model allows a systematic identification of firms' strengths and weaknesses, and a way of explaining differences in profitability of firms within the same industry. Thus the strategic group model provides a way of assessing the firm's competitive position in a fundamental way, another essential building block in business strategy development and an unanswered question in many of the strategic planning concepts of the 1970s.

The final element of the core competitive strategy framework is a model of industry evolution. This model starts from the premise that the product life cycle theory lacks generality, and its approach is to identify the economic processes underlying industry evolution, and examine how they interact to change structure over time. This analysis allows predictions of industry structural change given the circumstances in a particular industry.

From the generalizable analytical techniques described above, the competitive strategy framework goes on to make more specific the analysis of strategic problems in two broad ways. The first is to divide industries into generic "structural settings" based on key elements of industry structure such as seller concentration, state of development and degree of globalization. The framework then examines a number of particularly industry generic structures in detail to expose their particular competitive characteristics, the types of strategic alternatives available, and the pitfalls that firms can encounter from a strategic point of view.

The final broad part of the framework is an examination of each of the major forms of strategic decision that occur in an industry, including entry, divestment, vertical integration and major capacity expansion. The generalized analytical techniques described above have implications for each decision that is developed, and thus are combined with a drawing together of research on the particular economic and administrative considerations involved in each decision.

Philosophically, then, the competitive strategy framework begins with a very broad core model of competition that is generalizable to any industry. By applying the framework, the particular economic and competitive issues crucial in the particular competitors of significance can be identified. The framework then provides analytical tools to delve deeper into these and develop strategic implications. Based on type of generic industry structure the firm is in and any strategic decisions it may face, additional elements on the framework can be brought to bear as well to make the analysis richer. Thus the model begins at the very fundamental, broad level and gets increasingly specific and deep as the analysis proceeds.

Application of the competitive strategy framework thus leads to a comprehensive assessment of industry attractiveness and the competitive position of the firm, prominently unanswered questions in the strategic planning concepts discussed above. The competitive strategy framework also places central importance on in-depth competitor analysis and forecasting of behavior, another missing link in previous models. The framework provides the analytical tools to select concrete strategic moves that will improve the position of the firm, that go beyond broad statements such as "hold" or "build." The breadth of market boundaries, another unanswered question in the models reviewed above, is treated centrally through the examination of potential entry, shared costs and substitution.

Thus the competitive strategy framework offers at least beginnings of the answers to many of the unanswered questions posed above. While far from complete or exhaustive, then, the bridge between industrial organization and business strategy may be ushering in a third phase in the development of strategic planning concepts, based on more complex models of competition and a broader conception of the role of strategy than the models described above.

The Promise of Contemporary Industrial Organization Research

The competitive strategy framework as developed thus far is only a beginning. Much more remains for further elucidation, more rigorous modeling, and empirical testing to place quantitative dimensions on what is still a subtle and judgmental analytical process. Fortunately there are ample signs that research is underway to extend the framework, involving both industrial organization economists, economic theorists and business strategy researchers.

Important elements of industry structure that have received little attention in the economics literature are being examined with increasing frequency. Rigorous research is probing the strategic implications of the learning curve, including recent papers by Spence (1981) and Dolan and Jeuland (1981). Willig (1979), Willig and Panzar (1977) and Teece (1980) have begun analytical modeling of the implications of multiproduct economies of scale, a careful theoretical formulation of the issue of shared costs.

Recent work is ongoing to further specify and test the strategic group model. Oster (1981) has worked with strategic groups defined by differences in marketing strategy, and found substantial support for the premises of the model. Hayes, Spence and Marks (1981) have used an intriguing statistical technique to define strategic groups in the investment banking industry. Caves and Pugel (1980) have shown how intra-industry differences in firm performance can be linked to the group model.

Increasingly, research is beginning to encompass dynamic models of industry evolution, some framed from the point of view of the strategic decision facing the individual firm. A number of models have explored additional aspects of firm investment and innovation in a dynamic context (for example, see Spence, 1979; Flaherty, 1976; Kamien and Schwartz, 1972). Michael Spence and I have modeled the dynamic capacity expansion problem facing the firm in a group oligopoly using actual data drawn from a comprehensive case study of the corn milling industry (1981). Marvin Lieberman is examining the process of capacity expansion in a large sample of chemical industries in doctoral thesis research at Harvard.

Research is also proceeding on generic structural settings and strategic decisions. John Stuckey and Roger Fergusen have recently completed thesis research on vertical integration and joint ventures, respectively. Hall (1980) has studied the problems of mature industries.

CONCLUSION

I have only been able to sketch the outlines of the new link between industrial organization and business strategy here, and provide an indication of the research now underway. Nevertheless, the hope is that the promise of this research for ushering in a third phase in the development of the strategic planning field has been indicated. This third phase will be one where strategy models recognize the complexity of competition rather than abstract from it, where strategy research starts with the premise that competitive patterns differ from industry to industry, and where competitors are recognized as central and are viewed as living organizations with particular personalities, strengths and failings.

This third phase of strategic planning is one that strategic planners with a decade or more of accumulated experience with overly simplified strategic planning concepts should welcome with open arms. While the data requirements of this richer view of competition are formidable and the analytical questions complex, the payoff in more realistic and creative strategies should be well worth the price.

FOOTNOTES

[1]Originally a research project within General Electric and later a project of the Harvard Business School, PIMS became the basis of a non-profit consulting firm called the Strategic Planning Institute in the mid-1970s.

[2]These concepts have been widely described and discussed in the literature, and I will not attempt a summary here. See, for example, Abell and Hammond (1979) and Naylor (1981).

[3]Some of these questions have been discussed in the various critiques of the planning concepts. See, for example, Abell and Hammond (1979); Wind and Mahajan (1981).

[4]The determinants of each force are described in Porter (1980) Chapter 1.

REFERENCES

[1] Abell, D., and J. Hammond. Strategic Market Planning. Englewood Cliffs, N.J.: Prentice-Hall, 1979.

[2] Ansoff, I. Corporate Strategy. New York: McGraw-Hill, 1965.

[3] Bain, J.S. Barriers to New Competition. Cambridge, Mass.: Harvard University Press, 1956.

[4] Bain, J.S. Industrial Organization, 2nd ed. New York: Wiley, 1968.

[5] Bain, J.S. "The Comparative Stability of Market Structures," Essays on Price Theory and Industrial Organization. Boston, Mass.: Little, Brown, 1972, pp. 166-174.

[6] Caves, R.E., and M.E. Porter. "From Entry Barriers to Mobility Barriers: Conjectural Decisions and Contrived Deterrence to New Competition," Quarterly Journal of Economics, May 1977, pp. 241-262.

[7] Caves, R.E., and T. A. Pugel. "Intraindustry Difference in Conduct and Performance," Monograph 1980-2, Monographs on Economics and Finance, Graduate School of Business, New York University, 1980.

[8] Dolan, R. J., and A. P. Jeuland. "Experience Curves and Dynamic Demand Models," Journal of Marketing, Volume 45, Number 1, Winter 1981, pp. 52-62.

[9] Fellner, W.J. Competition Among the Few. New York: Augustus M. Kelley, 1965. Original edition 1949.

[10] Ferguson, R. "The Economics of Joint Ventures." Unpublished Ph.D. dissertation, Harvard University, 1981.

[11] Flaherty, T. "Industry Structure and Cost Reducing Investment: A Dynamic Equilibrium Analysis." Unpublished Ph.D. Dissertation, Carnegie-Mellon University, Graduate School of Industrial Administration, 1976.

[12] Hall, W.K. "Survival Strategies in a Hostile Environment," Harvard Business Review, Volume 58, Number 5, September-October 1980, pp. 75-85.

[13] Hayes, S., A.M. Spence, and D. Marks. "Competitive Structure in Investment Banking," forthcoming (1981).

[14] Kamien, M. and N. Schwartz. "Timing of Innovations Under Rivalry," Econometrica, January 1972, pp. 43-60.

[15] Learned, E.P., C.R. Christensen, K.R. Andrews, and W. Guty. Business Policy. Revised Edition. Homewood, Ill.: Irwin, 1969. Original edition 1965.

[16] Mason, E.S. "Price and Production Policies of Large Scale Enterprises," American Economic Review, Vol. 39, March 1939, pp. 61-74.

[17] Oster, S. "Intraindustry Structure and the Ease of Strategic Change," Working paper, Department of Economics, Yale University, 1981.

[18] Panzer, J., and R.D. Willig. "Economics of Scale in Multi-Output Production," Quarterly Journal of Economics, Volume 91, August 1977, pp. 481-494.

[19] Porter, M.E. Competitive Strategy: Techniques for Analyzing Industries and Competitors. New York: Free Press, 1980.

[20] Porter, M.E. "The Contributions of Industrial Organization to Strategy Formulation: A Promise Beginning to be Realized," Revised 8/80, Harvard Business School Working Paper 79-60, Division of Research, Graduate School of Business Administration, Harvard University, Boston, Mass., 1980.

[21] Porter, M.E., and A. M. Spence. "The Capacity Expansion Process in a Growing Oligopoly: The Case of Corn Wet Milling," National Bureau of Economic Research, forthcoming

[22] Schelling, T.C. The Strategy of Conflict. Cambridge, Mass.: Harvard University Press, 1960.

[23] Spence, A. Michael. "Investment Strategy and Growth in a New Market," Bell Journal of Economics, Volume 10, Number 1, Spring 1979, pp. 1-9.

[24] Spence, A. Michael. "The Learning Curve and Competition," Bell Journal of Economics, Volume 12, Number 1, Spring 1981, pp. 49-70.

[25] Stuckey, J. "Vertical Integration in the Aluminum Industry." Unpublished Ph.D. dissertation, Business Economics Committee, Harvard University, 1981.

[26] Teece, D.J. "Economics of Scope and the Scope of the Enterprise," Journal of Economic Behavior and Organization, Volume 1, 1980, pp.223-247.

[27] Von Newmann, J., and O. Morgenstern. Theory of Games and Economic Behavior. Princeton, N.J.: Princeton University Press, 1953.

[28] Willig, R.D. "Multiproduct Technology and Market Structure," American Economic Review, Volume 69, May 1979, pp. 346-350.

[29] Wind, Y., and V. Mahajan. "Designing Product and Business Portfolios," Harvard Business Review, Volume 59, Number 1, January-Feburary 1981, pp. 155-165.

BIBLIOGRAPHY

A BIBLIOGRAPHY ON STRATEGIC PLANNING AND MODELING

Thomas H. Naylor

Department of Economics
Duke University
Durham, North Carolina
U.S.A.

I. STRATEGIC PLANNING

Abell, Derek F. Defining the Business: The Starting Point of Strategic Planning. Englewood Cliffs, N. J.: Prentice-Hall, 1980.

Ackoff, Russell L. A Concept of Corporate Planning. New York: John Wiley, 1972.

Allen, M. "Competitive Business Strategies," in Strategic Leadership: The Challenge to Chairmen. London: McKinsey & Co., 1978, pp. 14-22.

Allen, M. "Corporate Strategy and the New Environment," in Strategic Leadership: The Challenge to Chairmen. London: McKinsey & Co., 1978, pp. 23-30.

Allio, Roert J., and M. W. Pennington. Corporate Planning: Techniques & Application. New York: AMACOM, 1979.

American Hospital Association. The Practice of Planning in Health Care Institutions. Chicago: American Hospital Association, 1973.

Andrews, K. R. The Concept of Corporate Strategy. Homewood, Ill.: Dow Jones Irwin, 1971.

Ansoff, H. Igor. Corporate Strategy. New York: McGraw-Hill, 1965.

Ansoff, H. Igor. Business Strategy. Middlesex, England: Penguin Books, 1969.

Ansoff, H. Igor, et. al. "Does Planning Pay? The Effects of Planning on Success of Acquisitions of American Firms," Long Range Planning, III (1979, pp. 2-7).

Ansoff, H. Igor, et. al. From Strategic Planning to Strategic Management. New York: John Wiley, 1976.

Ansoff, H. Igor. Strategic Management. New York: John Wiley, 1979.

Anthony, Robert N. Planning and Control Systems: A Framework for Analysis. Boston: Harvard Business School, 1965.

Anthony, Robert N., and John Dearden. Management Control Systems. Homewood, Ill.: Dow Jones Irwin, 1976.

Argenti, John. Corporate Planning. Homewood, Ill.: Dow Jones Irwin, 1971.

Ashton, David, and Leslie Simister. The Role of Forecasting in Corporate Planning. London: Staple Press, 1970.

Bell, D. J. Planning Corporate Manpower. London: Longman Group, 1974.

Bower, Joseph L. Managing the Resource Allocation Process. Homewood, Ill.: Richard D. Irwin, 1970.

Branch, Melville C. Planning: Aspects and Applications. New York: John Wiley, 1966.

Brion, John M. Corporate Marketing Planning. New York: John Wiley, 1967.

Burack, E. H. Strategies for Manpower Planning and Programming. Morristown, N. J.: General Learning Corp., 1972.

Buzzell, Robert D. Note on Market Definition and Segmentation. Cambridge, Mass.: Harvard Business School, 1979.

Buzzell, R., B. Gale, and R. Sultan. "Market Share--A Key to Profitability," Harvard Business Review, LIII (Jan.-Feb., 1975), pp. 97-106.

Byrnes, W. G., and B. K. Chesterton. Decisions, Strategies and New Ventures. New York: Halsted, 1973.

Cannon, J. Thomas. Business Strategy and Policy. New York: Harcourt, Brace & World, 1968.

Caves, R. E., and M. E. Porter. "From Entry Barriers to Mobility Barriers: Conjectural Decisions and Contrived Deterrence to New Competition," Quarterly Journal of Economics, May, 1977.

Chandler, Alfred D. Strategy and Structure: Chapters in the History of the American Industrial Enterprise. Cambridge, Mass.: M. I. T. Press, 1962.

Chevalier, M. "The Strategy Spectre Behind Your Market Share Goal," European Business, XXXIV (Summer, 1972), pp. 63-72.

Cohen, K. J., and R. M. Cyert. "Strategy: Formulation, Implementation, and Monitoring," Journal of Business (July, 1973).

Cotton, Donald B. Company-Wide Planning. New York: MacMillan, 1971.

Davis, Stanley M., and Paul R. Lawrence. Matrix. Reading, Mass.: Addison-Wesley, 1977.

Day, George S. "Strategic Market Analysis: Top-Down and Bottom-Up Approaches," Research Report No. 80-105. Cambridge, Mass.: Marketing Science Institute, August, 1980.

Dennings, Basil W. Corporate Planning. New York: McGraw-Hill, 1971.

Dill, W. R., and G. K. Popov. Organization for Forecasting and Planning: Experience in the Soviet Union and the United States. New York: John Wiley, 1979.

Eliasson, Gunnar. Business Economic Planning. London: John Wiley, 1976.

Emery, James C. Organizational Planning and Control Systems. New York: Mac-Millan, 1969.

Ewing, David W. Long Range Planning for Management. New York: Harper & Row, 1972.

Farmer, David H., and Bernard Taylor. Corporate Planning and Procurement. New York: John Wiley, 1975.

Forsyth, W. E. "Strategic Planning in the 1970s," Financial Executive (Oct., 1973), pp. 96-102.

Fulmer, Robet M., and Leslie W. Rue. The Practice and Profitability of Long Range Planning. Oxford, Ohio: Planning Executives Institute, 1973.

Gambino, Anthony J. Planning and Control in Higher Education. New York: National Association of Accountants, 1979.

Glueck, W. Business Policy, Strategy Formation and Management Action. New York: McGraw-Hill, 1976.

Goodwin, Craufurd, et. al. National Economic Planning. Washington, D. C.: U. S. Chamber of Commerce, 1976.

Gray, Edmund R. Business Policy and Strategy. Austin, Texas: Austin Press, 1979.

Hall, W. H. "SBUs: Hot, New Topic in the Management of Diversification," Business Horizons (Feb., 1978), pp. 17-25.

Hamermesh, Richard G. "Responding to Divisional Profit Crises," Harvard Business Review (March-April, 1977).

Hedley, Barry. "A Fundamental Approach to Strategy Development," Long Range Planning (Dec., 1976), pp. 2-11.

Henderson, Bruce D. Henderson on Corporate Strategy. Cambridge, Mass.: Abt Books, 1979.

Herold D. M. "Long Range Planning and Organizational Performance," Academy of Management Journal, XV (1972), pp. 91-102.

Hilton, Peter. Planning Corporate Growth and Diversification. New York: McGraw-Hill, 1970.

Hofer, Charles W. "Towards a Contingency Theory of Business Strategy," Academy of Management Journal, December, 1975.

Hofer, Charles W., and Dan Schendel. Strategy Formulation: Analytical Concepts. St. Paul: West Publishing, 1978.

Hussey, David E. Corporate Planning. Oxford, England: Pergamon, 1974.

Irwin, Patrick H. Business Planning--Key to Profit Growth. Hamilton, Ontario: Society of Industrial Accountants of Canada, 1969.

Jain, Subhash, and Surendra S. Singhvi. Essentials of Corporate Planning. Oxford, Ohio: Planning Executives Institute, 1973.

Jain, Subhash, and Surendra S. Singhvi. An Overview of Corporate Planning. Oxford, Ohio: Planning Executives Institutes, 1974.

Jain, Subhash, and Surendra S. Singhvi. Planning for Corporate Growth. Oxford, Ohio: Planning Executives Institute, 1974.

Jantsch, Erich. Technological Planning and Social Futures. New York: Halstead Press, 1972.

Karger, D. W., and Z. A. Malik. "Long Range Planning and Organizational Performance," Long Range Planning, VIII (1975), pp. 60-64.

Kastens, Merritt L. Long Range Planning for Your Business. New York: AMACOM, 1976.

Keichel, W. "Playing by the Rules of the Corporate Strategy Game," Fortune, XLIX (Sept. 24, 1979), pp. 110-121.

Kotler, Philip. Marketing Management: Analysis, Planning, and Control. Englewood Cliffs, N. J.: Prentice-Hall, 1977.

Kudla, Ronald J. "The Components of Strategic Planning," Long Range Planning (Dec., 1978).

Kudla, Ronald J. "The Effects of Strategic Planning on Common Stock Returns," Academy of Management Journal, XXIII (March, 1980), pp. 5-20.

Kudla, Ronald J. "Strategic Planning and Risk," Review of Business and Economic Research (Fall, 1981).

Lindsay, William M., and Leslie W. Rue. Environmental Complexity in Long Range Planning. Oxford, Ohio: Planning Executives Institute, 1976.

Lofthouse, S. "Strategy, Cross Subsidization and Business Portfolio," Long Range Planning, XI (August, 1978), pp. 58-60.

Lorange, Peter. Corporate Planning: An Executive Viewpoint. Englewood Cliffs, N. J.: Prentice-Hall.

Lorange, Peter, and Richard F. Vancil. Strategic Planning Systems. Englewood Cliffs, N. J.: Prentice-Hall, 1977.

Mace, Myles L. "The President and Corporate Planning," Harvard Business Review (Jan.-Feb., 1965).

McLean, E. R., and J. V. Soden. Strategic Planning for MIS. New York: John Wiley, 1977.

MacMillan, Ian C. Strategy Formulation: Political Concepts. St. Paul: West Publishing, 1978.

Madden, Donald L. People Side of Planning. Oxford, Ohio: Planning Executives Institute, 1980.

Miller, Ernest C. Advanced Techniques for Strategic Planning. New York: American Management Association, 1971.

Mockler, Robert J. Business Planning and Policy Formulation. New York: Appleton-Century-Crofts, 1972.

Moskow, Michael H. Strategic Planning in Business and Government. New York: Committee for Economic Development, 1978.

Mulvaney, J. E., and C. W. Mann. Practical Business Models. New York: Halsted, 1976.

National Association of Accountants. Long Range Profit Planning. New York: NAA, 1964.

Naylor, Thomas H. The Politics of Corporate Planning and Modeling. Oxford, Ohio: Planning Executives Institute, 1978.

Naylor, Thomas H. "Organizing for Strategic Planning," Managerial Planning (July-August, 1979).

Naylor, Thomas H. Strategic Planning Management. Oxford, Ohio: Planning Executives Institute, 1980.

Naylor, Thomas H., and Kristin Neva. "The Planning Audit," Managerial Planning (Sept.-Oct., 1979).

Naylor, Thomas H., and Kristin Neva. "Design of a Strategic Planning Process," Managerial Planning (Nov.-Dec., 1979).

Niehaus, Richard J. Computer Assisted Human Resources Planning. New York: John Wiley, 1979.

Paine, Frank T., and William Naumes. Strategy and Policy Formation. Philadelphia: W. B. Saunders, 1974.

Patel, R., and M. Yougner. "A Frame of Reference for Strategy Development," Long Range Planning, XII (April, 1978), pp. 6-12.

Peters, Joseph P. Strategic Planning for Hospitals. Chicago: American Hospital Association.

Porter, Michael E. Interbrand Choice, Strategy and Bilateral Market Power. Cambridge, Mass.: Harvard University Press, 1976.

Porter, Michael E. "Please Note Location of Nearest Exit," California Management Review (Winter, 1976).

Porter, Michael. "How Competitive Forces Shape Strategy," Harvard Business Review (March-April, 1979), pp. 137-145.

Rhenman, Eric. Organization Theory for Long Range Planing. New York: John Wiley, 1973.

Ringbakk, K. A. "Organized Planning in Major U. S. Companies," Long Range Planning (1969), pp. 46-57.

Rosen, Stephen. Long Range Planning. New York: The President's Association, 1973.

Rothschild, W. E. Putting It All Together: A Guide to Strategic Thinking. New York: AMACON, 1976.

Rothschild, W. E. Strategic Alternatives. New York: AMACOM, 1979.

Rudwick B. H. Systems Analysis for Effective Planning. New York: John Wiley, 1969.

Rumelt R. Strategy, Structure and Economic Performance. Cambridge, Mass.: Harvard University Press, 1974.

Sackman, Harold, and Ronald L. Citrenbaum. On Line Planning Towards Creative Problem Solving. Englewood Cliffs, N. J.: Prentice-Hall, 1972.

Said, Kamal, and Robert E. Seiler. Implementation of Long Range Plans through Current Operating Budgets. Oxford, Ohio: Planning Executives Institute, 1978.

Salter, M., and W. Weinhold. Diversification through Acquisition. New York: Free Press, 1979.

Schendel, Dan E., and Charles W. Hofer. Strategic Management. Boston: Little, Brown, 1979.

Schoennaure, Alfred W. The Formulation & Implementation of Corporate Objectives & Strategies.

Simmons, W. W. Exploratory Planning--Briefs of Practices. Oxford, Ohio: Planning Executives Institute, 1977.

Simmons, W. W. So You Want To Have A Long Range Plan. Oxford, Ohio: Planning Executives Institute, 1978.

Singhvi, Surendra, and Subhash Jain. Planning for Corporate Growth. Oxford, Ohio: Planning Executives Institute, 1974.

Steiner, George A. Top Management Planning. New York: MacMillan, 1969.

Steiner, George A. Comprehensive Managerial Planning. Oxford, Ohio: Planning Executives Institute, 1972.

Steiner, George A. Pitfalls in Comprehensive Long Range Planning. Oxford, Ohio: Planning Executives Institute, 1972.

Steiner, George A. Strategic Managerial Planning. Oxford, Ohio: Planning Executives Institute, 1977.

Steiner, George A. Strategic Planning: What Every Manager Must Know. New York: The Free Press, 1979.

Stemp, Isay. Corporate Growth Strategies. New York: American Management Association, 1971.

Stone, Merlin. Product Planning. New York: Halsted, 1976.

Taylor, Bernard. "Introducing Strategic Management," Long Range Planning, V (Sept., 1973), pp. 34-38.

Taylor, Bernard, and Kevin Hawkins. Handbook of Strategic Planning. London: Longman Group, 1977.

Taylor, Bernard, and John R. Sparkes. Corporate Strategy and Planning. New York: Halsted, 1977.

Thorelli, Hans B. Strategy Plus Structure Equals Performance. Bloomington, Ind.: University of Indiana Press, 1977.

Thune, S., and R. J. House. "Where Long Range Planning Pays Off," Business Horizons (1970), pp. 81-87.

Tsurmi, Yoshi. Multinational Management: Business Strategy and Government Policy. Cambridge, Mass.: Ballinger, 1977.

Warren, Kirby. Long Range Planning. Englewood Cliffs, N. J.: Prentice-Hall, 1966.

Wright, R. "A System for Managing Diversity," Cambridge, Mass.: Arthur D. Little, 1975.

II. ANALYTICAL PORTFOLIO PLANNING MODELS

Abel, Derek F., and John S. Hammond. Strategic Market Planning. Englewood Cliffs, N. J.: Prentice-Hall, 1979.

Abernathy, W., and K. Wayne. "Limits of the Learning Curve," Harvard Business Review, VII (Sept.-Oct., 1974), pp. 109-119.

Bodde, D. "Riding the Experience Curve," Technology Review, LXXVIII (March/April, 1976), pp. 53-59.

Boston Consulting Group. "Experience Curves as a Planning Tool," Boston Consulting Group, Feb. 23-29, 1970.

Boston Consulting Group. "The Product Portfolio," BCG Perspectives, No. 66, 1970.

Boston Consulting Group. "The Market Share Paradox," BCG Perspectives, No. 72, 1970.

Boston Consulting Group. "Growth and Financial Strategies," Boston Consulting Group, 1971.

Boston Consulting Group. "Perspectives on Experience," Boston Consulting Group, 1972.

Boston Consulting Group. "Cash Traps," BCG Perspectives, No. 102, 1972.

Boston Consulting Group. "The Experience Curve Reviewed: The Concept," BCG Perspectives, No. 124, 1973.

Boston Consulting Group. "The Experience Curve Reviewed: History," BCG Perspectives, No. 125, 1973.

Boston Consulting Group. "The Experience Curve Reviewed: The Product Portfolio," BCG Perspectives, No. 135, 1973.

Boston Consulting Group. "The Experience Curve Reviewed: Why Does It Work?", BCG Perspectives, No. 128, 1974.

Boston Consulting Group. "The Experience Curve Reviewed: Price Stability," BCG Perspectives, No. 149, 1974.

Boston Consulting Group. "Payoff on the Corporate Portfolio," BCG Perspectives, No. 195, 1976.

Boston Consulting Group. "Anatomy of the Cash Con," BCG Perspectives, No. 198, 1976.

Boston Consulting Group. "Market Share," BCG Perspectives, No. 200, 1977.

Carter, E., and K. Cohen. "Portfolio Aspects of Strategic Planning," Journal of Business Policy, II (1972), pp. 8-30.

Catry, B., and M. Chevalier. "Market Share and Product Life Cycle," Journal of Marketing, XXXVIII (Oct., 1974), pp. 29-34.

Channon, D. "Use and Abuse of Analytical Techniques for Strategic Decisions," presented at TIMS XXIII International Meeting, Athens, July, 1977.

Conley, P. "Experience Curves as a Planning Tool," BCG Special Commentary, 1972.

Cox, W. "Product Portfolio Strategy: A Review of the Boston Consulting Group Approach to Marketing Strategy," Proceedings of the American Marketing Association, 1974, pp. 465-470.

Abernathy, W., and K. Wayne. "Limits of the Learning Curve," Harvard Business Review, VII (Sept.-Oct., 1974), pp. 109-119.

Bodde, D. "Riding the Experience Curve," Technology Review, LXXVIII (March/ April, 1976), pp. 53-59.

Boston Consulting Group. "Experience Curves as a Planning Tool," Boston Consulting Group, Feb. 23-29, 1970.

Boston Consulting Group. "The Product Portfolio," BCG Perspectives, No. 66, 1970.

Boston Consulting Group. "The Market Share Paradox," BCG Perspectives, No. 72, 1970.

Boston Consulting Group. "Growth and Financial Strategies," Boston Consulting Group, 1971.

Boston Consulting Group. "Perspectives on Experience," Boston Consulting Group, 1972.

Boston Consulting Group. "Cash Traps," BCG Perspectives, No. 102, 1972.

Boston Consulting Group. "The Experience Curve Reviewed: The Concept," BCG Perspectives, No. 124, 1973.

Boston Consulting Group. "The Experience Curve Reviewed: History," BCG Perspectives, No. 125, 1973.

Boston Consulting Group. "The Experience Curve Reviewed: The Product Portfolio," BCG Perspectives, No. 135, 1973.

Boston Consulting Group. "The Experience Curve Reviewed: Why Does It Work?", BCG Perspectives, No. 128, 1974.

Boston Consulting Group. "The Experience Curve Reviewed: Price Stability," BCG Perspectives, No. 149, 1974.

Boston Consulting Group. "Payoff on the Corporate Portfolio," BCG Perspectives, No. 195, 1976.

Boston Consulting Group. "Anatomy of the Cash Con," BCG Perspectives, No. 198, 1976.

Boston Consulting Group. "Market Share," BCG Perspectives, No. 200, 1977.

Carter, E., and K. Cohen. "Portfolio Aspects of Strategic Planning," Journal of Business Policy, II (1972), pp. 8-30.

Catry, B., and M. Chevalier. "Market Share and Product Life Cycle," Journal of Marketing, XXXVIII (Oct., 1974), pp. 29-34.

Channon, D. "Use and Abuse of Analytical Techniques for Strategic Decisions," presented at TIMS XXIII International Meeting, Athens, July, 1977.

Conley, P. "Experience Curves as a Planning Tool," BCG Special Commentary, 1972.

Cox, W. "Product Portfolio Strategy: A Review of the Boston Consulting Group Approach to Marketing Strategy," Proceedings of the American Marketing Association, 1974, pp. 465-470.

Cox, William E. "Product Portfolio Strategy, Market Structure, and Performance," in Strategy Plus Structure Equals Performance (Hans B. Thorelli, editor). Bloomington, Ind.: University of Indiana Press, 1977.

Cyert R. M., R. L. Van Horn, and J. R. Williams. "Concepts of Management Strategy for Organizations," Carnegie-Mellon University, June, 1979.

Day, George S. "A Strategic Perspective on Product Planning," Journal of Contemporary Business, IV (Spring, 1975), pp. 1-34.

Day, George S. "Diagnosing the Product Portfolio," Journal of Marketing, XLI (April, 1977), pp. 29-38.

Dhalla, N. K., and S. Yuspeh. "Forget the Product Life Cycle Concept," Harvard Business Review (Jan.-Feb., 1976).

Gale, Bradley T. "Planning for Profit," Planning Review (Jan., 1978).

Hamada, R. "Portfolio Analysis and Market Equilibrium," Journal of Finance, XXIV (March, 1969), pp. 13-32.

Hamermesh, R., M. Anderson, and J. Harris. "Strategies for Low Market Share Businesses," Harvard Business Review, LVI (May-June, 1978), pp. 95-103.

Hedley, Barry. "Strategy and the Business Portfolio," Long Range Planning, X (Feb., 1977), pp. 9-15.

Hirschmann, W. "Profit from the Learning Curve," Harvard Business Review, XLII (Jan.-Feb., 1964), pp. 135-139.

Hussey, David E. "Portfolio Analysis: Practical Experience with the Directional Policy Matrix," Long Range Planning, XI (Aug., 1978), pp. 2-8.

Levitt, T. "Exploit the Product Life Cycle," Harvard Business Review, XLIII (Nov.-Dec., 1965), pp. 81-94.

Lloyd, R. "Experience Curve Analysis," Applied Economics, X (June, 1979), pp. 221-233.

Naylor, Thomas H. "PIMS: Through a Different Looking Glass," Planning Review (March, 1978).

Schoeffler, Sidney. "Cross-Sectional Study of Strategy, Structure, and Performance: Aspects of the PIMS Programs," in Strategy Plus Structure Equals Performance (Hans B. Thorelli, editor). Bloomington, Ind.: University of Indiana Press, 1977.

Smallwood, J. "The Product Life Cycle: A Key to Strategic Market Planning," Business Topics, XXI (Winter, 1973), pp. 29-35.

Strategic Planning Institute. "The PIMS Program: Selected Findings," 1977.

Tilles, Seymour. "Segmentation and Strategy," Perspectives, Number 150. Boston, Mass.: The Boston Consulting Group, 1974.

Wind, Y., and H. Claycamp. "Planning Product Line Strategy: A Matrix Approach," Journal of Marketing, XL (Jan., 1976), pp. 2-9.

Zakopn, A. "Growth and Financial Strategies," Boston Consulting Group, 1968.

III. OPTIMIZATION PORTFOLIO PLANNING MODELS

Boston Consulting Group. "A Strategy-Based Resource Allocation Model."
Boston: Boston Consulting Group.

Coate, Malcolm B. The Boston Consulting Group's Portfolio Planning Model:
An Economic Analysis. Unpublished Ph.D. Dissertation, Duke University,
1980.

Cohen, Kalman J. "Dynamic Balance Sheet Management: A Management Science
Approach," Journal of Bank Research (Winter, 1972), pp. 9-19.

Farrar, D. E. The Investment Decision Under Uncertainty. Englewood Cliffs,
N. J.: Prentice-Hall, 1962.

Hamilton, W. F., and M. A. Moses. "An Optimization Model for Corporate
Financial Planning," Operations Research (May-June, 1972).

Heal, G. M. The Theory of Economic Planning. Amsterdam: North-Holland, 1973.

Intrilligator, Michael D. Mathematical Optimization and Economic Theory.
Englewood Cliffs, N. J.: Prentice-Hall, 1971.

Johnson, E. Studies in Multiobjective Decision Models. Lund, Sweden:
Student Litteratur, 1968.

Markowitz, H. "Portfolio Selection," Journal of Finance, VII (March, 1952),
pp. 77-91.

Markowitz, H. Portfolio Selection. (Cowles Foundation Monograph No. 16).
New York: John Wiley, 1959.

Naylor, Thomas H., and John M. Vernon. Microeconomics and Decision Models
of the Firm. New York: Harcourt Brace, 1969.

Sharpe, William F. "A Simplified Model for Portfolio Analysis," Management
Science, IX (Jan., 1963), pp. 277-293.

Theil, H. Optimal Decision Rules for Government and Industry. Amsterdam:
North-Holland, 1964.

Weingartner, H. Martin. Mathmematical Programming and the Analysis of
Capital Budgeting Problems. Englewood Cliffs, N. J.: Prentice-Hall,
1963.

IV. CORPORATE SIMULATION MODELS

Benton William K. The Use of the Computer in Planning. Reading, Mass.:
Addison-Wesley, 1970.

Boulden, James B. Computer Assisted Planning Systems. New York: McGraw-
Hill, 1975.

Chacko, George K. Computer-Aided Decision-Making. New York: American
Elsevier, 1972.

Gershefski, George. "Corporate Planning Models: The State of the Art,"
Managerial Planning (Nov.-Dec., 1969).

Grinyer, Peter H., and Jeff Wooller. Corporate Models Today. London:
Institute of Chartered Accountants, 1975.

Hamilton, W. F., and M. A. Moses. "A Computer-Based Corporate Planning System," Management Science (Oct., 1974).

House, William C. Interactive Decision Oriented Data Base Systems. New York: Petrocelli/Charter, 1977.

Livingstone, John L. Management Planning and Control: Mathematical Models. New York: McGraw-Hill, 1970.

Lucas, Henry C., Jr. The Implementation of Computer-Based Models. New York: National Association of Accountants, 1976.

Mayo, R. Britton. Corporate Planning and Modeling with SIMPLAN. Reading, Mass.: Addison-Wesley, 1979.

McCosh, A. M., and Michael Scott Morton. Management Decision Support Systems. New York: Halsted, 1978.

Naylor, Thomas H. Computer Simulation Experiments with Models of Economic Systems. New York: John Wiley, 1971.

Naylor, Thomas H. "Why Corporate Planning Models?", Interfaces (Nov., 1977).

Naylor, Thomas H. "The Integration of Corporate Planning Models into the Planning Process," Long Range Planning (Dec., 1977).

Naylor, Thomas H. Corporate Planning Models. Reading, Mass.: Addison-Wesley, 1979.

Naylor, Thomas H. "Corporate Simulation Models," in Current Issues in Simulation (N. R. Adam and A. Dogranaci, editors). New York: Academic Press, 1979.

Naylor, Thomas H. Simulation Models for Corporate Planning. New York: Praeger, 1979.

Naylor, Thomas H. (editor). Simulation in Business Planning and Decision Making. La Jolla, California: The Society for Computer Simulation, 1980.

Naylor, Thomas H., et. al. SIMPLAN: A Planning and Modeling System for Government. Durham, N. C.: Duke University Press, 1977.

Naylor, Thomas H., Betty Frezor, and G. S. McKensie. "SIMPLAN," Simulation (May, 1978).

Naylor, Thomas H., and M. J. Mansfield. "The Design of Computer Based Planning and Modeling Systems," Long Range Planning (February, 1977).

Naylor, Thomas H., and Horst Schauland. "Experience with Corporate Simulation Models--A Survey," Long Range Planning (April, 1976).

Naylor, Thomas H., and Horst Schauland. "A Survey of Users of Corporate Planning Models," Management Science (May, 1976).

Rosenkranz, Friedrich. An Introduction to Corporate Modeling. Durham, N. C.: Duke University Press, 1978.

Schrieber, Albert N. (editor). Corporate Simulation Models. Seattle: University of Washington, 1970.

Traenkle, J. W., E. B. Cox, and J. A. Bullard. The Use of Financial Models in Business. New York: Financial Executives Research Foundation, 1975.

Wheelwright, Steven C., and Spyros G. Madriadakis. Computer-Aided Modeling for Managers. Reading, Mass.: Addision-Wesley, 1972.